*Number Eleven: The Centennial Series of
the Association of Former Students,
Texas A&M University*

ASHBEL SMITH OF TEXAS

Ashbel Smith of Texas

PIONEER, PATRIOT, STATESMAN,

1805–1886

By

Elizabeth Silverthorne

Texas A&M University Press
COLLEGE STATION

To the memory of Clark and Steve

Copyright © 1982 by Elizabeth Silverthorne
All rights reserved

Library of Congress Cataloging in Publication Data

Silverthorne, Elizabeth.
　Ashbel Smith of Texas.

　(The Centennial series of the Association of Former Students, Texas A&M University; no. 11)
　　Bibliography: p.
　　Includes index.
　　1. Smith, Ashbel, 1805–1886.　2. Texas—History.
3. Statesmen—Texas—Biography.　4. Physicians—Texas—Biography.　5. Texas—Biography.　I. Title.　II. Series.
F391.S629S54　　976.4'009'92 [B]　　82-739
ISBN 0-89096-127-1 (cloth)　　　　AACR2
ISBN 0-89096-974-4 (pbk.)

Manufactured in the United States of America

First Paperback Edition

Contents

Preface   xi
Acknowledgments   xv

CHAPTER

1. A Mind on the Stretch (1805–1831)   3
2. Paris Interlude (1831–1836)   19
3. Surgeon General of the Texian Army (1837–1839)   37
4. A House in the Country (1839–1841)   57
5. Chargé d'Affaires to Saint James and Saint-Cloud (1842–1844)   72
6. The Final Act in This Great Drama (1845–1847)   96
7. To Enter Battle (1848–1855)   114
8. The Connecticut Rebel (1855–1863)   134
9. Now is the Seed Time (1863–1872)   160
10. A Very Broad Stage (1873–1880)   183
11. Father of the University (1881–1885)   207
12. This World Is Not a Resting Place (1885–1886)   226

Bibliography   235
Index   249

Illustrations

frontispiece
Ashbel Smith, 1876 (*Courtesy Lee D. Kittredge, Cary, North Carolina*)

following page 94
Ashbel Smith's commission as surgeon general of the Texas Army
Sam Houston's residence in Houston
Ashbel Smith's residence in London
Invitation to a ball at Buckingham Palace
Evergreen, Ashbel Smith's home
Ashbel Smith in Confederate uniform
Revolver, pistol, and spurs of Ashbel Smith
Letter from Ashbel to Sam Houston
Ashbel Smith—Paris, 1878
Anna Allen Wright
Desk of Ashbel Smith
Certificate from the first Houston State Fair
Ashbel's perpetual calendar shelf clock

following page 226
Ashbel's appointment to the Board of Regents of the University of Texas
Laying the cornerstone of Old Main
West wing of Old Main at the University of Texas
Cornerstone of Old Main
Old Red at the University of Texas Medical Branch
Bust and plaque at the University of Texas Medical Branch
Medallion of the Distinguished Alumnus, University of Texas Medical Branch
Rubbing of the gravestone of Ashbel Smith

Preface

ON a Monday evening in the winter of 1886 a young student at Stuart Seminary, in Austin, sat down to add a supplement to the weekly letter that she had dutifully written the day before. "My dear Mama," she began,

> I will write you a few more lines telling you of the death of Col. Ashbel Smith. . . . You know he was the Pres. of the board of trustees of our school . . . so we had to draw up the resolutions. His remains were brought up from Houston on a special car Saturday, they lay in state at the Capitol from then until 2 o'clock P.M. yesterday, then it was brought out here and interred in the State Cemetery. After he was buried the Austin Greys shot three times over his grave, so this was the end of a great and useful life. Our house is draped in mourning.[1]

For the rest of that cold January week black crepe draped many other buildings in Texas as a symbol of Texans' respect, affection, and appreciation of the little Connecticut Yankee who had adopted Texas as his own.

In addition to the girls at Stuart Seminary, the highest-ranking leaders in state government, education, religion, medicine, business, agriculture, and civic affairs praised Ashbel Smith's character. He was called "the best-educated man in Texas," the "sage of Evergreen," "the Ben Franklin of Texas," and a "Texas institution." All of this was high praise for a man who in life had so enraged his fellow citizens that they had three times burned him in effigy. Ashbel Smith's own character, the conditions of the times, and chance had parts to play in the decisions that led to his transformation into a devoted "Texian," as he invariably spelled it. Once he established Texas as his home, the ver-

---

[1] Ada Wallace to her mother, January 25, 1886. Unless otherwise indicated, all personal letters cited are in the Ashbel Smith Papers, Barker Texas History Center, University of Texas, Austin.

satility of his mind and his multifaceted personality enabled him to serve his adopted land exceptionally well in a remarkable number of ways.

With a medical degree from Yale and study at hospitals and schools in New York and Paris, he was far better trained than most other nineteenth-century American physicians. His published works on cholera and yellow fever were praised by eminent men in medicine. He worked to establish higher standards for medical practice in Texas and to found a state medical society. F. E. Daniel, the founder of the *Texas Medical Journal*, called Ashbel Smith the "Nestor" of Texas medicine and the "father of Texas medicine."

From the time he was a young man, Ashbel Smith had a lively interest in politics. Besides acting as the Republic's minister to France and England and as its secretary of state, he served three terms in the Texas legislature. He helped organize the Democratic party in Texas, attended its meetings faithfully, often playing a leadership role, and several times served as a delegate to national Democratic conventions. He took an active part in many political campaigns, using his eloquent tongue and pen to support or oppose candidates, sometimes openly in letters to editors and in speeches and sometimes quietly in private letters.

In times of war Ashbel Smith could not sit on the sidelines. During the Mexican War he served under General Zachary Taylor in Mexico. At the commencement of the Civil War, in spite of his northern heritage and his age (fifty-six), he entered the Confederate service. He raised a company and led it at Shiloh, where he was seriously wounded and at Vicksburg, where he was captured. Toward the end of the war he was in charge of the defense of Galveston Island. When the war ended, he served as one of the two commissioners sent by Governor Pendleton Murrah to help arrange terms of surrender with the federal officials in New Orleans.

In between his other activities, Ashbel Smith was a planter and a stockman. He learned everything he could about agriculture and stock raising in his area, studying crops, farming methods, and equipment; participating in agricultural fairs; and writing detailed papers on the culture of cotton, sugarcane, sheep, hogs, and grapes—with instructions for making wines. He was in charge of the first state fair of Texas and was a United States representative to the Great Exhibition in London in 1851 and to the Paris Exposition of 1878.

Believing that "it is the duty of the state to educate its citizens," he worked persistently to help establish a system of free public schools in the state. The last years of his life were spent in an amazing burst of energy as he led the way in founding Prairie View State Normal School, the University of Texas, and the university's medical school at Galveston. He also worked diligently for the causes of transportation and immigration in Texas.

Because Ashbel Smith was the physician, friend, and confidant of all the presidents of the Republic of Texas, he was often asked to write their biographies. Except for a short sketch of Sam Houston and a few scattered statements about the others, he refused. His reasoning was that if one discusses the sun he must also talk about the spots on the sun, and then people may concentrate on the spots instead of the light shed by the sun.

I have had the same problem in writing about Ashbel Smith, a man more complicated and contradictory than most. For seven years I followed in his footsteps from Hartford to Yale; to the Texas Legation in London; to the British Museum; to Paris; to Salisbury, North Carolina; to Galveston; and to the site of Evergreen on Galveston Bay. On those travels, reading and rereading his journals, papers, and letters, I became so impressed by his accomplishments that I may have failed to emphasize his faults sufficiently to please some. What I have tried to do is see his world through his eyes. According to late-twentieth-century thinking, he had some ideas, particularly concerning slavery and evolution, that are no longer defensible. But seen against the tapestry of his times, they are understandable.

I hope that many will agree with me that this man lived within the framework of his time as purposefully and as creatively as nature and circumstances would allow. My concern has been to attempt the almost impossible task of doing justice to Ashbel Smith, A.B., A.M., M.D., Knight of San Jacinto, scholar, linguist, diplomat, soldier, statesman, scientist, physician, editor, writer, farmer, rancher, philosopher, educator, and humanitarian.

Acknowledgments

I am happy to have this opportunity to express my gratitude to the many people who have assisted me in my long search for information that would make this the most factual story possible.

It is so much more fun to research than to write that I might be happily investigating still had not William A. Owens strongly urged that it was time to begin the writing and encouraged me to continue after I had written several chapters under his direction.

The many days I have spent in the Barker Texas History Center at the University of Texas in Austin have been made pleasant and profitable by the assistance of the staff. I would especially like to thank Chester Kielman, former director of the center, who gave me helpful advice at the beginning of my research; archivist Ralph Elder, whose enthusiasm for my project and practical advice helped keep my motivation high; archivists Victoria Reed Bailey and Jeanne R. Wilson for their able assistance; and all the other librarians and staff members in the Barker Center who have helped me on so many occasions.

I acknowledge with thanks the capable research assistance of Mrs. Karl E. Fransson of West Hartford, Connecticut. I thank Ethel Wright, widow of one of the sons of Anna Allen Wright, for telling me anecdotes and passing along family impressions of Ashbel Smith. Other members of the Wright family who have given me invaluable help are Robert and Glenda Wright of Baytown. Larry Joe Enderli and Anna Pearl Wright Thomas let me see artifacts that belonged to Ashbel Smith and shared information with me.

I am grateful for the information given me by Dr. Lee D. Kittredge, and I am grateful to the members of the Shebay family, descendants of Ashbel Smith's sister, Caroline Smith Kittredge, for their kind assistance. I appreciate the help that local historian Isaac M. ("Deacon") Jones of Baytown and James S. Brawley of Salisbury, North Carolina, have given me in sharing the results of the their own research.

My appreciation goes to Weldon Green Cannon, historian, for his help in a number of ways, including sharing the gleanings of references to Ashbel Smith that he gathered from many tedious hours of viewing newspapers on microfilm. I thank my friends Tom Scott for generously lending material and sharing references and Marsha Talley for proofreading.

I am indebted to Larry J. Wygant, associate director for History of Medicine and Archives at the University of Texas Moody Medical Library in Galveston, for his aid. Dr. Amos Christie, Professor Emeritus of Vanderbilt University, gave valuable assistance in interpreting medical data.

Without the competent, interested help of the staffs of many museums, including the Reading Room of the British Museum and the San Jacinto Museum, as well as the staffs of numerous libraries, including the Texas State Library in Austin, my task would never have been finished. I received valuable assistance from archivists Judith A. Schiff and Patricia L. Bodak of the Yale libraries.

I would especially like to thank Rose Anne Brasher and Paul Haire of the Temple Junior College Library; Judy Kuykendall and the staff of the Temple Public Library; Jane Kenamore at the Texas Collection, Rosenberg Library, Galveston; Katherine McDowell, the Daughters of the Republic of Texas, Texas History Research Library, San Antonio; and Patricia G. Rosenthal, Rowan Public Library, Salisbury, North Carolina.

My love and thanks go to my sister, Geneva Fulgham, and to my aunt, Ada Sharpe, for their help and also to my daughter, Carol, and the many other relatives and friends who have tolerated and even encouraged my endless rhapsodizing about "that man" for more than a half-dozen years.

ASHBEL SMITH OF TEXAS

. . . life has duties to perform to its last moment; this world is not a resting place. Man to be true to his destiny should die in harness.

―◆{ CHAPTER ONE }◆―

A Mind on the Stretch
(1805–1831)

ASHBEL SMITH made sporadic attempts throughout his mature life to trace the roots of the Smith, Adams, and Seymour families from which he was descended. It would have delighted him to find a royal skeleton in the family closet. In fact, at one time while he was still at Yale, he told friends that he had traced the Seymour branch (from which he was descended on his father's side through two lines) back to Henry VIII's third wife, Jane Seymour. He must have felt some doubt about the connection, however, for he omitted this reference when discussing his heritage in later years.

Although other members of the family believed that their branch of the Adams family was connected with the presidential strain, Ashbel did not make this claim, nor does it seem to be substantiated by any evidence so far uncovered. The records show that George Adams, an English glover, came to America with his wife, Frances, in 1645. He settled in Watertown, Massachusetts, in 1664, and was killed there some years later by a falling rock. The Adamses' begats come down through Daniel, Joseph, and Matthew to Abel, who married Rosene Cossitt, the daughter of a couple of French descent whose forebears had fled France during the French Revolution. Abel Adams and his wife had ten children, one of whom was Phoebe Adams, Ashbel Smith's mother.[1]

On his first trip to England, Ashbel delved into the Smith family lineage and concluded that he could trace it back to Sir William Smith,

---

[1] Ashbel said that Cossitt was an erroneous spelling of Cossé. Ashbel Smith to Henry G. Kittredge, April 11, 1869 (letter in possession of Dr. Lee D. Kittredge, Cary, N.C.); *Commemorative Biographical Record of Hartford County* 1901, p. 814.

a knight who lived before the time of Henry VIII. In America the Smith line from which Ashbel is descended can be traced back to Joseph Smith, of Hartford, Connecticut, who married Lydia Huit (or Hewitt), the daughter of the Reverend Ephraim Huit, of Hadley. Their son Simon had a son, Elisha, who became a doctor. Elisha married Ruth Seymour. One of the sons of this couple was Moses Smith, Ashbel Smith's grandfather.[2]

Moses Smith also married a Seymour, Mabel, whose father, Daniel, was a captain in the Hartford Continental Guards, First Connecticut Regiment, in 1778. Moses had a shoemaking shop that apparently caused him considerable grief. In October, 1769, he ran an advertisement in the *Hartford Courant* for a journeyman shoemaker. Six months later he ran another advertisement asking for help in finding a *runaway* journeyman shoemaker. The next year he published a notice to his debtors and creditors, and a month after the notice appeared, he announced that he had been robbed.[3] It is not surprising to find that he changed professions and became a small merchant.

The people of Hartford were proud of the wooden bridge over the Park River (sometimes called the Little River). A few small shops were clustered in the area, and it was near this bridge, in what is now West Hartford, that Moses had his home, from which he conducted his business. He offered to exchange "shoe leather, salt, empty rum hogsheads or cash for wheat, rye, good flour or cider."[4]

Some years later Moses's son and namesake, Moses Smith, Jr., set up a small hatmaking business in the family home and advertised "hats of all kinds and sizes very cheap."[5] He did well enough to employ an apprentice and to marry. A son, Curtis, was born to the couple in 1802, but soon after his birth the mother died.

Two years later, on November 11, 1804, Moses Smith, Jr., married again. His second bride was Phoebe Adams. Nine months and two days later, on August 13, 1805, Ashbel Smith was born. It was common in the nineteenth century to give the firstborn son a biblical name (the Ashbelites are mentioned in the Bible as one of the tribes of Benjamin), and Ashbel was a family name. Over the next twelve years

[2] Unpublished Smith files prepared by Connecticut Historical Library.
[3] *Hartford Courant*, October 23, 1769; April 23, 1770; October 30, 1770; November 20, 1770.
[4] Ibid., October 14, 1777.
[5] Ibid., January 12, 1803.

young Ashbel was joined by a brother, a sister, and another brother: Henry Grattan, Caroline, and George Alfred.

For several years Moses Smith, Jr., served as constable, an office to which he was appointed by the town council. His duties included, in addition to levying and collecting state taxes, receiving and serving warrants and "putting forth hue-and-cries orders after murderers, peacebreakers, thieves, robbers, burglarians." He was also responsible for apprehending "such as are guilty of profane swearing, drunkenness, or sabbath-breaking."[6]

Life in Hartford at the beginning of the nineteenth century was well regulated and predictable. At twelve noon Christ Church bell rang, and people went to dinner. At nine in the evening Center Church bell rang, and people drank their cider, raked up their wood fires, and went to bed. As young men Ashbel and his cousin Daniel Seymour flippantly referred to the Hartford community as "the land of steady habits."

The Smiths were deeply religious, doting parents, and Ashbel and his sister and brothers grew up in a warm and loving atmosphere. Because Ashbel was a frail child susceptible to illness of the chest and digestive tract, Phoebe and Moses gave him extra attention and concern. There was much visiting back and forth with the Seymour, Cossitt, and Adams cousins and sharing of holidays and picnics. In this simple, orderly environment Ashbel Smith spent his early years.

Because he was considered to have a "weak constitution," Ashbel had to spend a great deal of time indoors, especially during the severe Connecticut winters. This confinement, plus his own inclination, led him to acquire a love of reading, an interest that brought him pleasure and comfort all his life and resulted in his eventual accumulation of a personal library of hundreds of volumes.

In the early years of the nineteenth century Connecticut was fortunate to have a large permanent school fund, produced from the sale of the Western Reserve Lands in 1795. The public school, which accepted children from three to sixteen, was housed in a two-story stone building not far from the business district. The schoolyard, about twenty-two square yards, was separated into two areas "for each of the two sexes" and contained a well of good water, furnished with a pump.

---

[6] *The Public Statute Laws of the State of Connecticut, as Revised and Enacted by the General Assembly in May, 1821.*

Inside, in the large rooms, where they were again separated by gender, the pupils sat at desks arranged in rows so that each desk accommodated five students. Each student had a seat, which was simply a square box without a back, fixed to the floor with one side open, to provide a place to stow a hat. At the front of the room was an eighteen-inch-high platform for teachers and visitors, and in the center of the room was a large woodburning stove. The school was in session throughout the year except for three one-week vacations.

In this school Ashbel studied spelling, defining, reading, writing, mental and written arithmetic, grammar, geography, modern and ancient history, and natural philosophy. The students were also required to study newspapers so that they could relate the important events of the day. There were frequent examinations, both by their teachers and by members of the awesome visiting district committee.[7]

Evidently Ashbel completed his studies at the elementary school satisfactorily, for he was admitted to the Hartford Grammar School, a preparatory school for college or for a business career. To be admitted to the school, one must be able to read and spell well, "write a good, round and running hand and cypher the ground rules of arithmetic."[8] The school day started at nine o'clock with the reading of a prayer by the master. It ended at five o'clock after each scholar had read one or more Bible verses, and another prayer had been offered by the master. Any student guilty of "light or trifling" behavior during these religious activities was subject to punishment.[9]

Decades later one of Ashbel's teachers had a vivid memory of Ashbel as an ambitious student who volunteered to solve all the examples in his algebra book so that they would be available for use with other students. The teacher had made use of Ashbel's solutions for about sixty years.[10]

Ashbel was fortunate to have assigned to him as his tutor an excellent young scholar named Solomon Stoddard, who undertook to prepare him to enter Yale. Stoddard gave Ashbel a thorough background in the basic subjects with emphasis on the study of Greek and Latin. In the late summer of 1822, at the age of seventeen, Ashbel Smith pre-

---

[7] William A. Alcott, *A Historical Description of the First Public School in Hartford.*
[8] "Hartford Grammar School System of Rules," December 5, 1815.
[9] Ibid.
[10] Lyman Cohmane to Ashbel Smith, October 23, 1877.

pared to leave home for the first time. He was not sure where his path would lead—with his love of learning, perhaps to a teaching career.

By good fortune Solomon Stoddard received a tutorship at Yale and was able to work with Ashbel during the fall of 1822 and the following spring to prepare him for acceptance as a candidate for graduation. In May, 1823, Ashbel Smith was officially matriculated in the Yale School of Liberal Arts.

During his first term Ashbel lived on campus in one of the dormitories, where he indulged in the common pastime of making sugar candy in his fireplace to sweeten his labors as he pored over his books. For recreation he walked the long elm-shaded streets with small groups of friends to such local attractions as the Judges' Cave, Wintergreen Falls, and Maltby Park and even to Mount Carmel, ten miles from the college.

A senior student bequeathed Ashbel his store of fireworks, and Ashbel probably joined in the popular sport of stealing into the halls in the dead of night to set off firecrackers with a "hellish" roar. Most likely, too, his quick temper led him to participate in the frequent clashes on the green between the town groups and the collegians that were considered a routine part of life at Yale.

In spite of the stimulations in New Haven, Ashbel was at times "rendered miserable" by a melancholy for which he could name no physical cause, other than the colds and respiratory problems from which he often suffered. His concern about his health, augmented by the anxiety of his parents for him, was so evident that one of his cousins called him a hypochondriac. It is possible that his moodiness was encouraged by the impact that Lord Byron's more melancholic poetry was having on Yale undergraduates at the time. The tragic life of the romantic poet was much discussed by Ashbel and his friends, and reading his poems was a popular pastime. Whatever the cause of Ashbel's dark moods, his antidote for them was to become absorbed in his studies.

He did well in all his subjects, excelling in the study of languages. Knowing that his course work would be even heavier during his second semester, he decided to take a room alone in a boardinghouse near the college.[11] Friends and professors alike were impressed by the intensity

---

[11] Catalogue of Officers and Students, Yale College, 1822, 1823.

of his scholarship. One friend teasingly accused him of being an "eccentric genius . . . fond of nice speculations and intricate problems in mathematics, philosophy, and chemistry." Among the classmates who remained lifelong friends were Elias Warner Leavenworth, who became a New York congressman; Ashbel's cousin Daniel Seymour; Adrian Terry, who became a physician; and Benjamin D. Silliman, who became a lawyer.

The professor who made the greatest impression on Ashbel was Benjamin Silliman, the uncle of Ashbel's classmate of the same name. Silliman, who was instrumental in founding Yale's medical school, started the *American Journal of Science*, which became one of the world's most important scientific journals. In addition to being the most outstanding scientist in America at the time, Silliman was a highly personable and deeply religious man of varied talents. Besides teaching Ashbel chemistry and natural history, he fostered in him an abiding interest in geology and mineralogy.

On August 2, 1824, Ashbel Smith was initiated into Phi Beta Kappa, and he wore his key conspicuously for the rest of his life. He was also awarded the Berkelian Premium for having made the best showing on an examination in Latin and Greek literature, an honor which carried with it a prize of fifty dollars.[12]

The commencement exercises on September 8, 1824, lasted all day, with orations, dissertations, colloquies, disputes, and poetry recitations, interspersed with prayers and sacred music. After the noon break Ashbel and a friend presented a colloquy Ashbel had written on the true causes of the "obliquity of the Equator to the Ecliptic." In spite of the heaviness of the subject matter, it was treated with humor and lightness, and Ashbel had enough pride in it to send copies to friends and relatives.

In the class album of a friend Ashbel recorded these words on the value of their school days:

> Forget not then our childish hours,
> The spirit of our joys,
> Like music past and gathered flowers,
> Each fleeting hour destroys.
> Too lovely were they to be lost,
> And wisest they who prize them most.[13]

[12] *Historical Register of Yale University, 1701–1937.*
[13] Class Album, 1824, Yale University.

At nineteen, Ashbel Smith had two degrees from Yale, the A.B. and the A.M., but he was still not prepared for a profession, except as a teacher in the lower grades. Both law and medicine attracted him, but he and his parents agreed that while he was deciding on a career it would be good for him to earn his own living, for Henry and George would soon have college expenses, which would further strain the family budget.

When President Jeremiah Day of Yale received a request from Colonel Charles Fisher, a prominent citizen of Salisbury, North Carolina, to recommend a teacher for a "private and select" school there, he suggested Ashbel Smith, the Berkelian graduate of the year. The offer included traveling expenses to Salisbury, room and board, and three hundred dollars for the term. Ashbel agreed to accept the position for a year and after a brief vacation set out to travel by stagecoach and steamboat to North Carolina.

Soon after he left home, his mother, discovering that she had forgotten to pack the calomel and opium she had intended to give him, sent them after him by a family friend who expected to overtake Ashbel. Both remedies were widely used in the early nineteenth century, though calomel, through much abuse and overuse, had acquired a bad reputation. A piece of doggerel of about twelve verses and in many versions included this question about doctors:

> How many patients have they lost
> How many thousands they make ill
> Of poison, with their *Calomel?*

Phoebe suggested to Ashbel that if he took too much calomel he could take some opium to counteract its effects. She also advised him to take opium for his cough, saying that "a little will be good for your breast."

Salisbury, the county seat of Rowan County, North Carolina, had become an important trading post late in the eighteenth century. When Ashbel Smith arrived a quarter of a century later, he found a small town whose ancient trees shaded a few stately colonial mansions, including one that was a combination bank and residence. On the town square stood the courthouse, an imposing brick building erected in 1800. There were several inns, or ordinaries, the most fashionable of which were the Mansion House and the Rowan House, where George Washington had stayed overnight and where Andrew Jackson had gained a reputation for gambling and other sports during the time he roomed there while he was studying law in Salisbury. Situated on a small creek that connects with the Yadkin River, Salisbury offered natural attractions for outings from the city. Charles Fisher, who was to become Ashbel's mentor in politics, owned an entire city block, and the new teacher came to feel at home in the Fishers' elegant two-story home.

In his school Ashbel taught both sexes, and since most of his girl students were of Moravian ancestry, he sometimes referred to "My Moravian School for Young Ladies." He was a conscientious teacher who won the approval of parents and established lasting friendships with many of his students. When he left the position, his successor found himself judged by the high standards set by Ashbel and often heard a chorus of "Mr. Smith did so" or "Mr. Smith didn't do so."

One advantage of Ashbel's work was that he had time to pursue his own studies. He had decided on law as a career and began a reading program which included a thorough study of *Blackstone's Commentaries*. He intended to return to Yale to study law after he completed his teaching assignment.

Phoebe and Moses worried about the long distance that separated them from their son and wrote him letters that were affectionate and sometimes witty. At the end of a long sermonette about his health and conduct, Phoebe signed off, "Thus endeth the first lesson of your mother." Moses added a note beginning dryly, "I had calculated to give you some advice but your mother has wrote enough allready." Nevertheless, Moses proceeded to pass along to his son some Polonius-like counsel:

Keep out of loose company; beware of flattery; associate with none but those of respectability; use all mankind alike in alike situations and you will gain the good will and esteem of all; gain the esteem of your schollars by mildness and kind treatment; don't deprive yourself of things necessary but be prudent.

The letter was signed "Your most affectionate friends and parents."[14]

In a small community like Salisbury it was inevitable that the new schoolmaster would come to know most of the inhabitants. His intelligence and personal charm won him the friendship of some of the leading families in the town and in the county, including the Fishers, the Beards, the Craiges, and the Hendersons. He received frequent invitations to their homes, where political talk flowed as freely as the

[14] Moses and Phoebe Smith to Ashbel Smith, December 9, 1824.

tea. Colonel Charles Fisher, who served at various times as senator and as representative in the North Carolina General Assembly and as a representative in the United States Congress, was a natural leader. Long after he left Salisbury, Ashbel continued to exchange ideas on state and national affairs with the colonel.

As a schoolmaster Ashbel was looked up to by the citizens of the small community. It soon became known that he could be depended on to deliver a graceful speech on almost any subject on any occasion. Consequently, he was called upon to give the July 4 oration in 1825. His stirring speech was the first of many Fourth of July declamations that he would deliver during his long life, and it demonstrated his ability to use his knowledge of history to suit his purposes. Reminding his audience that America had gained her freedom not quite a half a century earlier, he contrasted the "happy" condition of Americans with that of Europeans. He told his listeners that one-ninth of Britain's population were paupers; that Spain was ruled by "an impotent imbecile," and that France still had a Bourbon "on her neck."[15] The speech was published in the *Salisbury Western Carolinian* and later copied in the Hartford papers—to the gratification of Ashbel's parents and relatives.

When his teaching year ended, Ashbel was invited to stay on with an increase in salary. He asked his parents: Should he teach another year, and, after that, should he choose law or medicine as a career? Moses advised against staying more than six months longer in Salisbury, but he declined to give his opinion on careers.

In accordance with his father's suggestion Ashbel decided to leave Salisbury at the end of the spring term in 1826. He had finally chosen his profession. Believing that the study of law was injuring his health, he made plans to return to Yale to take a medical degree. Colonel Fisher wrote Ashbel a letter of recommendation praising his management of the school and commenting that "all concerned most seriously regret his leaving us."

During the next year Ashbel read the medical texts required by the conventions of the state of Connecticut for a doctorate in medicine. In the summer he attended New York Hospital and literally lived on bread and water to save money for his graduate work. To gain further training, he served as an assistant apothecary at the Retreat for the Insane, near the home of an aunt in Hartford. In the fall of 1827 he was

---

[15] *Salisbury Western Carolinian*, July 12, 1825.

accepted as a medical student by Yale, where he again came under the influence of the great scientist Benjamin Silliman.

One enduring friendship that Ashbel formed at this time was with Henry Barnard, whose family were also natives of Hartford. Since Ashbel was six years older than Barnard, their acquaintance in their earlier years had been slight, but now the two young men found that they had a great deal in common. Their correspondence over the years reveals the complete trust and confidence they had in each other. Ashbel's comment to a mutual friend summed up his opinion of Henry Barnard: "He has the best balanced head and heart of all our acquaintances. [Henry] combines so happily the utilitarian, the practical, philanthropic and liberal gentleman."[16]

While he was at Yale, Ashbel kept his ties with Salisbury. He corresponded with former students, who wrote to him affectionately, giving him news of his friends in North Carolina and asking for further direction in their studies. He answered them thoughtfully and in detail, always urging the importance of a thorough grounding in the liberal arts no matter what career they intended to pursue.

Two of his former students who came to Yale under his sponsorship, Archibald Henderson and Warren Huie, caused him problems. Both boys were eventually suspended for misbehavior. Ashbel tactfully wrote to the Huies that Warren's chief fault was "too much playfulness and lack of attention to his books," adding that his dismissal was caused by "some boyish actions, committed in the exuberance of good feelings on his birthday night." That Warren had a pretty sister named Antoinette undoubtedly had something to do with the interest Ashbel took in the wayward scholar.

To help pay his expenses, Ashbel did some part-time secretarial work in President Day's office. His precise, graceful handwriting probably helped him obtain the position. His friends often commented on his beautiful writing, and even in his old age it remained firm and handsome.

As Ashbel became more engrossed in the study of medicine, he felt lifted out of his previous self-concern and rejoiced that he was outgrowing the "moody melancholy that formerly preyed upon my happiness." In addition to his medical courses he studied French to improve his fluency for his own satisfaction.

[16] Ashbel Smith to George Bulkley, February 2, 1839.

A Mind on the Stretch

In the spring of 1828, Ashbel received his M.D. degree from Yale in a ceremonious commencement, which he described as a "dog" affair to a friend. After graduation he continued his studies at the Retreat for the Insane in Hartford to gain practical training while he looked around for a place to practice. The retreat, one of the first private establishments in the country for the care of the mentally ill, had an excellent reputation. If he had been able to secure a permanent position at the asylum, Ashbel might have settled in his hometown for life, for at that time he had more interest in mental illness than in any other branch of medicine. In his journal he wrote a description of the scene in the public room of the institution that shows his power of observation and his ability to dramatize—both himself and the patients:

> I saw the exulting maniac, imagining himself a king, commanding & directing every person & thing he met with—everything he saw belonged to him and every person was his subject. I saw another stealing away in moody melancholy, shunning everybody, frequently bursting into tears—& seeming desirous to escape from himself—I was particularly affected by the case of one—he noticed no one—talked incessantly. 'Twas the last ebbing of an expiring intellect—mere fragments of ideas mingled with single words in undistinguishable confusion. . . . I exclaimed with Lear "I would not be mad, Sweet Heaven, not mad."[17]

Ashbel's experiences at the retreat may have encouraged him to throw off his fits of depression, but they did not help him subdue his quick temper. One day while he was taking a walk, he was bitten by a dog. Outraged by the unprovoked attack, he beat the dog so hard that he killed it, and was fined for destroying an animal belonging to another person. A friend in Salisbury sympathized with Ashbel, rendering his judgment that it had been an act of "justifiable dogicide."

Colonel Fisher wrote to Ashbel asking him to return to Salisbury to practice his profession and as an added incentive offered him the opportunity to teach part time until his medical practice became profitable. With this added inducement Ashbel considered the opportunity a promising one, and in the late summer of 1828 he set off once more to seek his fortune in Salisbury. His parents did not try to persuade him to stay in Hartford but told him, ". . . we know your mind is ever on the stretch and if not well employed is rather on the down

---

[17] Ashbel Smith Journal, n.d., Ashbel Smith Papers, Barker Texas History Center, University of Texas, Austin.

cast." As Ashbel headed south once more, he expected to become a permanent resident of the Old North State.

With Ashbel's return to Salisbury in the role of physician he became the subject of careful scrutiny by the villagers. His physical appearance was not particularly distinguished. At twenty-four he was slender, five feet six inches, with prominent ears and a long face dominated by a rather large nose. His most attractive features were his chestnut hair and his hazel eyes, which had a piercing quality that sometimes caused acquaintances mistakenly to call them black. In dress he was neat and conventional, and he usually carried a cane. A great asset, and one he had learned to use well, was his vibrant voice. Its resonant tones, combined with his eloquence, could stir an audience to feelings of patriotism or make them quail under a scathing denunciation. The warmth of his hearty handshake and his sincere interest in others attracted people of all ages to him.

As usual, his parents were concerned about him. Moses wrote warning him to avoid dueling "above all," and Phoebe worried about his health and that he might ride his horses too fast and have an accident. Caroline kept Ashbel informed of the Hartford gossip and reported the news that their half-brother, Curtis, had a son and Ashbel was now an uncle.

Ashbel, who had strict ideas concerning the behavior of young ladies, warned his sister to beware of flatterers. Out of his medical knowledge came the advice to loosen her stays for the sake of her lungs, and she reported to him that she felt more energetic and healthier after doing so. In the midst of her new life she did not want him to forget her and told him, "When the memory of your sister steals over you, may you think of her as one who will never cease to love you."

While he sat in his room in Salisbury with his feet propped up against his chimney, waiting for the knock of a patient on his door or a summons to a sickbed, Ashbel passed the time reading medical books, studying languages, or entertaining friends. After a few months passed, he began making a modest living, but he felt an increasing dissatisfaction with his situation. He realized that the prospect of earning a very good income in his profession was limited unless he could obtain more training. He thought of returning to Hartford to practice and perhaps attending school in New York. Moses wrote: ". . . you know that here is a home for you at any and all times & in all circumstances."

Moses even built an office, intended for Ashbel's use, on the front of the family house. Hartford, however, was overstocked with physicians, some of whom were barely earning their expenses.

Ashbel considered other possibilities. He could move to New Orleans or to Mobile, Alabama. Or he might join the French army. The outbreak of the Revolution of 1830 in France led him to believe that there might be a war in Europe, and being involved in it appealed to him. Prudently he did not reveal this idea to his parents but tried it out on a friend, who agreed that Ashbel with his "contempt of danger might win glorious fame" by this route. Ashbel continued to postpone making a decision, however.

In the fall of 1830 he noted the passing of his twenty-fifth year by beginning again the journal that he kept intermittently over many years. On a clean page he outlined a plan for his life:

I am now a man in the prime of life & of intellectual vigor. This is the time to make those acquisitions in knowledge which shall conduct me to competency & fame. Much time is now at my command—I will waste no more of it on trifles. Every night shall find me having made some acquisition in medical knowledge—some advancement in Latin, Greek or French literature & by the grace of God, some moral improvement. Light, miscellaneous reading shall occupy but little of my time.

There shall be more *certainty* in my information.

Truth. I will always speak the truth—even in jest—nay more, I will not jest—Many good friends have been separated by words uttered in jest. Perhaps a person never attempts to jest i.e. to throw ridicule on an esteemed friend.

Temperance. I will be more temperate in eating. Satiety oppresses & torpifies the intellect.

Silence. When I have nothing to say I will say nothing.

Propriety. My conversation shall always be chaste—no obscene allusions—no profanity—language always elegant & grammatical in defiance of the sneers of the ignorant.

Punctuality. In this I often fail—letter writing.

Courteous to all, servile to none.

Conduct to Patients—I will be as attentive to the needy & helpless as to the rich & powerful.

Will God in his goodness grant me his grace to observe the preceding determinations.—Amen.[18]

During the winter of 1830, Ashbel suffered a serious illness, probably malaria, with fever lasting several days. His inability to think

---

[18] Ashbel Smith Journal, October 25, 1830.

clearly and the delusions he suffered during the bouts of fever alarmed him and conjured up visions of what it would be like to be mad—a fate he thought would be the "most exquisite" of all tortures. To his great relief he was feeling himself again by mid-January.

Ashbel was popular with people of his own age and stood as groomsman to several friends. His wit and chivalrous manners toward women made him a desirable guest, and he frequently attended teas, balls, weddings, and dinner parties. In the spring of 1830 he began visiting Warren Huie's sister, Antoinette, frequently. She was extremely romantic, a quality that intrigued him, even though he considered her too sentimental. One of their pastimes was reading and discussing books, though he found some that she recommended "sickeningly stupid." He was baffled by the charm she had for him because, as he told Henry Barnard, "I feel neither love nor lust for her," and he shared with her one of his darkest secrets.

Ashbel and his male friends made the conventional distinction between "pure" women and those who were not. The word "sex" had not yet come to have the meaning D. H. Lawrence would give it, and Ashbel often used the term "the sex" to refer to women. On February 21 he had penned a cryptic entry in his journal: "I made a compromise with Peter T——— for a release from all responsibility on account of his daughter's bastard, by giving him two notes for $30 each."[19] He confessed his "sin of passion" to his brother Henry and to Antoinette. Henry condemned his behavior severely, and Ashbel replied that in Henry's "castigatory epistle" he found cause for rejoicing because "the severity where withal you lash some vices over my back is a pleasing evidence of the detestation in which you hold them. . . . I see clearly the dark and rotten parts of my conduct."[20]

Still searching for a way to improve his situation, he considered accepting a job as a physician among the miners at a place called Gold Hill, about twelve miles south of Salisbury. He went so far as to visit the mines and asked his family's opinion of the opportunity. Moses very much disliked the idea, and brother Henry warned Ashbel that rumors had it that the mines were not making a profit, adding that he did not expect Ashbel to pay attention to his advice, for he doubted that Ashbel would take the counsel of an "angel." Moses suggested that

[19] Ibid., February 2, 1831.
[20] Ashbel Smith to Henry G. Smith, April 10, 1831.

Ashbel come home for a time and then decide what to do. Ashbel followed his father's advice and left Salisbury for Hartford about the middle of May.

In Hartford, Ashbel visited his many relatives and friends, read a great deal, and studied Latin with Henry Barnard. He was delighted by an exhibition of ventriloquism and wrote a long analysis of the physical mechanism involved in the process.[21]

He wrote a long letter to Antoinette, describing the new fashions of "low bosoms without chemisettes" and short dresses "that show the hosiery." Commenting on the books for sale in New York and Boston, he called them "the wildest, strangest, the most prurient and incestuous." He told her that he had had several *affaires du coeur* but assured her they had left no permanent traces. At the end he expressed surprise at himself for writing such a letter to a lady, but he nevertheless sent it, asking her to burn it after she read it. He made a copy of it in his journal.[22]

On August 13 he noted the passing of his twenty-sixth year with a prayer that rather peremptorily commanded: "God! Have mercy on me. Direct me in the path of Virtue. Continue to me that good health wherewithal I have been blessed for some years."[23]

After several family conferences it was decided that the best plan was for Ashbel to obtain more medical training, especially in surgery. In the early nineteenth century the mecca for medical students was Paris, where the world's most brilliant scientists practiced and taught the latest techniques and skills. Passage to Europe on a small freighter was cheap, and a single male student of frugal tastes could live abroad inexpensively. Moses, who was again town constable, generously agreed to finance the trip, for he and Phoebe were sure that their oldest son would not waste the opportunity.

In August, Ashbel went to New York City to arrange for his passage to France. While he waited, he visited New York Hospital regularly and read medical books. With the Seymours and his cousin Lydia Avery, he went sightseeing, toured museums, and attended the theater. One evening Ashbel made a visit alone to the "five points" (red-light) district in New York. He was horrified by the degradation:

[21] Ashbel Smith Journal, June 29, 1831.
[22] Ashbel Smith to Antoinette Huie, July 12, 1831.
[23] Ashbel Smith Journal, August 13, 1831.

". . . blacks and whites, sailors and landsmen, hes and shes all jumbled together. . . . the females are tenfold worse than the men."[24]

Characteristically he seized every opportunity to gain new experiences. In contrast to the sordidness of the red-light district was the sublimity of a trip to Bunker Hill that he made on the Fourth of July. The journey evoked feelings that he described in poetic language:

A silent, sober strong swelling emotion seemed to pervade my whole body—my soul within me seemed enlarging and I felt a rich quiet & haughty pride in being one of the same race with those who 50 years ago fought where I was then standing. The very soles of my feet burned as tho I were treading on holy ground.[25]

Ashbel's last concern before leaving the States was to pack his books carefully and leave them with his Uncle Seymour in New York. Then he was free to go.

[24] Ashbel Smith to Henry Barnard, September 13, 1831.
[25] Ashbel Smith to J. Beard, Jr., n.d. (ca. September 15, 1831).

─◆{ CHAPTER TWO }◆─

Paris Interlude
(1831–1836)

EARLY in the afternoon of October 12, 1831, Ashbel sailed for France on the *Mary Howland*, a ship of 575 tons. On the second day out he became seasick and continued to suffer for several days. With clinical precision he noted his symptoms, for which he prescribed exercise in the open air on the deck and a moderate diet. After twenty days at sea he arrived in France and took lodgings in Paris in the Rue et Hotel Corneille near the Odéon.

"Paris has on me the effect of magic," he wrote to his friend Eugene Rousseau in North Carolina. He felt overwhelmed as he remembered that Caesar had stood where he was standing and had described the scene before him. He had letters of introduction to Rousseau's French relatives and friends, who gave the newcomer a cordial welcome to their city homes and country estates and also furnished him with an entry into Parisian society. In addition he had a number of letters of introduction to men of importance in the professions. Some of them he had solicited from people like President Day of Yale and his Uncle Seymour, who was a well-known New York merchant.

Ashbel ironically contrasted his present situation with his recent past, telling a friend, "When in America I sighed . . . after opportunities for improvement; here on the contrary I have only to regret that I can avail myself of but few comparatively of the almost innumerable facilities which this metropolis affords." He was aware that he was studying with some of the medical immortals of France, including the distinguished pioneer surgeons Baron Guillaume Dupuytre and Jacques Lisfranc.

Among his other outstanding professors were Baron Dominique

Jean Larrey, the military surgeon who, serving under Napoleon Bonaparte, had introduced field hospitals and first aid on the battlefield; Charles Alexander Louis, the founder of medical statistics; François Magendie, a pioneer in experimental physiology; Claude Récamier, a noted gynecologist; Baron Georges Cuvier, the founder of comparative anatomy and paleontology; and René Laennec, the inventor of the stethoscope, who is considered the father of chest medicine.

Ashbel was impressed by the intensity with which these learned men pursued their medical careers. He told his cousin Daniel: "They whom science has crowned with its honors & threescore & ten sprinkled with its snows are no less industrious than they who have but commenced their career. Barons Larrey and Dupuytren etc. examine their patients in the hospitals by candlelight in the morning."[1] He was also impressed by the bickering among these distinguished scientists, listening in amazement as Lisfranc publicly called Dupuytren a "brigand" and labeled his writings "vomit from the water front." Dupuytren answered the outburst by retorting that Lisfranc had the "heart of a grovelling dog." But the personal animosities of these geniuses did not affect their medical ability, and Ashbel eagerly absorbed as much as he could of their knowledge and techniques.

He settled into a strenuous round of activity in the wards, lecture rooms, and operating theaters of the various hospitals, including the Hôtel Dieu, La Pitié, Necker Hospital, and Hôpital des Invalides, and at the École de Medicine and the Sorbonne—from six in the morning until five in the afternoon. At times he endured physical discomfort in his pursuit of knowledge: the scramble for a seat at a lecture by a particularly well known doctor might result in torn clothes and bruises. On one icy January day he was forced to stand for three hours in a cold, blustery wind waiting for the hospital doors to open so that he could obtain a seat in the pit to observe an operation. After watching operations performed by master surgeons, he practiced the same operations on corpses, for which he paid five dollars. Except for this fee, the hospital facilities and equipment were available to him free of charge.

In spite of his heavy schedule of medical and surgical studies, he made time to see the sights of Paris—the gardens, palaces, museums—and to attend the opera and the theater.[2] One week he visited

[1] Ashbel Smith Journal, November 5, 1831.
[2] Ashbel Smith to Daniel Seymour, February 6, 1832.

a cheap dance hall, where for twelve and a half cents one could obtain a ticket that could be exchanged for three dances or two bottles of beer.[3] A few days later he attended a dazzling ball at which the king and queen of France and the queens of Spain and Portugal were honored guests. For Caroline's amusement he described the dress of the ladies at the ball. They "glistened with gold & diamonds & jewels . . . all glowing in more than noonday brightness in the floods of light from huge lustres," he wrote, adding, "How I should have rejoiced to have promenaded before them all with you on my arm, dressed as plainly as when we used to walk to church."[4]

In his concern that he would not take every advantage of his opportunities, he worked to perfect his French, taking lessons and working at translations on his own. From time to time he resolved to spend less time with Americans and more with French friends. He studied French politics and watched individuals, trying to "penetrate the character of the nation." He observed that, although the French did things on the street that were not done on American streets, they were very private in their family circles. He noted that the present ministry was "deservedly unpopular" and concluded that in exchanging Charles X for Louis Philippe the government had gone from a "profligate to a pusillanimous & avaricious despotism." A decade later, when he returned to France as minister from Texas, his opinion of Louis Philippe changed radically, after he came to know the king personally. Perhaps his earlier impression was influenced by the ideas of Lafayette, for whom Ashbel had an immense admiration.

A few years before Ashbel was born, Lafayette had visited Hartford with George Washington and had received all the honors the city elders could bestow on him. When Ashbel's countryman James Fenimore Cooper introduced the venerable statesman to him in France, Lafayette was a legendary character of seventy-six, feared by his political opponents and beloved by the common people. He struck Ashbel as having a "noble simplicity" and one of the "largest hearts ever put into man." Ashbel concluded that English historians and authors such as Thomas Macaulay and Sir Walter Scott had dealt harshly with him.[5]

---

[3] Ashbel Smith Journal, December 25, 1831.
[4] Ashbel Smith to Caroline Smith, January 31, 1832.
[5] Ashbel Smith to John Beard, February 23, 1832.

To see and hear other political "lions," Ashbel visited the Chamber of Deputies. To make sure that he did not miss anything, he also visited the worst slums, as he had in New York. The drunkenness and prostitution in Paris astonished him. He was frequently accosted by streetwalkers with whom he sometimes bantered, but he felt pity for these wretched women, many with venereal diseases, who were treated like animals when they were examined by callous medical students in the hospitals. Ashbel was continually shocked by the French lack of concern for the dignity or privacy of patients, particularly women. When a fellow doctor uncovered a moribund woman simply to show Ashbel the shapeliness of her figure, the startled New Englander commented that France was the only country where such an incident could happen.

Frenchwomen were attracted by Ashbel's "whiteness," and several friends urged him to take a mistress to live with him in his chambers. One medical student brought a cousin for Ashbel to consider as a possible mistress, and another brought his sister. Ashbel resisted their overtures; however, in the free-and-easy atmosphere of the pre-Lenten carnival, he and the other young medical students attended masked balls and some of the wild street celebrations, where they participated in the sport of "kidnapping" young women for several hours.

Early in his stay in Paris Ashbel met the American novelist James Fenimore Cooper, who had also attended Yale. Cooper was on an extended stay in Europe, where he was seeing to the education of his son and four daughters. The two men became friends, and Ashbel spent many evenings in the Coopers' comfortable home in the rue Saint Domique, quartier Saint-Germain, dining with the family and spending long hours of talk with the famous writer. Ashbel disputed the popular conception of Cooper as eccentric and conceited, characterizing him as "a well bred gentleman, utterly fearless, a man of information extensive & minute, of strong common sense tho' a *romancier*."[6]

One of Cooper's favorite projects was the Polish Committee, a group organized for the purpose of giving moral and tangible support to Polish refugees of the Russo-Polish War huddled, starving and almost naked, in military enclosures. Americans sent shiploads of food and clothing for the Poles, consigning them to Lafayette for distri-

---

[6] Ashbel Smith to W. Hall, February 25, 1832.

bution. He in turn organized some of his American friends into the Polish Committee to direct the distribution. In addition to Lafayette and Cooper, another Yale man, Samuel F. B. Morse (who had already won acclaim as a painter) was a member of the group. Ashbel Smith felt honored to be accepted into the organization, which met in Cooper's home on Wednesday evenings.

After the business of the committee was concluded, the four men discussed the affairs of the world. Ashbel listened avidly to the ideas of the three older men, occasionally breaking in with a remark or an inquiry. Later he was surprised to recall his own temerity in such distinguished company.

Early in April, 1832, there was a violent outbreak of cholera in Paris. By mid-April the official bulletin was listing fifteen hundred new cases a day. During the first few days of the epidemic most of the victims were members of the lowest classes of the approximately one million inhabitants of Paris. This fact was so evident that people of the afflicted classes refused to believe that a disease was killing them and accused the government of being in league with the physicians in a plot to poison them all. For two or three days they were in a state of frenzy. Mobs roamed the streets and threw horses, carriages, and even human beings into the Seine River. The doors of the hospitals were besieged and had to be guarded night and day by armed soldiers. Some people, pretending to be sick, sent for physicians and attacked their supposed poisoners.[7]

Most Americans fled the city, but Ashbel and a fellow student and friend, Dr. James Jackson, Jr., of Boston, stayed on to help. Ashbel was appointed an extern at Necker Hospital, where nearly all the patients admitted with the disease died. The bodies of the dead were piled naked in a room until relatives could claim them. Ashbel himself had a light attack of cholera, with symptoms of diarrhea and colic that lasted three days. As soon as he recovered, he returned to Necker, where he spent long off-duty hours performing autopsies, trying to learn the nature of the disease. When Cooper's daughter Fanny contracted a mild form of cholera, Ashbel treated her successfully.

In May, after the disease abated, Ashbel left for England for a month's rest, but it was hardly a vacation. He spent most of his time at

[7] Ashbel Smith, *The Cholera Spasmodica in Paris in 1832*.

New Bethlehem Hospital studying mental diseases, and in his leisure hours he was so involved with "curiosities, society, theaters, and the houses of parliament" that he hardly had time to sleep. "I am completely exhausted," he wrote Barnard. He listened carefully to speeches by Sir Robert Peel and Thomas Macaulay, and he also listened carefully to the speech of the people on the streets, making notes on the differences he found in American and English use of his native language.[8]

Back in Paris, Ashbel gave a Fourth of July party for his American friends. Then he set to work writing a pamphlet in which he discussed the symptoms, pathology, and treatment of cholera. He illustrated his points by describing the cases he had observed, declaring in his preface: "I have described no symptom, no post mortem appearance, no treatment, which I have not myself witnessed."[9] The pamphlet (which he dedicated "To my father") was praised by eminent medical men for its painstaking detail and rational presentation, in which the author made no extravagant claims concerning treatments or cures.

Ashbel Smith became known in medical circles as something of an authority on cholera, and he had the satisfaction of being publicly thanked by the director of Necker Hospital for the service he had rendered during the epidemic. He made no profit from the sales of his booklet. By the time it was printed, the cholera scare in the United States had passed, and there was little market for it.

As Ashbel's frequent visits to the Coopers' home continued, he found himself greatly attracted to Cooper's daughter Susan. He began to dream of her and to include her in his plans for the future. "What shall I do? I am afraid I am on the point of acting very foolishly in the case of Miss Susan," he wrote in his journal. But he felt he had nothing to offer her—neither wealth nor fame. He decided to allow himself three years to become worthy of her and vowed: "Every day shall bear testimony of something learned or some good deed performed. I will have to leave my children what I never received, a name."

Meanwhile, friends in Salisbury were writing Ashbel that his patients were anxiously awaiting his return. An epidemic of scarlet fever had caused several deaths, and they feared an outbreak of cholera. One correspondent told him, "A great many think . . . that they would be

---

[8] Ashbel Smith to Henry Barnard, May 25, 1832.
[9] Smith, *Cholera Spasmodica*.

perfectly safe if you were only back."[10] Ashbel's funds were getting low. He had even borrowed money from Samuel Morse (which he later repaid), and he hated to draw on Moses for more money. Therefore, although he wanted badly to stay longer in France and "burned" to see Italy, he wrote to his friends in North Carolina asking them to insert an announcement in the Salisbury paper announcing his return by early fall.

The year that Ashbel Smith spent in Europe influenced the rest of his life. He had improved his medical knowledge and skills under the greatest living physicians and had come through the trial by fire of the cholera epidemic. He had added valuable medical books to his library, though he lamented that he could not afford many that he would have liked to own. He had written a well-received medical pamphlet. He had witnessed history in the making by the most distinguished legislators in France and England. He had hobnobbed with the legendary Lafayette and had made lasting friendships with such men as Cooper and Morse and with many American doctors. He had experienced with all of his considerable emotional and intellectual capacities the cultures of the two countries, including their languages. And he had acquired a permanent infatuation with travel. Last but not least to his thinking, he had fallen in love.

By the end of September, Ashbel was again in North Carolina. He put the plaster casts of Venus de Medici and Apollo Belvedere, which he had bought in Paris, in his room, where they could scandalize by their nudity his friends who were "delicate beyond what is required."

Immediately he put his new skills to work, taking three medical students to train in dissection and other techniques, giving lectures on anatomy and surgery to groups of half a dozen students preparing to enter medical school, and keeping a casebook describing his own dissections. He found himself in demand for all kinds of operations as word spread of the surgical training he had acquired in Paris.

New medical books were sent to him occasionally by friends in New York and London, and he wrote reviews of some of them. His reviews were published in medical journals such as the *Cyclopedia of Practical Medicine and Surgery* and the *American Journal of the Medical Sciences*. He had met Dr. Isaac Hays, the editor of the latter journal, in Paris. Over the years they corresponded and sometimes visited

---

[10] Will M. Locke to Ashbel Smith, September 4, 1832.

when Ashbel was in Philadelphia. Between 1835 and 1838, Ashbel was listed as a collaborator in the journal. His reports included successful operations for rectovaginal fistula, depressed fracture of the skull, malignancy of the eye, and cancer of the breast.[11]

He bought the best medical equipment available to him, sending to Europe for some of his instruments. In certain areas of medicine he was handicapped by the limitations of knowledge of his time. Although he agreed with the controversial theory that cholera and yellow fever were not contagious, he shared and originated some of the bizarre ideas concerning the causes of intermittent fevers—particularly concerning malaria or "marsh miasmata"—blaming the disease on emanations from the drying of green timber, the burning of green logs, or the plowing of virgin soil. The vehicle of the malarious influences he thought was dampness or moisture, which was most dangerous at sunset or dawn.[12]

Ashbel's patience was often tried by rural patients who were uneducated and superstitious. Sometimes there was a mixture of danger and humor in his encounters. One day he was called to the home of a man who was drinking peach brandy and "talking political nonsense." The man had his servant bring pistols with the intent of shooting the doctor, who later described the scene: "He hugged me, cursed me, called me honest (and a viper), struck me, & said he hoped I would marry his cousin." Ashbel concluded, "I pray to God to preserve me from the dreadful folly of drunkenness."[13]

When a call took him some distance into the country, Ashbel often spent one or more nights at the patient's home, in this way developing a more intimate relationship with the patient and the family than would have been possible in the formal atmosphere of an office or a hospital. Sometimes whole weeks went by when he did not sleep at home. One day, on the way to visit a patient, he had a bad accident. While he was attempting to ford a swollen river, his horse and sulky were swept downstream, and he barely escaped drowning. He considered himself fortunate that he was only bruised and sore, even though he lost his watch, extra clothing, and instruments.[14]

[11] Pat Ireland Nixon, *The Medical Story of Early Texas, 1528–1853*, p. 330.
[12] "Memorandum concerning the Climate of Rowan and the Adjacent Counties," n.d., Ashbel Smith Papers.
[13] Ashbel Smith Journal, January 29, 1831.
[14] Ashbel Smith to Henry Barnard, August 23, 1833.

Paris Interlude

As his popularity increased, so did his income. Soon he was making the respectable sum of about $2,500 a year. Nevertheless, he again began experiencing deep dissatisfaction with his situation. "Here I am with a large practice to be sure," he told Barnard, "but every way cramped." In his leisure time he studied medical literature and translated French works into English, as well as parts of the New Testament from the Greek. He studied the Cherokee language and sent a copy of the *Cherokee Phoenix*, which was written partly in English and partly in Cherokee, to Sir Anthony Carlisle in England, commenting, "Though the printed language . . . is not very handsome, yet it is the model of a perfect language—each character has a single determinate sound, & for every sound in the language there is one and only one character."[15]

All natural phenomena interested Ashbel. One clear December night, returning late from a visit to a patient some distance from Salisbury, he saw a spectacular meteoric display. He wrote an account of it for the *Western Carolinian* and sent a copy of the article to Professor Denison Olmsted at Yale.[16]

When Henry Barnard planned a trip in the spring of 1833 that would take him to Washington, D.C., and through Salisbury on his way to visit some of the southern states, Ashbel was delighted. The friendship between the two men was very close: Barnard told Ashbel things he revealed to no one else. Although he was an eloquent public speaker, Barnard's diffidence was so overpowering that he sometimes felt paralyzed in social situations. Ashbel told him that "a right goodly share of modest assurance much promotes our 'comfortable getting along in this world'" and urged him to meet the political "lions" in Washington, citing his own experience that "hours of intercourse with those whom the world considers as its mighty intellects" is more worthwhile than "months of mere closet study." Ashbel also sent Barnard letters of introduction to prominent acquaintances in all the cities that Barnard would visit and procured other letters from his political friends.[17]

The visit was a great success, though at times Barnard doubted whether he would survive the "cursed roads" over which he had to travel to reach Salisbury. He accompanied Ashbel on trips in the coun-

---

[15] Ashbel Smith to Sir Anthony Carlisle, 1832.
[16] Ashbel Smith to Professor Olmsted, December 29, 1833.
[17] Ashbel Smith to Henry Barnard, January 8, 1833; January 25, 1833.

try to look after patients and observed that many of the slaves lived better than did the poor whites. The two friends also visited local attractions such as the natural basaltic rock wall five miles from the town. Barnard was impressed by the homes of Ashbel's friends, especially those of the Fishers, the Hendersons, and the Huies, and by their libraries and their hospitality.

It may have been on this visit that Barnard became infected with Ashbel's enthusiasm for foreign travel. At any rate, he was soon planning a trip abroad and asking Ashbel's advice, urging him to "think for me as you would for a younger brother." Ashbel, of course, gladly complied, telling Henry, among other things, to "learn the language, spend some time in the provinces, live in the quartier St. Germain and attend the Sorbonne and Ecole de Droit."[18]

Ashbel was living comfortably in Salisbury. He kept three horses, owned a "very fine" sulky, and had a Negro girl and boy to look after his needs. He added a room to his chambers to make them "more genteel and comfortable." George came to stay in Salisbury to study medicine with Ashbel to prepare to enter Yale. At first George caused his older brother considerable anxiety. But after a few months Ashbel told a friend with relief that George was growing rapidly, adding, "He studies more & thinks of unripe girls less than formerly."

Always enticed by politics, Ashbel became embroiled in the campaigns of his friends John Beard and Charles Fisher for the state legislature. The heat of the campaign brought an estrangement between Ashbel and several former friends, including Antoinette Huie's father. Ashbel's emphatic and didactic manner of denouncing politicians with whom he disagreed made bitter enemies for him, and several insulting pamphlets were issued against him.

Through his political activities Ashbel became a regular contributor to the *Western Carolinian*, a nullification paper. He eventually became half owner and editor of the paper. On March 7, 1835, a notice appeared on the editorial page addressed "To Our Patrons," informing them that Ashbel Smith and Joseph W. Hampton were the new proprietors of the paper. Readers were assured that the political character of the paper would undergo no change; that is, that it would continue a "bold advocacy of a strict construction of the Federal Constitution &

[18] Ashbel Smith to Henry Barnard, 1835.

Paris Interlude

consequently of the rights of states."[19] Ashbel used the editorial page to express his violent opposition to Andrew Jackson and Martin Van Buren, and he campaigned vigorously against them in the elections. The tariff issue in South Carolina concerned him deeply, as it did many North Carolinians. "The tariff *must be repealed*," he declared, "or there will be a dissolution of our glorious union." Owner Smith also made use of the paper for other than political purposes, using its columns to advertise that he was the agent for selling such apothecary items as "Doctor Price's Metalic Truss."

The legal and moral right of southerners to own slaves had become an increasingly heated issue ever since England had passed legislation in the early 1830s freeing its slaves. Ashbel wrote his views in an open letter in which he urged that southerners be allowed to resolve the problems involved with slavery without interference from the North. The letter, which was published in the Boston papers and in the *Washington National Intelligencer* under the title "Slavery and the Probability of Any Interference with It as Now Existing in the Southern States by the Abolitionists in the North," was credited by Henry Barnard as having a calming effect in "helping to give public sentiment a right direction." It was the first shot in a long war Ashbel Smith would wage with the abolitionists.

As was common in other small southern towns, the Protestant churches in Salisbury shared their ministers and sometimes their buildings for services. On Sundays, Ashbel attended church services frequently in the mornings and afternoons at the Episcopal, Presbyterian, Methodist, or Lutheran churches, and in the evenings after supper, he usually read from the Bible or from a book of sermons. He considered himself a student of the Bible but not a "religionist," in the sense of accepting exclusively the theology of one Protestant group over all the others. Nevertheless, he enjoyed discussions with the Reverend John Morgan, rector of Saint Luke's Episcopal Church, and became a member of that church on June 16, 1833, when he was baptized by the rector and confirmed by Bishop Levi Silliman Ives.[20]

Although he did not consider himself permanently settled in Salisbury, when a farm with forty Negro slaves was offered for sale at a low

---

[19] Editorial, *Western Carolinian*, February 28, 1835, microfilm, Salisbury Public Library.

[20] Ashbel Smith Journal, n.d. (ca. June 20, 1833).

price, Ashbel decided to buy it as an investment and became a land- and slaveowner. He continued to fret, however, that "so much of my time is spent unprofitably." Mobile, New Orleans, Nashville—all appealed to him as more "respectable theaters for exertion" than Salisbury. One of his reasons for hesitating to move any farther from Hartford was that Caroline might in some way need his help. As long as she remined single, he felt an obligation and a desire to be available to "my dear sister."

In spite of a resolve to stay out of local civic affairs, Ashbel was appointed a magistrate and ex officio a justice of the Court of Pleas and Quarter for Rowan County. In this capacity he frequently performed marriage ceremonies. As he approached thirty, he thought seriously, even a little desperately, of his own bachelorhood. "I am strongly possessed with the general determination to wed," he told Barnard. He often thought of Susan Cooper, but with less passion than before, and reasoned, "If I were fortunate enough to wed her . . . I must live in New York City—it would require exhaustless resources of mind to satisfy her; & with all my self-complacency I cannot regard myself as equal to this." Yet, he asked Barnard to sound out Dr. Eli Todd, director of the Retreat for the Insane, on the possibility of serving as a resident for a few years at the retreat to study "mind diseases." Ashbel added, "I have another reason which you will readily conjecture for wishing to be in the vicinity of New York."[21]

Meanwhile, Ashbel's ambiguous relationship with Antoinette Huie continued, even after her father refused to speak to him because of their political differences. Just before leaving on an extended trip to New Orleans with her family, Antoinette gave him a set of gold studs with his name engraved on them. "Antoinette is gone to New Orleans with all her sentiment—God bless her," he commented to Barnard.

In the spring of 1835, however, Ashbel met a young woman who made him forget that he had ever had romantic feelings for any other. He wrote his sister, Caroline, rhapsodically describing Mary Louisa Phifer, of Carbarras County: a beauty of good background, highly gifted and well educated and an heiress with twenty thousand dollars in her own right. *And* he believed that she returned his feelings. Rashly he told Antoinette of his love for Mary, and she jealously tried to convince him that he could not marry her. Antoinette's argument

---

[21] Ashbel Smith to Henry Barnard, October 12, 1833.

was that Mary was a "widow," because Mary had made a promise to a suitor as he lay dying that she would never marry. That pledge, according to Antoinette, made Mary ineligible to marry, since a person could have only one "real" love. However much Ashbel may have been flattered by Antoinette's reaction, he remained unconvinced by her logic.[22]

In March, just before leaving for a visit to the North, he determined to ask Mary to be his wife. She neither accepted nor declined his offer, telling him they were still strangers, that it was too soon to consider marriage. Hurt and dismayed, Ashbel was swept by such violent and powerful emotions that everything else seemed unimportant. He begrudged every mile that took him farther from Mary and wrote her passionate love letters in which he poured out his love: "Oh! Mary, would that you could hold my heart in your hand."[23] He worshiped her with a devotion bordering on idolatry and found thoughts of her "mingled" with his prayers.

In New York he was invited to dine at the Coopers and went only after learning that Susan Cooper was not well and would not appear at dinner. He rejoiced that he had never made any declaration of his feelings to Susan. He assured Mary that what he had felt for Susan was an *incipient* regard, which had faded in the brilliant light of the flame of his love for Mary, assuring her: "My love all violent as it is I have offered to you, *pure* and *whole*. My whole existence is merged in one great eternal feeling and that is *you*."[24]

When he arrived in Hartford, he enjoyed the relief of being able to discuss endlessly the charms of Mary Phifer with his sympathetic sister. Each day he looked eagerly for a letter from Mary. He begged her for a note—only a few lines that would give him a tiny hope that she missed him a little and wanted him to return to her—but no word came.

From Boston he wrote to Mary describing the entertainments and honors he had received from members of the medical profession and from other distinguished people he met, such as Nathaniel Bowditch, whom he compared to Plato. His letter concluded:

Time, distance, brilliant & cultivated society, warm friends & serious studies, are so far from banishing you Mary from my memory even for a short time, that

---

[22] Ashbel Smith Journal, April 1, 1835.
[23] Ashbel Smith to Mary Phifer, March 31, 1835.
[24] Ashbel Smith to Mary Phifer, April 17, 1835.

everything would pale were it not for the hope & belief that you sometimes think of yours
    forever & devotedly,
        Ashbel Smith [25]

Although Mary had sent no word in answer to his passionate outpourings, when he returned from his trip, he went at once to her home. The meeting was strangely unsatisfactory for them both. The next day Ashbel wrote Mary, apologizing for acting "coldly," explaining that he felt "sick at heart" and had learned to discipline his feelings.[26] Literally and figuratively his passion had been spent. It was Mary's turn to be puzzled and hurt. To his friend Adrian Terry, Ashbel tried to rationalize the change in his feelings:

My plebeian pride (I record my own disgrace) was wounded, tortured, maddened into a whirlwind of passion. . . . Your kind words coming to the aid of my reason laid the storm . . . [he had visited Terry in New York]. But in its fury it had swept away alas! my love. . . . My heart was left vacant.[27]

He discontinued his visits to Carbarras. On July 21, Mary wrote him a cool farewell letter and returned a ring he had put on her finger. "We part as friends," she told him.[28]

Ashbel was as active as ever, increasing his studies and his writing, but he admitted to his close friends that he carried on a normal life with great effort, in spite of "broken heartstrings" and a "haunted" pillow. He intensified his efforts to remove himself from "this graveyard of energy, North Carolina," and asked friends to recommend him for the position of director of the Retreat for the Insane at Hartford, left vacant by the death of Dr. Todd. One of his supporters for the post was his old Yale professor and friend Dr. Silliman, who wrote regretfully to tell him that the position had been given to another doctor.

Adrian Terry, Henry Barnard, and other friends who knew of the affair, urged Ashbel to try to renew his relationship with Mary. But Ashbel had been deeply shaken by the effect his emotions had had upon him. He wrote to Terry: "You can't well conceive the deep mortification I feel, when I recollect how I was subdued, how my mind was palsied, my little bookish & worldly knowledge despised & forgotten,

---

[25] Ashbel Smith to Mary Phifer, May 18, 1835.
[26] Ashbel Smith to Mary Phifer, June 25, 1835.
[27] Ashbel Smith to Adrian Terry, June 26, 1835.
[28] Mary Phifer to Ashbel Smith, July 26, 1835.

& my heart filled with dark, bitter, brooding imaginations." He was determined that no one would ever again have that much power over him.

When Antoinette heard that he was back in Salisbury, she sent word to him that she was on her deathbed, but the next day when he visited her, he found her much improved and as amorous as ever. She continued to pursue him, and he continued to visit her frequently. Their relationship progressed to embraces and kisses, and she would willingly have let it go further. He resisted the temptation, however, even when she told him of her "pretty" dreams in which he seduced her. After an evening with her, he prayed, "Save me O God from compassing her present & perhaps her everlasting ruin—it would of necessity involve my own."[29]

In the late summer of 1835, Ashbel's income was augmented by his appointment as surgeon to the Sixty-third Regiment, North Carolina Militia. He soon found use for the extra money. Moses had not been reelected constable of Hartford, the family had pressing debts, and there was scarcely enough money to keep George in school. Ashbel sent his father all the money he could spare and suggested that the family could move with him to whatever location he settled in when he left Salisbury.

Even though Ashbel no longer visited Mary, they continued to write to each other occasionally. Both were proud and stubborn, and both overreacted to rumors and reports that gossips and friends spread about them. Each was afraid that the other did not feel enough; each was mortified at the idea of being the one who loved the most. Ashbel accused Mary of being liberal in taunts that he was indifferent, yet in the same letter he told her that he had "come to love to be alone and to feel alone."

In his frustration and unhappiness Ashbel felt a stronger need than ever to leave Salisbury. In early spring of 1836 he borrowed money and wandered over much of the southeastern United States, visiting his brother Henry in Mobile, exploring the "wilds of Mississippi," and spending some time in New Orleans. He invested money in public lands for himself and some of his friends, believing that he was making a "splendid" speculation.[30]

[29] Ashbel Smith Journal, November 27, 1835.
[30] Ashbel Smith to Henry Barnard, August 16, 1836.

While he was in New Orleans, Ashbel met a friend, James Pinckney Henderson, a North Carolinian from Lincolnton, who was on a recruiting mission for the Texas army. Henderson's enthusiasm for Texas and the bright picture he painted of opportunities for fame and fortune in the new republic began to turn Ashbel's thinking in that direction. In June, Henderson wrote Ashbel a long letter from Velasco, Texas, describing events following the Battle of San Jacinto. He added: "This is a most delightful country . . . richest land in the country . . . at the lowest prices. . . . As you are now likely to be a rambler for some time, prepare & accompany me out in the fall. . . . Do me the favor to enlist as many in our cause as possible."[31] Memucan Hunt, a major general in the Texas army, was also in North Carolina recruiting against the expected invasion of Texas by Mexican forces. He too wrote encouraging letters to Ashbel, urging him to join the Texas cause.[32]

At last Ashbel Smith had heard a call that appealed to his restless spirit. He would try Texas. He cautiously decided to keep his Salisbury property, however, so that he would have something to fall back on if the adventure did not live up to its billings. Delighted, Henderson promised: "You *shall* be surgeon general of our division or anything else we can give you . . . success, honor & fortune is sure." Ashbel's salary was to be $2,500 a year plus rations and twenty thousand acres of land.

The reaction from Ashbel's family was mixed. George was excited and thought it would be a splendid life. Moses was cautiously approving, and Phoebe warned about the dangers to his health. Caroline was trying to decide whether to marry Thomas Kittredge, a doctor, and she deeply regretted not being able to gain Ashbel's opinion of him, which she said would have "determined my course instantly."

On August 6, Ashbel got into an argument with an old political enemy, D. F. Caldwell, a former senator from North Carolina. The argument led to a street fight, which ended inconclusively, each man feeling that he had been the victor.[33] The next day Ashbel received a letter from General Hunt addressed to "Dr. A. Smith of the Texian Army," informing him that the president of the Republic of Texas had ordered all officers of the army to return to their posts and to duty.

[31] James Pinckney Henderson to Ashbel Smith, June 10, 1836.
[32] Memucan Hunt to Ashbel Smith, August 2, 1836.
[33] Ashbel Smith to Henry Barnard, August 16, 1836.

Hunt offered Ashbel the choice of going to Texas by land with General Henderson or by boat from Charleston.[34] Ashbel arranged for an overseer to look after his slaves and property and prepared to leave with Henderson and the Tennessee Volunteers on October 15. He was already thinking about Texas's problems:

> As a citizen of Texas and of the U.S., I shall oppose the annexation at all hazards. If Texas can "conquer" her independence from Mexico, no good reason will exist for an union under this gov't, except to prevent the evils of a conquest & forcible subjugation of it by ourselves. I will resist those long-armed companies in the cities who are clutching at Texas to make it tributary to themselves.[35]

At the end of October, Ashbel was still in Salisbury. His friends' objections to his departure during a season of "general unhealthiness" and the serious illness of the mother of his friend John Beard had detained him until it was too late for him to leave with the Tennessee Volunteers. Again Ashbel wavered about what he should do. He felt pangs of conscience about not coming to the aid of his family at a time when Caroline was appealing to him for advice and Moses was in a precarious financial condition. He wrote home offering to abandon his plans to go to Texas, telling Caroline to postpone her marriage until he could get to Hartford. His letter arrived too late, however. Caroline and Thomas Kittredge were married on October 24; Ashbel's letter arrived the next day.[36]

George, whose respect for his brother had soared when he learned of the Texas venture, now wrote impatiently: "You will lose an opportunity of distinguishing yourself (which you will never meet with again) to save an old woman 80 years old from the grave. . . . If you intend leaving Salisbury, leave, don't talk and do nothing, leave *immediately*, or *never*."[37]

Yet Ashbel continued to remain "buried in Salisbury," as he described his situation, trying to bring his affairs to a conclusion, gradually giving up seeing his rural patients and referring his town patients to other doctors. He worked with the Whig party to support Tyler and defeat Van Buren in the November election. He attended parties and

---

[34] Memucan Hunt to Ashbel Smith, August 7, 1836.
[35] Ashbel Smith to Henry Barnard, September 27, 1836.
[36] George A. Smith to Ashbel Smith, October 27, 1836.
[37] Ibid.

visited Antoinette Huie, who wept over his leaving and permitted him to comfort her with kisses and embraces. On the day he received the news of Caroline's marriage, he went to Antoinette's in a state of depression. "She is dead to me," he exclaimed to Antoinette, who promptly offered to be his sister.

In the meantime, Henderson had reached Texas with the Tennessee Volunteers. He wrote Ashbel an encouraging letter, telling him, "I have travelled over much of this delightful region & never did man's eyes behold such in any other portion of the earth." He described to Ashbel the qualities of the leaders of the Republic—Houston, Austin, Rusk, Henry Smith, Lamar—and asked Ashbel to have them noted in the *Western Carolinian* as men of talent and fine character to counteract some of the misconceptions people had about Texas.[38]

Two more months passed. Henderson, now the secretary of state of Texas, was still telling Ashbel to come "*now.*" He assured Ashbel that if he would live in Texas for six months to qualify as a citizen he could almost certainly have the post of minister to France from the Republic.

When Ashbel finally left North Carolina in March, 1837, he told friends that after his sojourn in Texas he expected to settle in New Orleans or return to Salisbury to live.

[38] James Pinckney Henderson to Ashbel Smith, December 4, 1836.

― CHAPTER THREE ―

Surgeon General of the Texian Army (1837–1839)

THE journey to Texas took Ashbel over a month, for he went by way of Hartford and then New York, where he remained until April 10. From New York he wrote to James Fenimore Cooper at Cooperstown, New York, urging him to come to the aid of their friend Samuel F. B. Morse.[1] The impoverished Morse had counted on winning a commission to do one of the four large vacant panels in the rotunda of the Capitol in Washington, but the selection committee was reluctant to choose an American painter.

Cooper wrote a fiery blast condemning the members of the committee for not thinking American artists, and especially Morse, good enough for the commission. When the letter appeared without signature in New York papers, readers assumed that Morse had written it himself, and that may have cemented the committee's decision. At any rate, Morse did not get the commission and turned his attention to the development of his new invention, the electric telegraph.[2] Ashbel probably never realized that, although his effort to help Morse had had the opposite effect to what he had hoped for, it may have expedited the perfection of an invention of incalculable significance.

Leaving New York, Ashbel traveled by railroad, canalboat, and steamer to New Orleans. There he found several letters waiting for him, including one from Antoinette Huie and one from Henderson informing him that by the time of his arrival in Texas the capital would probably be moved from Columbia to Houston.

When he arrived at Galveston, Ashbel saw only one house. Trans-

[1] Ashbel Smith to James Fenimore Cooper, March 31, 1837.
[2] "Samuel Finley Breese Morse," *Dictionary of American Biography*, 1:247.

ferring to another steamer, he watched with interest as it glided past the burned remnants of the village of Harrisburg and the site of the Battle of San Jacinto. At last, on May 9, 1837, the thirty-two-year-old doctor arrived in the village of Houston, Texas.[3]

Less than a year earlier, two brothers, Augustus C. Allen and John K. Allen, had hired the brothers Tom and Gail Borden to survey and plat the site of a town on Buffalo Bayou. The Allens had shrewdly named the town for their friend Samuel Houston, the hero of San Jacinto and the leading candidate for the presidency of the Republic. As Henderson had predicted, during the month before Ashbel's arrival the seat of governent of the Republic had been moved from Columbia to Houston, a fast-growing frontier town of about fifteen hundred people, one hundred houses, and a disproportionate number of saloons.

In Houston one of the first people Ashbel met was Sam Houston. From the very beginning their acquaintance was one of mutual respect and liking, and Ashbel found his first home in Texas in the log cabin—two rooms and kitchen leanto (on present Caroline Street, between Preston and Prairie)—which served the president as quarters.[4] He shared the same bedroom with Houston, and in this day-by-day closeness and during their endless discussions in the long hours of the night, Ashbel got to know Sam Houston probably better than any of his other contemporaries ever knew him. When Houston fell ill in the summer with "congestive fever," Ashbel acted as Houston's physician and nurse, and the bond between them deepened.

Years later Ashbel wrote a sketch of Sam Houston, which he unfortunately never completed. It debunked some of the myths that had developed from the complexities and seeming contradictions in Houston's personality. Ashbel emphatically denied, for example, the rumors that Houston was a gambler; in all the time he spent with Houston, he said, he never saw him "have a card in his hand" or bet on "any other game." Both men appreciated fine horses and attended the local horseraces, but the only bet Ashbel ever knew Houston to make was for "a pair of gloves with a lady." Until Houston married Margaret Lea and had several children, he sometimes made a point of publicly scorning bookish learning. In the privacy of their room, however, he liked to have Ashbel read to him during the "quiet hours after midnight." If

[3] Ashbel Smith Journal, April, May, 1837.
[4] Edwin A. Bonewitz to Dr. Llerena Friend, October 21, 1962.

these sessions were "invaded by friends," the book was hastily concealed under Houston's pillow.

During this period of his life Houston drank heavily, but even when he drank to the point of physical incapacity, Ashbel noted, he never lost his "accurate appreciation of all that was said or done within his knowledge." On more than one occasion when Congress tried to take advantage of Houston's supposedly helpless state, Ashbel used his medical skill to restore the president to a state of sobriety in "the least possible time." Ashbel believed that Houston's drinking bouts were not motivated by a search for inspiration or courage in times of trouble, anxiety, or danger; on the contrary, at those times he avoided liquor completely. Nor, according to his physician, did Houston drink from a love of spirits or their intoxicating effect or from a desire to stifle thought. Houston drank, Ashbel said, "to spite opinion and to avoid the unpopularity of Aristides; it was deliberate policy in him not to appear to people generally to be morally faultless." Houston's seemingly inexplicable habit of making enemies of people who wanted to establish friendly relations with him Ashbel explained as his way of acting upon Talleyrand's strange maxim "Would you rise, make enemies."[5]

Ashbel came to have great respect for Houston's intellectual capacity, particularly his ability to analyze a subject "in all its parts and relations." He understood that, when Houston appeared to be concentrating on nothing but whittling a stick of wood into a crucifix or a winding spool for some lady, his mind was pursuing long, concentric trains of thought. He concluded that Houston's apparent outbursts of passion were all for show, that they were always a result of "judgment and calm calculation."

Ashbel came to believe that "the Old Chief is as wary and sagacious as he is patriotic." He found Houston's imagination "burning" and his memory "awful"—retaining with extraordinary vividness the minutest details of all circumstances he ever witnessed, heard, or read. When Houston left town for a few days, Ashbel told a friend, half seriously, that he was enjoying a "respite." When Houston was at home, he said, the two men lay awake until nearly dawn "four nights out of five" and "battled the watch with incessant vollies of winged words."[6]

The spring of 1837 was unusually rainy in Houston, and there

[5]"Life Sketch of Sam Houston," n.d., Ashbel Smith Papers.
[6]Ashbel Smith to Burton Craige, December 16, 1837.

were many cases of pneumonia, fever, and violent dysentery, which were blamed on bad hygienic conditions, bad food, bad whiskey, and bad water. Whatever the causes, Dr. Smith soon had many patients. During the first week in June, while calling on a patient thirty miles from Houston, he himself suffered a severe attack of diarrhea, which he thought had been brought on by "exposure and some carelessness, or rather imprudence by drinking large quantities of water."[7]

When he returned to Houston, he found that in his absence Sam Houston had sent a memorandum to a secret session of the senate nominating Ashbel Smith surgeon general of the Texas army and that the appointment had been confirmed on June 7.[8] Although he knew that he should rest for a few days to recover his strength, Ashbel set to work immediately to reorganize the medical department of the army according to his standards. As a consequence he became weak, feverish, and "greatly emaciated" and was unable to leave his bed for several days. Fortunately, along with his new position he acquired an able and energetic assistant, John H. Bowers.[9] Bowers soon became Ashbel's protégé, studying medicine under his instruction and later attending the University of Louisiana with Ashbel's financial assistance. There were only thirteen years' difference in the two men's ages, and the relationship developed into a lasting friendship.

As an army officer Ashbel wore a military uniform. He wrote to his brother George, "I think you would laugh could you see me. . . . I suspect that at times I resemble a soldier more than a grave, melancholy doctor." Apparently the role did not displease him, for he ordered a special sword with a gilt scabbard to wear with his uniform and specified that it must be "easily carried on horseback."[10]

The new surgeon general's first concern was to obtain medicines and medical stores both for the army and for his private practice. In a letter to a drug-supply company he rather extravagantly estimated that the army would need $5,000 to $8,000 worth of medical supplies a

---

[7] Ashbel Smith to Charles Fisher, July 5, 1837.

[8] E. W. Winkler, ed., *Secret Journals of the Senate, Republic of Texas, 1836–1845*, p. 64.

[9] John Henry Bowers was born in Alsace, France. He and others sometimes spelled his name Bauers.

[10] The sword, now in the Texas Memorial Museum on the University of Texas campus, Austin, is elaborately decorated and has his name and the title "Surgeon General" engraved on it.

year, payment to be made in orders on the treasury or in land script at fifty cents an acre. For his own use Ashbel wanted drugs and medicines both to use in his practice and to sell. There was no apothecary in Houston, and physicians were selling medicines at markups of 200 to 1000 percent. He asked the company to send him $3,000 worth of medicine and felt safe in offering to pay 6 percent above the list price and half of the profit on all sales above that amount. He was scrupulous in dictating which drugs were for the army and which for himself, explaining that he was not "entitled" to use the army stores in his private practice.[11]

Even with Bowers's help he soon found himself under heavy pressure with his official duties and his private practice, especially when he discovered that the finances of the medical department were in disarray and that supplies ordered by the army had been delivered to the navy. Bowers and Ashbel often "sweated away in their shirttails" past midnight, attending to the paperwork of the office of surgeon general.

At a fee of approximately $5 a call (doubled after 9:00 P.M.), his private practice averaged between $25 and $35 a day. That added to his annual salary of $2,500, plus other government stipends, made his income very good by the standards of the time. He also began almost immediately to speculate in real estate, purchasing a lot and building a small house, which he rented to the army as a medical-supply storehouse, and by mid-August he had a second house under construction.[12] The latter house, which he described as spacious and comfortable, he planned to share with his new friend Colonel Barnard E. Bee, the secretary of war, when Sam Houston moved into the new "White House." Like so many other newcomers to Texas, Ashbel erected his buildings as investments with the expectation of selling them for a large profit in the future. Thus far he was not thinking of Texas as his permanent home. He continued to assure his North Carolina friends that he intended to return to Salisbury eventually.

Dueling was a common if greatly deplored practice in Texas in the late 1830s. In June, 1837, Ashbel found himself involved in one of the most famous duels ever fought in the Republic, one that aroused great public indignation. The antagonists were Dr. Chauncey Goodrich, an army surgeon, and Levi L. Laurens, a young reporter from New York.

[11] Ashbel Smith to Lee and Butler, July 8, 1837.
[12] Ashbel Smith to Henry Barnard, August 7, 1837.

Goodrich, Laurens, and several other men lodged together at the Mansion House in Houston, a customary arrangement owing to the scarcity of rooms. When Goodrich discovered that he was missing a $1,000 bill from his pocketbook, he randomly chose Laurens from among his roommates to accuse of the theft. Laurens, who had come to Texas with excellent character references and had won the respect and friendship of a number of Houstonians, was horrified by the accusation. Although he knew little about dueling, being convinced that his honor was at stake, he challenged Goodrich. Goodrich chose rifles at twenty paces. Goodrich had already killed one man with a rifle, and Laurens was unfamiliar with the weapon. Ashbel was called upon to be the physician in attendance at the duel, which took place at 6:00 A.M. on June 25. Laurens fell on the first fire, shot through both thighs. Ashbel did what he could for him, but forty-eight hours later the young man died, and Ashbel reported that "the wound of the spirit was more fatal than that of the body."

On the day Laurens died, Ashbel presided as chairman at a meeting of the youth's friends. The group drew up resolutions asking Houstonians to wear crepe on their left arms for thirty days and appointing a commission to erect a monument to Laurens. Some time later, the real thief was arrested and imprisoned in London for another crime.[13]

One of the annoyances of living in the Republic was the difficulty of communication. Although Ashbel had left a substantial sum on deposit with a business house in New Orleans, which agreed to pay postage and forward his mail, it was not until August that he received any word from the United States. In the packet of nine letters were one from Mary Phifer and several from Kincaid, Ashbel's overseer, who was conscientiously attending to Ashbel's affairs in Salisbury, including selling Ashbel's share of their wheat crop; hiring out Ashbel's slaves, collecting and paying debts due or owed by Ashbel; and selling various pieces of medical equipment and furniture, as well as caring for Ashbel's livestock and books.[14]

Since his arrival in Texas, Ashbel had been sending letters to

---

[13] Ashbel Smith Journal, June 25, 1837; Andrew Forest Muir, ed., *Texas in 1837*; Ashbel Smith to N. N. Noah, June 27, 1837; Chauncey Goodrich to Ashbel Smith, June 30, 1837.

[14] Jesse Kincaid to Ashbel Smith, May 13, 1837; June 13, 1837; August 16, 1837.

Mary Phifer through a mutual friend in Salisbury. The friend reported to Ashbel that Mary was "delighted" when she received a letter and that she had grieved over his leaving. Yet in her letter to him Mary continued to show the same defensive tactics that had marked their earlier exchanges. She assumed an air of indifference: "If you wish to reply to this well—*if not it is still well*." But she enclosed a poem whose last stanza read:

> Thou canst not forget me—the past has been frought
> With emotions too deep to be lightly effaced
> In the core of thy heart—in the depths of thy thought
> In letters of lava that past is now traced
> In thy weal, in thy woe, in thy joy and regret—
> From afar I defy thee to live and forget![15]

Antoinette wrote to Ashbel frequently, sending long letters reporting the gossip about his departure from Salisbury and particularly the "dark allusions of an infant." Branding the insinuations "*utterly entirely & before God gratuitously false*," he alluded to his previous "sin" and added, ". . . the offspring of passion I have not denied—it yet lives, I hope."[16]

Before he had held his office many weeks, Ashbel began working out a new, tighter plan of organization for the medical division of the Texas army. In a closely written twelve-page report to Colonel Bee, the new surgeon general outlined his plans. He requested that a surgeon and an assistant surgeon be assigned to each of the three main garrisons at Galveston, Velasco, and Bexar, with a spare team available for service at frontier posts as they were needed. The surgeons were to be required to make monthly reports on the condition of the posts and the health of the men. In addition, Ashbel would ask them to keep "thermometrical tables and metrological tables" so that facts could be accumulated about the healthfulness of the climate of the various sections of the country.[17]

Ashbel also asked Colonel Bee to authorize him to set up a board of examiners to ascertain the qualifications of every candidate for appointment to the medical department. Ashbel would be in charge of the board. The way for the regulation of medical practitioners in Texas

---
[15] Mary Phifer to Ashbel Smith, 1837.
[16] Ashbel Smith to Antoinette Huie, September 16, 1837.
[17] Ashbel Smith to Barnard E. Bee, November 6, 1837.

had been paved by Dr. Anson Jones, who had tried in vain to get enabling legislation through the First Congress of the Republic.[18] In December, 1837, the Second Congress cooperated, setting up a board of eleven medical censors with Ashbel Smith as it head. The board was to examine all medical officers and issue licenses to those who passed its examinations.

In his efforts to find the missing medical supplies for his department, Ashbel entered into a correspondence with Gail Borden, the customs collector at Galveston, who helped Ashbel ascertain not only that the navy had misappropriated some of the army supplies at Galveston but also that some of the most valuable unclaimed boxes intended for the army had been shipped back to New Orleans and sold for freight charges there. Since the only means Ashbel had of paying for supplies was "drafts on the Treasury to be audited in military script which would purchase nothing," he was driven to purchasing some of the most desperately needed supplies with his own funds while he waited for Congress to make appropriations.

The summer of 1837 was a difficult time for the Texas army for many reasons besides the shortage of supplies. Hundreds of soldiers came to Houston to have their records audited so that they could obtain discharges. They traveled long distances, some as far as 200 miles under the burning summer sun, wearing scanty, ragged clothing and near starving. When they reached the capital, they camped in the open or in flimsy shacks, spreading whatever diseases they contracted. After a few days of rain most of them had malaria. Numbers of them died, and Ashbel realized that he could not wait for the sluggish legislators to provide funds for a desperately needed hospital. On the edge of town he had a temporary shed and two borrowed tents erected to serve as a military hospital. These rude facilities were soon overcrowded, and convalescent patients were dismissed prematurely to make room for the acutely ill. When one of the tents was reclaimed by its owner, Ashbel secured permission to set up cots on the open gallery of a house next to the shed. Eventually Congress provided the money to construct a building to accommodate about thirty patients. It was finished in late fall, and Ashbel rejoiced that the sufferers were at least protected from the weather, though it was a crude building, and a hole

---

[18] Herbert Gambrell, *Anson Jones: The Last President of Texas*, pp. 108–10.

Surgeon General of the Texian Army

had to be poked in the roof after it was finished to let out the smoke.[19]

Although it was not an official part of his job, Ashbel acted as the regular surgeon of the hospital, visiting it daily and prescribing for its inmates. He also visited and took care of officers and soldiers at other residences in Houston without charge and with the help of his clerk acted as apothecary general to save the army money. On one record day he saw and prescribed for 119 patients suffering from "violent, congestive fever." Another method he found of saving money was to eliminate "spirituous liquors & wines" from hospital purchases. He was convinced that "the sick for whom they are destined, seldom get a taste of them."

One of the "bigbugs" with whom Ashbel was on good terms, as he told Henry Barnard, was Mirabeau B. Lamar, a hero of San Jacinto and a kindred spirit to Ashbel in his love of literature and poetry. In December, 1837, Lamar invited a group of outstanding citizens of Texas to help him found a Philosophical Society of Texas to be patterned after the American Philosophical Society in Philadelphia. At the organizational meeting Lamar was elected president, and Ashbel Smith was elected first vice-president. Other members included David Burnet, Dr. Robert Irion, Dr. Anson Jones, Augustus Allen, and Attorney General John Birdsall. The society was to be both literary and scientific in character, and its stated purpose was to collect and diffuse knowledge. The first paper read to the society was a discussion of the diseases and management of health in Texas. The author was Ashbel Smith, who had high hopes for the new organization. He expected it to "elevate Texas among the civilized nations of the World & in great probability extend the borders of Science."[20]

Toward the end of 1837, Sam Houston ordered Ashbel to prepare for a trip to the United States early the next year to purchase medical supplies for the Texas Department of War and to confer unofficially with President Martin Van Buren on the delicate subject of annexation and other matters important to the Republic. Ashbel looked forward to visiting Hartford and Salisbury after his official business was taken care of, though his affairs in Texas were so prosperous that he regretted having to leave at the time. After little more than six months in the Re-

---

[19] Ashbel Smith to Dr. J. W. Copes, February 10, 1878; Nixon, *The Medical Story of Early Texas*, pp. 430, 287.

[20] Ashbel Smith to Dr. Thomas Mutter, December 6, 1837.

public his financial situation had improved immensely. He had made between $12,000 and $15,000; the rents of his houses in Houston amounted to $1,200 to $1,500 a year; and he owned 4,000 to 6,000 acres of land besides a "share of Galveston city." He wrote to Barnard asking him to alert their friends of the impending visit. His letter ended with an epigram on Texas: "Taxes light, soil fertile, climate delicious, ladies scarce."[21]

Ashbel interrupted his travel preparations to spend New Year's Day 1838, with three of his new friends, Sam Houston, Albert Sidney Johnston, and Algernon Thurston. The day was so warm and pleasant that the four men sat on the bank of the bayou talking for a long time. Afterward they went to a "shanty" beside the bayou, where they had an oyster supper. Returning home at midnight, Ashbel resumed writing letters and instructions until he was again interrupted by Sam Houston, who came in at 3:00 A.M. to continue their discussion.[22]

Ashbel left careful instructions with his steward, John Bowers, and with Dr. James W. Copes, who was to act as surgeon general during his absence. He stressed keeping the office and storage magazine locked, because "the city of Houston abounds in thieves."[23] Ashbel took with him $4,000 of his own money in addition to a draft on the Texas treasury for $2,000, with instructions to "lay it out to the best advantage."

Traveling in the first half of the nineteenth century required fortitude, which fortunately was one of Ashbel Smith's strong characteristics. As long as he had with him a plentiful supply of reading and writing materials, he could ignore discomforts and delays. Nevertheless, just traveling from Houston to Galveston was not easy. On January 6, after an affectionate farewell from Sam Houston, he set out on a horse he had borrowed from Colonel Thurston. The horse was so unruly that Ashbel dubbed it the "mad Tiger," but he managed to get to Harrisburg on it. There he embarked on a barge. Because of blustery headwinds the barge had to be rowed down the bayou. At 9:00 P.M., Ashbel and three companions went ashore, built a fire, cooked their supper, spread blankets on the ground, and went to sleep. At 3:00 A.M. they got under way again and reached Morgan's Point in time for breakfast. While they were eating, a norther blew in with heavy rain,

[21] Ashbel Smith to Henry Barnard, December 22, 1837.
[22] Ashbel Smith Journal, January 1, 1838.
[23] Ashbel Smith to J. W. Copes, January 7, 1838.

Surgeon General of the Texian Army

but they managed after a "boisterous passage" to reach Galveston about sunset. There Ashbel boarded the steam packet *Columbia* bound for New Orleans, where he arrived on January 11.[24]

In New Orleans, where he had an unexpected delay of about a week, Ashbel took time to write an open letter to the public in which, speaking with the authority of Sam Houston's personal physician, he tried to lay to rest some of the ugly gossip that branded the general as a mental, moral, and physical wreck. The letter was printed in the *New Orleans True American* and the *Houston Telegraph and Texas Register* and was reprinted in several other papers, including the *Washington Chronicle*. In the letter Ashbel said of Houston:

His health has certainly been impaired by privations and exposures; but he possesses at this moment more physical force—despite his severe attack of the congestive fever last summer,—than ninety-nine able bodied men out of one hundred. . . . As regards his mind, he is still in the pride of his intellect. . . . The statements of his being a madman and cutting tall antics before high Heaven and man, are utterly and gratuitously false.[25]

Many of Ashbel's old friends and acquaintances were in New Orleans, and he spent his evenings visiting and dining with them. The Huies had moved there, and he had a meeting with Antoinette, which he recorded in his journal, using fictional names as he sometimes did when recounting the more romantic moments of his life. He was concerned that she had some expectation that he would eventually ask her to marry him, and during this meeting, in as kind a way as he could, he made it clear to her that he had no intention of doing so. They kissed like "brother and sister and parted—forever—forever." The next morning he received from her a Bible and a lock of her hair. He vowed, "I will read the Bible for my own sake, and retain the lock of hair as a memorial from one purely, ardently, nay most devotedly attached to me for long, long years even from childhood."[26]

Ashbel left New Orleans for Mobile on the steamer *Swan*, which ran into heavy seas, causing him to be seasick. Then the steamer ran aground and was out of commission for several days, causing him to miss his stage connection in Georgia. Apparently he did not manage to make a side trip to visit Andrew Jackson at the Hermitage in Nash-

---

[24] Ashbel Smith Journal, January 6–11, 1838.
[25] Letter to the editor, *New Orleans True American*, January 16, 1838; reprinted in *Houston Telegraph & Texas Register*, February 24, 1838.
[26] Ashbel Smith Journal, January 16, 1838.

ville, as Sam Houston had hoped he would. In expectation of this visit Houston had written to his "Venerated Chief" a letter of introduction in which he described Ashbel as "A Gentleman of useful, varied and elegant intelligence" and called him "my endeared personal friend."[27] It is unlikely that Ashbel revealed to Houston just how strongly he had opposed Houston's idol back in the days when he was involved in North Carolina politics.

When he finally reached Washington, D.C., on February 11, Ashbel found lodging with his friend General Memucan Hunt, who gave a dinner party in his honor. A letter of introduction from Sam Houston, which characterized Ashbel as "a gentleman of the purest honor and chivalry," earned him a cordial welcome from President Van Buren. In the course of several meetings and at an informal family dinner the president conveyed to him the attitude of the top United States administrators: "The present is not the time for urging annexation."[28] Politics make strange dinner companions, and Ashbel was also wined and dined by Secretary of War Joel R. Poinsett, a former antinullification leader.

Among the nation's leaders whom Ashbel met was John C. Calhoun, whose political and philosophical beliefs were close to Ashbel's own. Evidently Calhoun was also impressed by Ashbel Smith, for the two met and exchanged ideas on several occasions. On this trip Ashbel made a point of going to the Senate when Calhoun was scheduled to speak. Another person Ashbel was pleased to find in Washington was his friend Morse. The two dined together, and Morse showed Ashbel the progress he had made on his electric telegraph.

Reaching New York, Ashbel encountered difficulties in purchasing supplies; the credit of Texas was extremely low, and prejudice against Texas was extremely high. He finally completed his official business, however, and had time to spend with such friends as Henry Barnard and James Fenimore Cooper. On his own behalf Ashbel formed a partnership with his Uncle Seymour and Seymour's oldest son, Melancton, in a venture to sell clocks and stationery in Texas—items in short supply.

In another moneymaking scheme Barnard and Ashbel invested in

---

[27] Sam Houston to Andrew Jackson, January 4, 1836, in Sam Houston, *The Writings of Sam Houston, 1813–1863*, ed. Amelia W. Williams and Eugene C. Barker, 2:178.

[28] Ashbel Smith Journal, February 15, 1838.

Surgeon General of the Texian Army   49

a large supply of quinine at $1.875 an ounce, which Ashbel expected to sell in Texas for $8.00 to $10.00 an ounce. Ashbel also purchased a number of magazines and a set of encyclopedias, which he later sold to the Texas government for $250 as its first purchase toward a national library.[29] In spite of the strange ideas that some northerners had about Texas, almost all of them were convinced that land speculation in the new republic was a sure route to a fortune, and Henry Barnard and George Bulkley gave Ashbel money to invest in shares of the funded debt and in land.[30]

Ashbel had only a few days to spend in Hartford, and he was disappointed that he could not go to New Hampshire to see Caroline, who had named her first baby for him. He wrote to her, urging her to persuade Dr. Kittredge to move to the "delicious" climate of Texas, where the doctor could "amass a fortune."[31]

On the long journey back to Texas, Ashbel was accompanied by three young men: Henry Barnard's cousin George Barnard, who hoped to find a place in the mercantile business in Texas;[32] his own brother George, who wanted to see Texas for himself; and Radcliffe Hudson, the son of old family friends in Hartford, who was qualified as a surveyor and civil engineer. The Hudsons asked Ashbel to be their son's "friend and counselor" in his new life.

Stopping in Salisbury, Ashbel packed up some of his possessions—books, leather goods, and bedding. He also took along his favorite slave, Peter, forty-five years old. In New Orleans, Ashbel purchased three more slaves for $2,200: Robert and Albert, ten and twelve years old, and Eliza, seventeen years old, who was advertised as a good washerwoman.[33] He reasoned that hiring out the three would earn for him at least $90 a month.

That Ashbel was shipping to Texas both dutiable private goods and nondutiable public goods caused some confusion at the customs station, and the conscientious customs inspector, Gail Borden, refused to deliver some of the public consignment to Dr. Copes without official

[29] Ashbel Smith to Henry Barnard, March 29, 1839.
[30] Ibid., May 16, 1838; September 25, 1838; Ashbel Smith to George Bulkley, August 7, 1838.
[31] Ashbel Smith to Caroline Smith Kittredge, January 27, 1838.
[32] George Barnard became a successful trader and established several trading posts near the site of Waco.
[33] Manifest of slaves on board the S. B. *Columbia*, April 16, 1838; Ashbel Smith to Henry Barnard, May 6, 1838.

authorization from the surgeon general. Ashbel was offended by the inference that he might be using public cover to import private goods. After a slightly heated exchange of letters between Ashbel and Borden, each man acknowledged the integrity of the other, and feelings of mutual trust and respect were established that would prove important in their future relationship.[34]

Some of the inaccurate ideas about Texas that Ashbel had tried to dispel on his trip to the United States had to do with the Indians. He assured his northern friends that the Indians of Texas were not formidable in numbers or in valor. Nevertheless, the raids of small bands and the occasional murders they committed were a threat to immigration. Sam Houston, who knew the Indians as well as or better than most other Texans, tried to deal with them through talks and treaties. A few weeks after Ashbel's return to Texas, Houston commissioned him along with the secretary of state, Dr. R. A. Irion, to negotiate and sign a treaty of peace with the Comanche Indians.

As a linguist Ashbel was intrigued by the differences in the languages spoken by the Indians he met. He observed that the Bidais (from the east) communicated with the Comanches (from the west) entirely by signs or through interpreters. Writing to his old friend George Bulkley, Ashbel described the Texas tribes as being inferior in intelligence to the Creeks and Seminoles of the United States and related an experience he had while the treaty negotiations were going on. Visiting the Comanche camp one morning, he found the old chief Mugarrah, or Buffalo Bull, who was about seventy years old, walking about perfectly naked, as "unselfconscious as a young child." In the afternoon Buffalo Bull returned the call, bringing along his wives, who immediately began searching the heads of Ashbel's slaves for lice to eat. Ashbel reported that the women had "no luck" on this occasion, for he did not "sufficiently fancy that sort of vermin to indulge my servants in raising them."[35]

After the commissioners had given the Indians gifts, the white men signed their names to the treaty, the Indians made their marks, and the new peace pact was affirmed with an exchange of embraces. The treaty, dated "Houston, May 29, 1838," specified that the Indians would refrain from any depredations against the property or persons of

[34] Ashbel Smith to Gail Borden, June 14, 1838; Gail Borden to Ashbel Smith, August 15, 1838; Joe B. Franz, *Gail Borden: Dairyman to a Nation*, pp. 144–145.

[35] Ashbel Smith to George Bulkley, February 2, 1839.

Surgeon General of the Texian Army 51

citizens of the Republic of Texas, that each year on the second Monday of October they would send chiefs to talk with the president, and that they would make war on any other tribes who attacked white traders. In return the Texas government would appoint an Indian agent to superintend their business and protect their rights and would guarantee the Indians safe conduct through and from the nation. The treaty warned: "Peace is never to die between the parties that make this agreement. . . . the Great Spirit has looked down and seen their actions. He will curse all Chiefs that tell a lie before his eyes and Their Women and Children cannot be happy."[36] Before a year had passed, however, the treay was violated, and the bloody war resumed between the red and white "brothers."

Even for south Texas the heat was extreme in June, 1838, and the transplanted Yankee, along with the natives, could do nothing in the middle of the day but "lie in the shade and pant." At least that is what Ashbel told his friends, but in reality he continued to work at his usual strenuous pace with the result that about the middle of the summer he became ill with a debilitating fever.[37]

On July 2 he accompanied Sam Houston to Liberty, about fifty miles from Houston, and then returned home while Sam Houston continued his journey to Nacogdoches. A few days later Ashbel received a summons from Houston to attend his private secretary, John Ross, who had fallen ill some fifty miles farther along on their trip. The letter was addressed "EXPRESS!!!" and the messenger had been sent on Houston's favorite and seldom-lent horse, Sam Patch, so Ashbel knew the need was urgent. In spite of his own weakness he made the arduous trip and cared for Ross until he was convalescent.[38] After his second return to Houston, Ashbel suffered a recurrence of fever, from which he did not recover for several weeks. Barnard Bee scolded him for yielding too much to the president's whims, telling him that Houston would "*use but not serve*" his friends.[39]

The strong-minded Bee's thinking was undoubtedly colored by the fact that he was a bitter political enemy of Sam Houston. In this instance, as in others, Ashbel exercised his dexterity in diplomacy, managing to maintain warm friendships with both obstinate men.

---

[36] Texas Indian Papers, Texas State Archives, Austin, Texas.
[37] Ashbel Smith to J. W. Copes, June 25, 1838.
[38] Sam Houston to Ashbel Smith, July 10, 1838.
[39] Barnard Bee to Ashbel Smith, July 17, 1838.

Further evidence of Ashbel's tact was his skill in supporting the candidacy of Lamar for the presidency that year without losing Houston's friendship. In addition to their membership in the Philosophical Society, Lamar and Ashbel had other common interests, and they frequently visited and dined together. Ashbel acted as a kind of unofficial manager for Lamar during the campaign, exchanging ideas with Bee for promoting Lamar in letters marked "strictly confidential." After Lamar won the election, Ashbel conferred with him about his cabinet selections.

Some of Ashbel's friends suggested the possibility that he would be named to a position in Lamar's cabinet. Some of Ashbel's enemies implied that this hope was the motivation of his efforts in Lamar's behalf. Stung by this accusation, Ashbel publicly announced that he *did not* want *any* office in the new government. Afterward, however, when he did not receive an appointment, he felt some disappointment and in his journal penned some political wisdom as a reminder to himself for the future: "It appears to me that I might have had an office of decided honor under General Lamar, if I had not expressed a disinclination to accept any." That was, he admitted, "a lack of political generalship. A stronger position decidedly would have been to decline after it should be tendered." Other friends pointed out, however, that it would have seemed strange for him to be taken into Lamar's confidence immediately after having "so long enjoyed an intimate & confidential intercourse with Houston, the enemy of Gen. Lamar." Ashbel consoled himself with the thought that he had kept his independence and vowed, "I shall not permit myself to hang on Princes' favors."[40]

In September a series of recurrences of fever nearly took Ashbel's life. He suffered "horribly" and dosed himself with quinine, which he loathed. Twice he thought that he was dying and was surprised to find that he did not recoil from the idea. "I am not so much attached to this life as I thought I was," he told Barnard. The person he longed to see most in his illness was his father, Moses. He recovered slowly and emerged into convalescence emaciated, "a mere shadow of myself."

Toward the end of October, when he thought that he was well along in recovery, he suffered another severe episode of illness, with excruciating pain in the muscles, bones, and joints; headaches; and ex-

---

[40] Ashbel Smith Journal, October 23, 1838.

citement and confusion of mind amounting almost to delirium. He recovered from this attack only to have yet another relapse in November. He almost wished that he *would* die: "I am tired, wearied, disgusted, vexed out of all patience by these eternally recurring indispositions. Life is a burthen if passed in suffering as mine has been for months." Toward the end of November, however, he could finally say, "God be thanked that I now have the prospect of better health."[41]

As 1838 drew to a close, Houston was filled with bustle and activity. Business of all kinds was brisk, even though the principal streets were often ribbons of mud. Ashbel estimated the population at 3,000 and "rapidly growing." He was pleased that transportation was improving:

Some four or five steamboats ply regularly between this place and Galveston, and the jingling of bells and the discharge of small cannon which announce their arrival and departure and the new faces of passengers and the unexpected meeting with old ones enliven the scene and compensate . . . in a good degree for the many discomforts we have still to submit to in this new country.[42]

One of the amusements he enjoyed was the fall racing, sometimes in the company of the colorful Dr. Branch Archer, of Brazoria. Although Ashbel did not participate in the betting, he enjoyed equally watching the "pretty running of the well-bred geldings" and the promenading of the "elegant ladies and high-bred gentlemen" at the large balls given by the clubs after the races.

He also was involved in the festivities connected with the changing of administrations. When retiring President Houston gave a levee for an overflow crowd in the executive mansion, Ashbel noted approvingly that it was "a far less promiscuous assemblage than is commonly seen on such occasions." An "excellent" orchestra played softly as the crowd promenaded or stood quietly conversing. As always, Sam Houston dominated the stage, and Ashbel felt it worthwhile to behold his "elegant form and manly proportions" and to listen to the "promptness and variety of his colloquial powers, his facility and great tact at appropriate compliments."[43]

[41] Ashbel Smith Journal, September–November, 1838; Ashbel Smith to Henry Barnard, September 10, 1838; Ashbel Smith to Bulkley, November 6, 1838.
[42] Ashbel Smith to Will Locke, December 20, 1838.
[43] Ibid.

The inauguration ceremony was held on the concourse in front of the capitol, where Houston upstaged Lamar by delivering a lengthy valedictory address. Ashbel had helped arrange for the inaugural ball. It took place in the senate chamber, from which the seats had been removed to provide a dance floor, and in the hall of representatives, where a bountiful supper was spread. Unfortunately, as the night wore on, the free-flowing liquor undermined the dignity of the occasion, and there were "some excess of rioting and some shameful spreeing toward the breaking of the day."

Gambling, drinking, and fighting were a way of life for many in the boom town. So, although Ashbel joined in the formation of a Bible Society under the auspices of the American Bible Society of the United States, he was not optimistic about its influence. He feared, he said, that there did not exist "in this community a sufficient regard for virtue in which religion and a well-based morality can take root and attain a permanent stand."

True to his paradoxical nature, soon after he joined the Bible Society to promote morality, Ashbel became the central figure in a well-publicized scandal caused by his inevitable fiery reaction to any real or imagined slight to his honor. For some months there had been hostility between Ashbel and Senator Stephen H. Everitt, also a doctor. During a gathering one evening while Houston was still president, Everitt spoke disparagingly of Houston in the presence of Ashbel and President-Elect Lamar. As Ashbel described it, he rebuked Everitt for his "baseness & falseness, and charged home on him his duplicity in speaking disparagingly of General Houston in his absence, as I had been a witness of his frequent attempts at gross flattery and fawning sycophancy offered to General Houston at the very time he was backbiting this gentleman."[44]

Early in the congressional session that winter Ashbel heard rumors that Everitt was saying derogatory things about him as well. Then a friend told him of seeing a confidential letter that Everitt had sent to President Lamar on January 4, which said in part: "I shall be under the necessity of opposing two nominations that I have Reason to presume You intend to make. . . . The first is Doct. A Smith as Surgeon General he has no claims on the country—and he has not talent,

---

[44] Ashbel Smith to James Armstrong, Esq., June, 1839.

merit or political honesty as will be shewn if an investigation be had."[45] The morning after he was told about the letter, Ashbel encountered Everitt in the senate chamber. Ashbel challenged the senator over the insulting letter. Everitt answered by calling Ashbel a liar, whereupon Ashbel began beating Everitt with a horsewhip he happened to be carrying. He continued striking the senator until the two were separated by onlookers. As was his custom, Ashbel was also carrying a pistol and a knife, but he used only the riding whip in his assault.[46]

Subsequently there was, in Ashbel's words, "an outburst of awful indignation & wordy wrath" in the senate, and a committee of five members was appointed by the house to investigate the matter. After their investigation four of the members defended Ashbel, and the fifth remained silent. Not satisfied with this outcome, Everitt initiated and pushed through resolutions in the senate to require the president to censure Ashbel—which Lamar refused to do.

Everitt then raised questions about Ashbel's honesty and efficiency in running the medical department and demanded a committee of investigation. The senate granted his request and created a committee with Everitt as its chairman. But Ashbel Smith's books were meticulously kept, and the committee could find no basis for bringing any charges against him, though Ashbel accused the members of acting with "infinite virulence and malignity." As an army officer he demanded and got a court of inquiry, which found "no charge nor cause of complaint" against his conduct of the office.[47]

Against Lamar's wishes Ashbel resigned his post as surgeon general to avoid causing any further embarrassment to the president. The horsewhipping story was reported with embellishments by northern papers, and Ashbel expended a considerable amount of time and ink setting the record straight for his astonished friends and relatives.

Although Ashbel put up a front of being undismayed by the incident and casually told friends, "I horsewhipped an honorable Senator most sufficiently," he was deeply affected by what he felt to be the "malignant" persecution by Everitt and his supporters. Privately Ashbel admitted, "For a short period during its progress my vast spirits &

[45] S. H. Everitt to Lamar, January 4, 1839, in Mirabeau Buonaparte Lamar, *The Papers of Mirabeau Buonaparte Lamar*, ed. Charles A. Gulick et al., 2:401–402.
[46] Ashbel Smith to Select Committee of Senate, January 10, 1839.
[47] Ashbel Smith to James Armstrong, Esq., June, 1839.

most solid self-confidence were shaken—I was maddened nearly to desperation."[48] After it was over, however, he felt relief at being free of public office and refused Lamar's offers of his old position or of another one in the government. He planned to practice his profession and tend to his business affairs until he became a wealthy gentleman in that land of opportunity.

[48] Ashbel Smith Journal, 1839.

CHAPTER FOUR

A House in the Country
(1839–1841)

IN January, 1839, Lamar discussed with Ashbel the possibility of sending an expedition to Santa Fe, New Mexico, for the purpose of occupying this territory, which the Texas Congress had declared to be under the jurisdiction of Texas. The expedition was to have the further objectives of stopping the Indians' depredations along the frontier and opening up trade between Texas and the Santa Fe area. Lamar offered Ashbel the chance to be one of the four commissioners to accompany the expedition, with the assignment of diplomatically persuading the New Mexicans to join the Republic.[1]

When young Radcliffe Hudson was appointed an engineer to go with the expedition, Ashbel wrote to Radcliffe's father that he thought it was a promising opportunity and expected that it would occasion "more privation" than danger for its members. In fact, he told Mr. Hudson, "it is sufficiently probable that I shall form one of the party."[2] In the spring of 1839, Ashbel could not know that by the time the ill-fated expedition left Kenney's Fort on Brushy Creek in June, 1841, he would be involved in other state business that would prevent his joining it and that he would deeply regret having encouraged his young friend to take part in the venture.

After his resignation as surgeon general Ashbel had time to explore his region of Texas with the idea of establishing a home outside Houston. He made short trips up the Brazos and Bernard rivers and visited the Velasco area. He was pleased by the crops he saw—especially the cotton, which he believed to be superior to that raised in Ala-

[1] Ashbel Smith Journal, January 27, 1839.
[2] Ashbel Smith to Henry Hudson, March 31, 1839.

bama or Mississippi. He predicted that Texas would soon be growing an "important" quantity of the cotton produced in the world.

When wintery blasts and rain, sleet, and mud kept him confined to his rooms, one of his pastimes was to analyze in his journal the quirks and foibles of the Republic's political leaders. He mused that Lamar required "a good deal of *docility* in his friends," and since Barnard Bee was as frank as he was inflexible, it was best for those two to stay apart. Albert Sidney Johnston he thought an "honorable" man but found him "painfully" slow in grasping ideas. Moseley Baker's defects as a speaker, Ashbel believed, were mainly from a neglect of preparation, for Baker possessed "a copious and inventive" mind. Lamar made an error, Ashbel thought, when he broke his political relationship with Baker.[3]

Among the social events that Ashbel attended during the spring of 1839 was the wedding of Dilue Rose to Ira A. Harris in a log house on Brazos Bayou. One of the bridesmaids was Mary McCrory, a young widow whom Ashbel would come to know well as Mrs. Anson Jones.[4]

In May, when the French fleet arrived in Galveston from Mexico, Ashbel's facility in the French language earned for him the role of interpreter and companion for the admiral. Wining and dining and listening to the French band on board the admiral's flagship, Ashbel felt himself "almost in France" again.

He was astonished to discover how much Galveston had grown— from the single house he had observed upon his arrival two years ago into a bustling town "twice as large as Salisbury" (which had about 1,000 inhabitants), with twenty-five or thirty sailing ships in the harbor at all times and a dozen or so steamboats moving in and out during the day. The change, he wrote Charles Fisher, was like "the magic of the Arabian Nights stories."[5] He also felt that the sea air and sea bathing at Galveston made it one of the healthiest places in the world. Accordingly, after he had nursed President Lamar through a violent attack of "bilious fever," he ordered the president to go to Galveston to recuperate.

Since his own health was not robust, Ashbel decided to follow his

---

[3] Ashbel Smith Journal, January–February, 1839.
[4] "The Reminiscences of Mrs. Dilue Harris," *Quarterly of the State Historical Association* 4–7 (1903–1904).
[5] Ashbel Smith to Charles Fisher, May 24, 1839.

own prescription and spend a long time in Galveston trying to recoup his strength. He could not, however, refuse to attend Lamar's mother when she became critically ill at Oak Grove, the president's country home near Houston. Touched by the affection between Lamar and his mother, Ashbel wrote Bee, "I never have seen Mother and son who were more completely all in all to each other and whose existence seemed more entirely bound up in that of the other's."[6] He remained at Mrs. Lamar's bedside until she died.

Ashbel had a warm relationship with all the members of Lamar's family in Texas, including Lamar's sister Lauretta, to whom Ashbel sent a book entitled *The Gentleman of the Old School*. Some of Ashbel's friends expected him to propose to Lauretta Lamar, but he told Barnard that his affections did not "wash" in that direction. Lamar's young daughter Rebecca was being reared by her aunts in Georgia. While she was visiting her father in Texas, she became ill, and Ashbel took care of her. An affectionate, teasing relationship developed between the doctor and the lively child. He advised her to study botany because it is "a beautiful and interesting study that improves the memory and makes for clearness in thinking." Rebecca scolded him for writing her letters that were too businesslike and commanded him to publish something she could read, since she could not understand his medical writings. As Rebecca matured, she became a lovely replica of her mother, but tragically, also like her mother, she succumbed to tuberculosis at an early age.[7]

During the early summer of 1839, in spite of being himself only "one remove" from sickness, Ashbel kept up his practice and took part in civic affairs, serving as foreman of a grand jury and as an alderman for the city of Houston. Finally, in July, he was able to take a vacation in Galveston, where he stayed at Evergreen, the plantation of his friend General Baker. The rest was not as complete as he desired, for he found himself "annoyed with a pretty extensive practice." His patients included the family of General Baker, who in gratitude presented Ashbel with one of the best lots in Galveston, worth about $2,000.

Ashbel bought another two lots in Galveston for $1,000 each,

---

[6] Ashbel Smith to Barnard Bee, July 26, 1839.
[7] Ashbel Smith to Rebecca Lamar, January 27, 1840. Rebecca Lamar to Ashbel Smith, January 4, 1840; Farrell and Silverthorne, *First Ladies of Texas*, pp. 42–43.

planning to build a small house and an office on them.[8] Until his proposed plantation became profitable, he decided, he would practice medicine in the flourishing town of Galveston, as soon as he regained his health. He was beginning to consider Texas his permanent home, for he wrote Kincaid that he would come to Salisbury soon for a long visit and to settle up his affairs there.

As another demonstration of his confidence in the future of the Republic, he continued to collect property of "different kinds." In September, 1839, the tax assessor estimated Ashbel's holdings in Houston to be worth $16,790, and Ashbel estimated that his other holdings in the Republic amounted to "more than as much more." But he complained to friends in the United States that the continued depressed state of Texas's currency made it difficult to obtain cash. When Texas notes depreciated to twenty-five cents on the dollar, Ashbel gave up the idea of making a trip to the United States. He was not discouraged, however, for he felt sure that the economy would soon improve: Texas would either get the loan it was negotiating for in Europe or change to a sounder currency. In the meantime, to obtain money to send to Moses, Ashbel had Henry Smith sell some of Ashbel's Mississippi land.

Brother George, who was studying medicine, stayed in Houston to look after Ashbel's "establishment" there, including the Negroes, who were working for wages, and Ashbel moved into comfortable quarters in Galveston, where he had a horse and buggy and servants to look after his comfort. While his health improved, he spent his time riding on the beach, bathing in the salt water, reading Shakespeare, eating oysters, and enjoying the "delicious sea breeze."

Toward the end of September this idyllic life ended abruptly when an epidemic of yellow fever broke out in Galveston. For the next six weeks, while the epidemic raged, Ashbel Smith was furiously busy. Some of the large property owners and merchants in Galveston tried to suppress the news that yellow fever had spread to the island, and they tried to put pressure on the newspapers and on the doctors to keep silent. Dr. Smith was not an easy man to silence, however, and in his own words "set them at defiance" by publishing truthful accounts of the extent of the disease and making the citizens aware through the papers of the progress of the epidemic. He did not know what caused

[8] Ashbel Smith to Daniel Seymour, September 3, 1839. Ashbel Smith to Memucan Hunt, August 21, 1839.

the outbreak, but he observed that all the cases were from the vicinity of the Strand, along which ran a low, marshy area that extended parallel with the shore almost the length of the city.[9] He believed that exhalations from this "malodorous fetid area," plus those from the decomposition of various animal and vegetable matter, were the "local" causes of the disease. He did not realize that mosquitoes were the transmitters of the fever, but if the city had followed his urgent pleas to clean up the filthy areas and fill in the marshy area with sand and lime, the epidemic would undoubtedly have ended sooner. The cost of this work, however, would have been over $1,000, and since many of the local leaders refused to admit the presence of a yellow-fever epidemic, the project was postponed.[10]

A letter written by one of his patients to her mother in New England shows the confidence Ashbel inspired in his patients:

We are fortunate in having an excellent physician, Dr. Smith. . . . Dr. Smith says it is the most manageable of all the fevers which prevail in a hot climate. There are ten resident physicians on the island, two at the garrison and one on board each of the men-of-war in the harbor, and among so many there must be some good ones, but we think we have found the best.[11]

As Ashbel made his rounds in his buggy, he did not overlook the opportunities the epidemic presented to him as a scientist. He summoned George from Houston to observe the effects of the disease, and he himself studied it from every possible angle, keeping careful notes with an eye to publishing his findings. In a letter to Dr. Casper W. Pennock, whom he had met in Paris, Ashbel admitted that one of his reasons for publishing the report in pamphlet form was a "sort of vanity to publish the first medical treatise *in* and concerning Texas."[12] The pamphlet was praised both by eminent scientists of Ashbel's own time and by outstanding scientists of later generations for its astute and succinct observations.

It begins with a preface that contains sharp criticism of those who

---

[9] Ashbel Smith, *An Account of Yellow Fever Which Appeared in the City of Galveston, Republic of Texas, in the Autumn of 1839; with Cases and Dissections.*

[10] "Dr. Ashbel Smith's Account of Yellow Fever Epidemic in Galveston in 1839," *Galveston News*, December 2, 1862.

[11] "Ashbel Smith Sketch," *University of Texas Medical Center News*, Mid-October, 1962.

[12] Ashbel Smith to C. W. Pennock, October 21, 1839. Actually Dr. Theodore Leger had published the first essay on medicine in Texas in 1838.

denied the existence of the disease and treated him as if he were "the author of the pestilence." The preface is followed by geographical, topical, and meteorological descriptions of Galveston Island. Descriptions of symptoms and stages and observations of the pathology of the disease are followed by discussions of treatment, prognosis, contagion, and mortality. Frankly and in detail Ashbel discussed the overharsh methods of treatment he and his fellow physicians had used with dismaying results in the early days of the epidemic. He described the improved results he obtained from a more conservative treatment, which eliminated dosing with the ubiquitous calomel. To prove that the disease was not contagious he reported:

I have made several post mortem examinations—handling every organ without squeamishness; immersing my hands freely in the black vomit and other fluids; smelling and viewing them closely; I have *repeatedly tasted black vomit*, when fresh ejected from the stomachs of the living, and I am not aware of ever having experienced further inconvenience or effect than fatigue.

He recorded his postmortem findings minutely, from the "intense yellow color" of the bodies while they were "not yet cold" to the condition of each organ, emphasizing the involvement of the liver and the stomach in the course of the disease. The booklet ends with twenty-one case histories, meticulously detailed.[13] As always, Ashbel acted as his own press agent, sending copies of his pamphlet to friends, relatives, journal editors, and doctors in the United States and in Europe, asking them to have it "noticed" in their papers. He also sent copies to the Yale library and to Professor Silliman. In his covering letter to Pennock, Ashbel assured the doctor that, apart from the epidemic, the Texas coast was healthy:

If you have any invalids send them among us. An abundance of sea food—an atmosphere unrivalled for balminess and salubrity—and novelty of scenes and the excitement of a virgin country are at the command of the dyspeptic. For rheumatics and consumptives the climate is particularly genial.[14]

The coming of the first norther on November 7 was a great relief to the people of Galveston, including their weary physicians. Ashbel was happy to be able to report to a friend, "We have just had a smart frost which renders our whole country perfectly healthy for 8 months to come."

[13] Ashbel Smith, *An Account of Yellow Fever*.
[14] Ashbel Smith to C. W. Pennock, October 21, 1839.

A House in the Country 63

No matter what else occupied his days, Ashbel found time for politics. Even though the Texas presidential election was still two years away, it was already a popular topic for discussion. Ashbel told Memucan Hunt, "Our party ought soon to be organized and organized too as it will be on the great principle of carrying out the measures which will benefit the country."[15] Hunt, who expected to be a candidate for the presidency, wrote a series of long letters to Ashbel marked "confidential," "strictly confidential," and "sacredly confidential" and told Ashbel that he revealed more of his opinion to him than to anyone else.

Two of Hunt's confidences were that Thomas Rusk's "habits" precluded the idea of running him for office and that Sam Houston, who had been in Nashville visiting Andrew Jackson during the summer, had been drunk almost every day and therefore was "out of the question."[16] In turn, Ashbel told Hunt that David G. Burnet was trying to "appropriate Lamar's friends, but it won't take" and that Burnet would try to win the presidency by using the weight of government patronage. "He is a sold man," said Ashbel, who also reported, "General Houston is very popular but has no manager."[17] Despite his friends' opinions of his drinking habits and his lack of organization, Houston was elected by the people of San Augustine to be their representative in the next Congress.

The Texas capital had been moved to Austin in the fall, and in early December, Ashbel eagerly accepted an invitation to make a trip to see the new town. His traveling companions were his old friend Barnard Bee and a new acquaintance, James Hamilton, who was going to the capital to be appointed a commissioner to Europe to try to secure a loan of five million dollars for the Republic. Ashbel found the outgoing Hamilton an agreeable and entertaining companion on this trip, though before many months he would have occasion to be annoyed by Hamilton's forwardness.

The fertility, variety, and beauty of the "frontier country" delighted Ashbel. And he felt satisfied with *himself*. Writing from Austin, he summed up his view of his situation to Charles Fisher:

My position here in Texas is very agreeable. . . . I may without impropriety add that it is an enviable one. I enjoy the confidence of all the leading men of the country. I dined with the President [Lamar] on the day of my arrival—I am

---

[15] Ashbel Smith to Memucan Hunt, August 21, 1839.
[16] Memucan Hunt to Ashbel Smith, September 5, 1839.
[17] Ashbel Smith to Memucan Hunt, August 21, 1839.

to dine with the Vice President [Burnet] today. General Houston and I are on the most intimate terms. And I have acted a pretty important part in some important matters here. I got into hot water last year by striking a Senator in the Senate Chamber—but this has done me no damage in any quarter.[18]

Ashbel's observation of Houston's behavior in Austin contradicted the report that Hunt had made from Tennessee, and he wrote to Moseley Baker that he regarded Houston's election as president as certain. Ashbel told Baker that Houston's health and deportment were as good as he had ever known them to be, though "he sometimes engages in a small spree at night but never so as to expose himself to general observation."[19] If Houston confided to his old roommate the reason for his improved behavior—that he was engaged to be wed—Ashbel did not report it to Baker, one of Houston's old foes.

By the time Ashbel returned from Austin, he was determined to establish a plantation home for himself on Galveston Bay. His intention was "to have a house in the country with all the profusion, the hearty comforts and appliances for field sports that such a life affords." He told his cousin Lydia Avery, "This settlement . . . will be my *home*, here will be my negroes, my books, horses, . . . my dogs and guns. Here I hope to see my friends and here to live with Mrs. S. if I ever marry!—Which of course I am determined to do."[20] He declined to engage in medical practice in Houston any longer lest it interfere with his plans to get the plantation underway.

From James Pinckney Henderson and others Ashbel bought several hundred acres of land adjoining the plantations of Moseley Baker and A. C. Allen on Galveston Bay. He also acquired more slaves until he had seven "good hands," and he bought a Dick China stud colt, telling Baker that it would be a convenience "to any of our neighbors who may wish to be breeders." He added, "It appropriately devolves on me being a bachelor to keep a fine stud." He traded two of his Houston lots for seventeen cows and calves.

During the winter months, while he waited to obtain clear title to his land, Ashbel engaged in two writing projects. One was a brief stint editing a paper, the *Houston Morning Star*. It was a task he enjoyed, finding it "far more pleasant to dictate to others than to hold an office

---

[18] Ashbel Smith to Charles Fisher, December 13, 1839.
[19] Ashbel Smith to Moseley Baker, December 28, 1839.
[20] Ashbel Smith to Lydia Avery, January 21, 1840.

where you may be exposed to the sneers of boobies or the calumnies of the unprincipled."[21] One of the causes that Ashbel supported vigorously in his editorials was the foreign-loan policy.

His second literary task was a series of letters to an officer of the French navy on the "history and condition of Texas," to fulfill a promise he had made when he visited with members of the French fleet the previous year. In the letters he included a firsthand account of the Battle of San Jacinto, which he had heard Houston relate in their lodgings in Houston.[22]

When Henderson arrived in Galveston in January with his new bride, whom he had married in London, Ashbel took part in the festive dinner and ball which the citizens of Galveston gave to welcome the couple. Frances Cox Henderson, a native of Philadelphia, charmed Ashbel with her brilliant mind and cultivated manners, and he wrote enthusiastically to several friends, praising her conversational skill and social grace. To prepare the new Mrs. Henderson for her meeting with Sam Houston in Austin, Ashbel told her many anecdotes about the "Old Chief."

Later that spring, when Sam Houston announced his plans to be wed also, to Margaret Lea, of Alabama, Ashbel exchanged with friends pessimistic prognoses about the marriage. Understandably, they had forebodings about the union of the worldly, restless veteran soldier with a pious, sheltered girl a quarter of a century younger than he. Ashbel would gladly have yielded to Houston's urgent invitation to accompany him to Alabama for the wedding, except that Ashbel had no available cash; he had put all he had into land for his plantation. Since he knew that Houston had no extra money to lend, he was forced to decline.

Upon Houston's return to Texas with his pretty young wife, Ashbel was astonished at the change in his friend. "His health is excellent," Ashbel noted, "as good or *better* than I have ever seen it. He indulges in no conviviality with his friends—but strange to say is a model of conjugal propriety." To Bee, Ashbel commented, "His health and ways are infinitely mended—will it last? I always hope for the best."[23]

[21] Ashbel Smith to Barnard Bee, January 15, 1840.
[22] Ashbel Smith to Sam Houston, January 5, 1840.
[23] Ashbel Smith to Barnard Bee, July 27, 1840.

Soon after Henderson's return, Ashbel was able to obtain title to his land, and he set his slaves to work building a log house and several small outbuildings. By the end of June, "Headquarters," as Ashbel called his home, was virtually finished. While Ashbel's medical practice kept him busy in Galveston, his brother George supervised operations at the plantation, buying chickens, planting corn, and building fences. When the novelty wore off, however, George found business to take him elsewhere, and Ashbel had to hire an overseer—the first in a long line of overseers on the plantation, some of whom stayed only a few days. The overseers complained that Ashbel's slaves were "spoiled" and difficult to manage, and the slaves found other supervisors, who did not take the same personal interest in them that Ashbel did, harsh and uncaring. It was never a satisfactory arrangement, but it was the only way that Ashbel could have the kind of life he wanted and his plantation too.

During July and August medical duties kept Ashbel from his new home, for the serious illnesses of Henderson and Margaret Houston occupied him for several weeks. Henderson became ill on board a steamboat as he was traveling from Saint Augustine to Houston. Ashbel was called and had his friend put to bed, for weeks filling the roles of nurse and doctor. No sooner was Henderson convalescent than Ashbel was called to the interior, thirty-five miles from Houston, where he spent several days taking care of Mrs. Houston, who was suffering from an attack of fever.[24]

Consequently it was not until late fall that Ashbel was finally free to spend time at Headquarters, superintending the preparations for planting. He put in two strawberry beds, each one hundred feet long, and made plans to plant thirty acres to cotton. Game was bountiful, and he enjoyed successful hunting. These pastoral pursuits were interrupted by an urgent letter from his faithful overseer in Salisbury. Kincaid had been struggling to look after Ashbel's interests in North Carolina, paying notes as they came due, trying to collect money owed to Ashbel, and looking after his property and servants. As Texas paper money, called "red backs," became more depressed and cash more scarce, Ashbel was reluctant to send money to the States, where it would be worth only a fraction of its value. He had $10,000 in good notes due him but found it extremely difficult to realize any cash from

[24] Ashbel Smith to Jesse Kincaid, August 30, 1840.

A House in the Country

them. Moreover, it had become almost impossible to sell land for cash. His optimistic expectation of an improvement in the state of the currency had not come true. As the months passed, the Texas dollar fell until it reached a low of sixteen cents on the dollar. Kincaid, who was desperately pressed to pay some of Ashbel's debts in cash, finally was forced to sell Ashbel's slaves with the option of redeeming them in ninety days.

The day after he received this news, Ashbel started for North Carolina to reclaim his slaves and settle his affairs in Salisbury. As a matter of profit it would have been to his advantage to let the slaves go, but he felt "much attached to them" especially since a number of them had been born "his."[25]

Setting out for the United States during the last week of December, 1840, Ashbel made the trip by way of Tennessee to visit brother Henry and his wife at Somerville. While he was in that city he dined with Sam Houston's brother William and his wife and satisfied Mrs. William Houston's curiosity about her new sister-in-law. Ashbel described the new Mrs. Sam Houston as having "a fine person, handsome and intellectual countenance, a well-cultivated mind" and as being devoted to her husband. In deference to Houston this time Ashbel had the stage wait for him at the Hermitage in Nashville long enough to pay his respects to the aging General Jackson, whom he found in good health, though feeble.[26]

By mid-February, Ashbel had settled his business in Salisbury and was on his way to Hartford by way of Washington and New York. In New York he found awaiting him an urgent request from Henry Stuart Foote, a Mississippi lawyer, journalist, and politician (later to become governor of his native state). Two years before, in the spring of 1839, Foote had gone to Texas. At that time Ashbel had joined a group of citizens who publicly and privately memorialized Foote to "prepare for the world a History of Texas."[27] Foote had agreed to undertake the work. Settling in Velasco, he had become a friend of many prominent Texans, including Ashbel. Foote had taken his completed manuscript to Philadelphia, where he discovered that his prospective northern readers were eager to have, in addition to a history of Texas, informa-

[25] Ibid.
[26] Ashbel Smith to Sam Houston, January 23, 1841.
[27] E. W. Winkler, ed., *Manuscript Letters and Documents of Early Texians*.

tion on the climate, soil, natural resources, productions, and flora and fauna. Knowing that Ashbel was on a trip to the North and believing that he was best qualified to supply the needed information, Foote turned to him for help.

Ashbel complied with a long descriptive article that he told Foote he had written in New York, "eighteen hundred miles from home, without the aid of any book and relying wholly on my memory." The article became an appendix in Foote's book, *Texas and the Texans*. It is a remarkably thorough account, laden with facts linked with bits of lyric description. The article includes temperature ranges, weather variations, elevations of terrain, and qualities of the soils and natural features from the coasts of Texas to its mountains. Ashbel described the great variety of scenery, including "prairies clothed with a most luxuriant growth of grasses gorgeously enamelled with flowers," skies of "transparent clearness," and the "open champagne character" of the country, free of swamps and lagoons, and he dwelled on the advantages to the farmer of the long growing season and the "amazing fertility of the soil." The tomato grew "spontaneously" on the prairie, Ashbel reported, and pecans, hickory nuts, persimmons, wild grapes, wild plums, and blackberries "flourish in high perfection." In addition to these foods he noted the presence of wild animals, such as buffalo and deer and turkey, ducks, geese, partridges, and other game birds, as well as the choicest seafood, including oysters, shrimp, and crabs. He also mentioned the herds of wild horses available for transportation.

Among Texas's natural resources he listed its trees and undeveloped deposits of gold, silver, coal, and salt. He not only described the present condition of the Republic but managed to include a number of suggestions for its future, such as breeding the rangy longhorn cow with the Durham to create a "more perfect race of cattle," increasing the yield of sugarcane and wheat and other grains, and improving rivers and roads, as well as encouraging railroad building.[28]

In the East, Ashbel found time to visit friends, including Maria, the charming sister of Radcliffe Hudson. Before he left Texas, Ashbel had announced that he might bring back a wife to be the mistress of Headquarters. Several of his friends urged him to do so, and one of them pointed out, "No man who is as fond of children, and wants them as bad as you do can be happy without them." But he did not ask Maria

---

[28] Henry Stuart Foote, *Texas and Texans*, app.

Hudson to become Mrs. Smith, though she and Ashbel began a correspondence that lasted until his death.

Ashbel longed to visit Caroline, who now had two children, but he did not make the long trip to New Hampshire in the snow and ice. His namesake, Ashbel Smith Kittredge, had learned to say that he was "going to Texas" and to know his uncle by the portrait of Ashbel that Caroline kept in her bedroom. The Kittredges' daughter, born a few months earlier, was named Antoinette Huie Kittredge—partly, as Caroline explained, because Antoinette was a family name that she liked and partly for Ashbel's "interesting friend" about whom she had heard so much.

On the return trip, by railroad, steamboat, and stagecoach, it took Ashbel eighteen days to reach Somerville, Tennessee. As usual he amused himself by keeping a list of his fellow passengers, noting their occupations and family connections. He got into a long discussion with a Mormon named James, who enlightened Ashbel on the history and beliefs of the sect. Ashbel listened politely and recorded the discussion in his journal, noting: "Mr. James . . . is a sensible man enough on other subjects, has his temper under excellent control, and is quite well-behaved. . . . It appears to me a case of when rational belief is utterly lost in a sea of credulity, when the mind has cast loose from common sense."[29]

When he reached Texas, Ashbel immediately plunged into politics. He urged Houston to run for the presidency "untrammelled"— that is, without a vice-presidential candidate—encouraging him to "Ball against the field and the Devil take the hindmost." The Houstons now had a home at Cedar Point, not far from Headquarters, and the two men met frequently to plan strategy to defeat Houston's opponent, Burnet.

The election was as scorching as the Texas summer. Under pen names Houston and Burnet wrote vitriolic articles about each other, and Houston sent copies of his anonymous articles to Ashbel to have published in the Galveston papers to answer the anonymous articles that Burnet had published in the Houston papers.[30] Ashbel himself got into a hot debate with a Lamar man named John G. Chalmers, who published articles attacking Ashbel on such personal grounds as lacking

---

[29] Ashbel Smith Journal, April 19, 1841.
[30] Sam Houston to Ashbel Smith, August 4, 1841.

an aristocratic background and "starving" his household. Ashbel gave him back the taunts with interest, avowing that, although he had not inherited a fortune from his father, he had "received at his hands what must ever command from me a devotion and affection which knows no limit," and accusing Chalmers of poking his nose into a "bachelor's kitchen" to divert the public gaze from his own misdeeds. Ashbel threatened that, if Chalmers continued his insults, he would "array before the public such damning proofs of his guilt [as a swindler] as shall make him howl on his deathbed at his folly in having provoked me."[31] At this point the matter seems to have been dropped.

At one stage in the campaign George felt called upon to be the keeper of his brother's honor and got into a fight in a bar with a man who he believed had insulted Ashbel. George was fined twenty-four dollars for disturbing the peace, but he was satisfied because he received only a scratch while his opponent suffered a black eye and a gash over his temple and "confessed himself whipped."[32] When the smoke of the campaign cleared after the September vote, Sam Houston had won by a large majority, to the delight of the Smith brothers.

In October, Ashbel had thrust upon him painful professional and personal duties in connection with the suicide of his friend George C. Childress, the author of the Texas Declaration of Independence. On his trip east Ashbel had visited George Childress and his family in Nashville and had offered Childress and his wife lodgings at Headquarters when they returned to the Republic.[33] When Childress returned to Texas, he found it almost impossible to make money practicing law because of the glut of lawyers in the country, the tight money situation, and squabbles among judges over jurisdiction. He applied to Lamar for a job as his private secretary but was turned down.

On October 6, Ashbel arrived in Galveston at 6:00 A.M. to learn that Childress had stabbed himself several times in the abdomen with a bowie knife. The doctor found his friend in critical condition with his intestines protruding through three wounds. He did all that he could to make Childress comfortable, replacing the intestines and sewing up the wounds. In answer to Ashbel's question about why he had stabbed himself, Childress answered, ". . . it is the effect of an oversensitive

---

[31] Ashbel Smith Journal, October, 1841.
[32] George Smith to Ashbel Smith, September 1, 1841.
[33] George C. Childress to Ashbel Smith, March 26, 1841, in Winkler, ed., *Manuscript Letters and Documents*.

A House in the Country

mind," and added that he had no money to bring his wife to Texas or to return to her. After Childress died, three hours later, Ashbel performed an autopsy to establish that Childress was not suffering from any physical disease. In an envelope addressed to Ashbel, Childress had placed several letters to be forwarded to friends and relatives in Nashville and elsewhere. Before forwarding them by the uncertain mail service, Ashbel carefully copied them into his journal. He wrote detailed and sympathetic covering letters to Childress's relatives, describing the circumstances of the tragic death of the great Texas statesman.[34]

Ashbel did not attend the inauguration ceremony and celebration that took place in Austin in December, 1841, but he kept in close touch with Sam Houston as the Old Chief resumed the leadership of the Republic, which was beset with many serious problems. Red backs had sunk to a low of three or four cents on the dollar, and Texas's credit was for most purposes nonexistent. The Indians were causing problems on the frontier, and the Mexicans were threatening an invasion.

In addition, Texas's relations with other countries needed skillful attention. Treaties negotiated with England had not been ratified, and the French chargé d'affaires, Count Alphonse de Saligny, was on the point of breaking off diplomatic relations with Texas. His garden had been invaded by an Austin innkeeper's pigs. The pigs had been shot by a servant at the French embassy, whereupon the innkeeper had beaten the servant. Finding that he could not get the Texas courts to punish the innkeeper without a trial, the indignant count demanded his passport and left in a huff for New Orleans on his way home to France.

Sam Houston obviously needed a man of great tact, personal persuasiveness and the ability to speak French fluently. Only such a man could handle the delicate negotiations required to win the goodwill and support of France, as well as of other European nations. Houston's choice naturally was his old roommate. And so Ashbel Smith gave up his dream of enjoying his own strawberries and cream in the spring and prepared to undertake the mission that would make him, whether he wished it or not, one of the key figures in the complicated international maneuverings that preceded the annexation of Texas by the United States.

[34] "Copies of Letters left by Col. Childress. . . ," Ashbel Smith Journal, October 4, 1841.

CHAPTER FIVE

Chargé d'Affaires to Saint James and Saint-Cloud (1842–1844)

As Ashbel began preparations for the mission to Europe, he received news from Radcliffe Hudson's family that his young protégé was in a dangerous situation. In a note smuggled out of Mexico, Radcliffe had informed them that, along with other members of the Santa Fe Expedition, he had suffered near starvation and then betrayal into the hands of the Mexicans, who had stripped him of his clothes and money and were preparing to march him and the other prisoners to Mexico City.[1] The distressed doctor could only write sympathetic letters to the family and wish that he had never heard of the venture.

Both President Houston and his secretary of state, Anson Jones, went to Galveston in February, 1842, to confer with the new chargé. Day after day, during morning and afternoon sessions and over long dinners at the Tremont House, the three men plotted the strategies by which Ashbel could best accomplish his difficult tasks. These included smoothing over relations between Texas and France, securing ratification of a treaty of amity and commerce between England and Texas, working for friendly mediation by the European powers to stop Mexican threats of war, obtaining recognition of Texas by Spain, making a treaty with Belgium, encouraging immigration to Texas, and learning in an unofficial manner the "dispositions" of other European governments toward Texas—especially Russia, Prussia, and Austria.[2]

In between business meetings Ashbel found time for a brief flirtation with a young Frenchwoman, Mlle de Philibeaucourt, "one of the

[1] Hannah M. Hudson to Ashbel Smith, February 16, 1842.
[2] Ashbel Smith Journal, March 2, 1842.

Chargé d'Affaires to Saint James and Saint-Cloud 73

sweetest of her sex," traveling with her father and a group of French noblemen who were bringing laborers to settle in Texas. One member of the group was a suave Frenchman who called himself the "Count de Narbonne," a name Ashbel would have cause to remember in the future.[3]

Ashbel made arrangements for his old friend John Bowers to act as his overseer at Headquarters. With bachelor fussiness he explained exactly how his furniture, curtains, and counterpanes should be cared for, stipulating that Bowers was to reserve the mahogany bed for "gentleman strangers" and that his moss mattress was not to be used. His instructions included every detail, down to breeding the boar ("anyone sending a sow must send a plenty of provision with it or she must be turned out").[4] In packing the possessions he planned to take, he was most concerned for the care of his precious books.

With some pride Ashbel wrote to his relatives and friends about his assignment. Antoinette Huie sent a self-contradictory and somewhat bitter reply. She congratulated him, adding, "'Tis well you are rewarded—that your ambition is partially gratified—for it you have lived and 'tis the shrine at which you have sacrificed every feeling." She assured him of her everlasting friendship but demanded the return of all her letters.[5] Antoinette, who knew Ashbel well, correctly read between the lines to conclude that his self-esteem had been raised. Further evidence is that from this time on his journal entries were written in the third person, and he referred to himself as "Ashbel Smith."

The new minister plenipotentiary sailed from Galveston on March 15, 1842. In New Orleans he stayed at the Saint Charles Hotel with Henry de Castro, Texas's new consul general to France. Castro, who was to travel to Europe with Ashbel, would cause him a number of problems over the next three years.

In New Orleans, Ashbel began his diplomatic duties by calling on the disgruntled Saligny, who was en route to France following the "pig war" in Austin. Ashbel delivered to Saligny a letter from Anson Jones in which the secretary of state invited the French diplomat to return to his post. The new chargé paid many compliments to the ruffled diplomat on behalf of the president and the secretary of state. The French-

[3] Ashbel Smith to Sam Houston, February 20, 1842.
[4] Ashbel Smith to John Bowers, March 12, 1842.
[5] Antoinette Huie to Ashbel Smith, February 29, 1842.

man was mollified, and Ashbel was pleased to be able to inform Jones that Saligny would return to Texas "by the next *Neptune* without fail." Ashbel also told Jones that Saligny had revealed to him that a French squadron was in the Gulf of Mexico "subject to his orders" and that the French government had directed Saligny to proceed to a position off Galveston harbor and send the Texas government his ultimatum. Whether or not Ashbel took this threat seriously, he concluded, "I cannot but regard this termination of the misunderstanding between the two governments as fortunate, and at least as preventing *quite opportunely* an *awkward* position."[6]

Arriving in London on May 10, Ashbel took lodgings with his cousin Daniel Seymour at 103 Jermyn Street, a few doors from the Texas legation. For a parlor and two bedrooms the cousins paid four guineas a week.

The chargé's first step was to obtain an interview with the American minister to London, Edward Everett, and through him to arrange a meeting with George Hamilton Gordon, Lord Aberdeen, the British secretary of state for foreign affairs. While he waited for the interview, Ashbel renewed his acquaintance with London and attended the reviewing of the troops, part of the celebration of Queen Victoria's birthday. He noted that the Duke of Wellington reminded him of Sam Houston.

Ashbel informally tested the attitude of the British public toward Texas and found the people generally unfriendly to the Republic. "Texas has numerous active enemies," he reported to Houston and Jones, adding, "Everything American is here regarded with unconcealed dislike." He noted in his journal that he had heard that two steamers of war were being built for the Mexicans in England—one in Liverpool and the other on the Thames in London—and commented, "Ashbel Smith must inform the government of this fact."

The first interview with Lord Aberdeen was set for May 16. Promptly at 2:00 P.M. that Monday, Ashbel was introduced to the British foreign secretary by Everett, who soon left the two alone. In reply to an inquiry by Ashbel, Lord Aberdeen expressed his government's dislike of the way James Hamilton, who had preceded Ashbel in England under the title "diplomatic agent," had handled matters pertaining to trade between the two countries. Knowing that Sam Houston did not ap-

[6] Ashbel Smith to Anson Jones, March 15, 1842.

prove of Hamilton, who had been close to Lamar, Ashbel assured Lord Aberdeen that Hamilton's actions in England had not been authorized by the current administration.

He then brought up a subject close to his heart: the wretched condition of the Santa Fe prisoners, who were still in chains. He pointed out that some of the prisoners were British by birth. Aberdeen promised that the British government would make an appeal to the Mexican government in the interest of humanity. Before the meeting ended, Lord Aberdeen told Ashbel that he would let him know something definite about the treaty ratification, but he expressed doubt that Britain would be able to mediate effectively between Texas and Mexico, since Santa Anna had already declined an offer of British mediation.

The next morning Ashbel wrote a report of the interview to Anson Jones, informed him about the two steamers of war, and suggested that Texas should maintain an efficient blockade of Mexican ports. He also emphasized the hostility toward Texas of the antislavery party in England, whose meetings he attended incognito.[7]

While he waited to hear from Lord Aberdeen about the treaties, Ashbel set out to learn what he could about the steamers being built for Mexico. He managed to get on board the *Montezuma* at the Indian Docks in London and to stay long enough to get a good idea of her capabilities. He found her "a noble, stout vessel of upwards of a thousand tons, drawing about ten feet of water and admirably constructed as a vessel of war." He thought that if she were well manned, the Texas navy had nothing that could cope with her singlehandedly. He solicited reports from friends in Liverpool on the second ship, the *Guadalupe*. His informants reported she was approximately 800 tons, "splendidly equipped and armed" and about in the same state of completion as the *Montezuma*.[8] The chargé expressed his anxiety to the Texas leaders: "Let me beseech you, *most earnestly* to give your care to these steamers. They *must not be* permitted to *reach the harbor of Vera Cruz. Capture them.*"[9]

When Ashbel mentioned the two steamers in his second interview

---

[7] Ashbel Smith to Anson Jones, May 17, 1842, in G. P. Garrison, ed., *Diplomatic Correspondence of the Republic of Texas*, p. 955.

[8] Ashbel Smith to Anson Jones, June 3, 1842, in ibid., p. 961; Ashbel Smith to Sam Houston, May 31, 1842; Robert Russell to Ashbel Smith, June 4, 1842; Matthew Russell to Ashbel Smith, June 15, 1842; August 30, 1842.

[9] Ashbel Smith to Anson Jones, June 8, 1842.

with Lord Aberdeen, the earl denied knowledge of them but suggested that Texas also was at liberty to have ships built for it in England. To Ashbel the reason for the cautious policy of the British cabinet in the affairs of Texas was obvious. As the chargé told Jones, "There exists at this time a very good understanding between England and Mexico, which is quite favorable to the interest of British commerce and manufacturers and the Cabinet will take no step which might interrupt this good understanding."[10]

One of the most delicate problems that Ashbel inherited when he became chargé was the British attitude toward slavery. He found that antislavery feeling pervaded every class. In letters to Houston, Jones, Bee, Calhoun, and Van Zandt, Ashbel expressed his great concern about the British and Foreign Anti-Slavery Society. To Van Zandt, Texas's chargé to the United States, he said, "The establishment of a free state on the territory of Texas is a darling wish of England,"[11] and he asked Calhoun, "The abolition of slavery in Texas is fraught with infinite danger to the South—Will the South look to it?"[12]

Ashbel waited impatiently for Lord Aberdeen to summon him for the formal ratifications of the treaties between Texas and Great Britain. He was eager to move on to France. On June 23 he noted irritably in his journal: "No reply from Lord Aberdeen. The conduct of England toward Texas is very ungracious. *To be remembered.*"

Finally the meeting was arranged, and on June 28, 1842, the ratifications were signed at the Foreign Office by Lord Aberdeen and Ashbel Smith. Ashbel then invited the attention of the foreign minister to the urgent desire of Texas' leaders that England mediate with Mexico to recognize Texas' independence. But he received the same negative response that he had received in their previous meetings.

The following day Ashbel wrote to Houston about the successful conclusion of that part of his mission connected with the treaties and included further warnings about the steamers. Ashbel suggested that Houston allow him to investigate the availability of steamers in France that Texas might purchase to use against Mexico. He promised to take

---

[10] Ashbel Smith to Anson Jones, June 3, 1842, in Garrison, ed., *Diplomatic Correspondence*, p. 961.

[11] Ashbel Smith to Isaac Van Zandt, January 25, 1843, in ibid., pp. 1103–1107.

[12] Ashbel Smith to John Calhoun, June 19, 1843, cited in Harriet Smither, "English Abolitionism and the Annexation of Texas," *Southwestern Historical Quarterly* 32 (January, 1929): 203.

no action without instructions, adding plaintively that he had had no word from Texas in more than two months and begging to be kept informed about the situation there. Ashbel was also concerned that the blockade of Mexico, which he had insisted upon the English government observing, was only a "paper blockade." He told Houston, "It is *very* important it should be maintained in full force and vigor."[13] He suggested that Texas issue letters of marque against Mexico so that the steamers could be seized. After some delay the letters were sent to him to issue at his discretion, but by that time the steamers had left England.

In spite of the knotty problems that remained, Ashbel found that after the wide publicity given to the signing of the ratifications the hostile feelings that he had found on his arrival in England were "manifestly giving place to more favorable feelings and a much better appreciation of our country."[14]

At Ashbel's suggestion Lacklan Macintosh Rate was appointed general consul for the United Kingdom and Ireland to replace William Kennedy, who had resigned. Rate, a London merchant, had become a close personal friend of Ashbel. Ashbel stated that one of Rate's most important official assignments would be to furnish potential emigrants to Texas with accurate information and encouragement. Rate's unofficial assignment—keeping Ashbel informed about important diplomatic developments in London—was even more valuable to Ashbel.

Before he left London, Ashbel asked Lord Aberdeen for permission to present his respects to Queen Victoria on a suitable occasion after he returned from France. Lord Aberdeen replied that he would present the chargé to her majesty at the first levee she held after Ashbel's return.[15]

When Ashbel arrived in Paris, he found a pall over the city. On the previous day the Duke of Orleans, the oldest son and heir of King Louis Philippe, had died. Ashbel found the general silence and grief "dramatic," but the strangest thing of all was to find himself, dressed in mourning, standing in the Ambassadors' Tribune among men who were shaping history. The king's speech, interrupted by his sobs, was listened to in profound silence. Outside the Palais Bourbon some

---

[13] Ashbel Smith to Sam Houston, June 29, 1842.
[14] Ashbel Smith to Anson Jones, July 3, 1842.
[15] Lord Aberdeen to Ashbel Smith, July 7, 1842.

20,000 soldiers were massed, and beyond them Ashbel could see a moving ocean of multitudes upon multitudes of people paying tribute to their dead prince.[16]

George McIntosh, the Texas chargé d'affaires to France whom Ashbel was replacing, was delighted to be relieved of his position. McIntosh had not received any salary or expense money since the preceding fall, and, having pawned his watch and other valuables, had been living on credit. For the sake of Texas's reputation, Ashbel assumed McIntosh's debts, which amounted to more than $2,000.[17]

Another embarrassment to the chargé was the infighting in the Texas consular office in Paris, which was the talk of the foreign diplomatic corps. Henry Castro, the new consul, had been unable to get his *exequatur* (written authorization for his position) from the French government, and the incumbent consul, Theodore Barbey, refused to accept the letter of recall from the Texas government. Ashbel "extricated" Texas by explaining that President Houston often had to make assignments when he did not possess accurate information in regard to individuals.[18]

In Paris, Ashbel's fluency in French was invaluable to him. Without it, as he said, he would have been a "cypher." Also important in that city where knowledge was revered was his familiarity with classical literature and his reputation as the author of several medical articles and pamphlets. These accomplishments opened as many doors to him as did his diplomatic standing. Too, his scholarly inclinations did him no harm in his relationship with the French foreign secretary, François Guizot, who was himself a professor of history and a writer.

In addition to his diplomatic duties Ashbel found time to take advantage of the valuable opportunity to study his profession again in Paris. He arose early and went at dawn to the hospitals, where he stayed until 10:00 A.M. He occasionally attended lectures and viewed autopsies, making notes of his observations. And he enjoyed the unique pleasures that the city offered, visiting the Louvre, strolling in the Tuileries, and attending high mass at Notre Dame, where he heard a choir of 700 voices.

Through Rate and other friends he kept in touch with progress on

[16] Ashbel Smith to Maria Hudson, July 20, 1842; August 4, 1842.
[17] George McIntosh to Ashbel Smith, May 18, 1842; Ashbel Smith to Anson Jones, July 30, 1842.
[18] Ashbel Smith to Anson Jones, August 1, 1842.

the Mexican steamers. He continued to protest to Lord Aberdeen and to members of Parliament. He dug into dusty tomes of English law, trying to find a legal way to keep the ships from leaving England. All his efforts failed, however. The *Guadalupe* sailed in July, "armed to the teeth," and then the *Montezuma* attempted to leave in September.[19] Ashbel's urgent remonstrances caused the government to detain the *Montezuma* until the armament was removed, but the chargé had little faith in this act, feeling sure that large quantities of small arms were hidden on board and that the heavy armament would follow in another ship and be restored to the *Montezuma* when the vessels reached the open sea.[20] His erstwhile friend James Hamilton arrived in London and jumped into the affair of the steamers, writing letters and talking to government leaders. Ashbel decided that Hamilton was doing more harm than good and also that he was claiming credit for what Ashbel had already done. The chargé commented scornfully to Houston that "General Hamilton made a great parade about the steamers."[21]

Even after the steamers had left England—for the record and perhaps to have the last word on the subject—Ashbel sent a thirteen-page letter to Lord Aberdeen explaining emphatically why it was a violation of British law and of the "Laws of Nations" for England to have permitted the building and dispatching of the war ships.[22]

Sam Houston, fearing that his minister was taking too high a tone with the British foreign minister, told Ashbel, "You were rather 'tight' on the Earl," and cautioned, ". . . when we get our hand in the Lion's mouth, my rule is to get it out just as easily as possible, but not to strike the Lion on its nose!" Ashbel answered the Old Chief that his words were well taken but that he believed that the British liked manly behavior and thought that Lord Aberdeen respected him for the firm stand he had taken in the matter of the steamers.[23]

Ashbel's worst fears concerning the steamers did not come to pass, though the ships did evade the Texas blockade and reach Veracruz.

---

[19] William Pringle to Ashbel Smith, July 8, 1842; Ashbel Smith to Anson Jones, September 19, 1842; Ashbel Smith to Lord Aberdeen, September 14, 1842; September 19, 1842.
[20] Ashbel Smith to Anson Jones, October 19, 1842.
[21] Ashbel Smith to Sam Houston, October 3, 1842.
[22] Ashbel Smith to Lord Aberdeen, October 10, 1842.
[23] Sam Houston to Ashbel Smith, December 9, 1842, in Houston, *Writings*, 3:222; Ashbel Smith to Sam Houston, April 11, 1843.

There they were manned by Mexican crews and British officers who had resigned their commissions in the Royal Navy to enter Mexican service. In May, 1843, both steamers were seriously damaged in a battle with Texas ships and ceased to be a threat.[24]

One of Ashbel's duties as chargé was to investigate the reputations and intentions of persons wishing to sign contracts for land grants in order to take emigrants to Texas. Spurious land titles were a problem, and Ashbel issued instructions to Texas consular agents to make every effort to prevent fraud in land deals. As honestly as he could he warned empresarios what to expect.

When Henry Castro (who had never received approval as consul by the French government) undertook a colonization project of a frontier area of Texas, Ashbel told him that it was not a safe area for settlers. When Castro persisted in sending the colonists he had recruited, Ashbel tried to impress on him the need for an efficient agent in Texas to receive them. Castro became angry when Ashbel refused to write a letter of recommendation that the Frenchman had requested, and Ashbel wrote George that Castro might try to harm his reputation in Texas. To avoid any appearance of bias, Ashbel did not permit himself to be "concerned nor interested . . . in any manner . . . in any sale of land whatsoever."[25]

Daniel Seymour was living with Ashbel in his lodgings at the Hotel Meurice, rue de Rivoli, and acting as his cousin's secretary. When Daniel planned a trip to Brussels, Ashbel sent along letters and personal messages to the Belgian foreign minister, inviting Belgium to enter into commercial agreements with Texas. The reply that Daniel brought back to Ashbel was that Belgium admired Texas for her "energy and brilliant prospects" but must postpone making formal treaties with the Republic because of commercial commitments with Mexico.[26]

Ashbel tackled the problem of winning Spain's recognition of Texas by having a preliminary interview with General Zicente Sancho, the Spanish minister to England. He then wrote a long letter for Sancho to transmit to the Spanish government, setting out the advantages to Spain of recognizing and trading with the Republic. Ashbel countered Sancho's opinion that Spain did not need to recognize the Texas blockade of Mexico since Texas was not a state by pointing out to

---

[24] Tom H. Wells, *Commodore Moore and the Texas Navy*, p. 152.
[25] Ashbel Smith to Sam Houston, October 3, 1842.
[26] Daniel Seymour to Ashbel Smith, August 21, 1842.

him that the recognition of Texas's independence by the United States, England, France, and Holland admitted her into the "family of nations."[27] Ashbel also wrote to Washington Irving, the American minister in Madrid, asking his help in persuading the Spanish government to recognize Texas and to respect the blockade of Mexico.[28]

After another invasion of Texas by Mexico and disastrous efforts at retaliation by Texan expeditions, Sam Houston pressed his minister to try again to persuade England and France to mediate peace between Texas and Mexico. Accordingly Ashbel sent formal requests to Guizot and Lord Aberdeen, urging them to act together in a triple mediation effort with the United States.[29] The result was the same as before: France expressed willingness to participate in the "triple interposition," but England preferred to act by itself. Lord Aberdeen told Ashbel that her Britannic Majesty's government believed that it could do a better job of mediation alone. Ashbel was inclined to agree with this opinion, but unfortunately the Mexican government did not, and no progress was made.

To carry out his duties as minister to both England and France, Ashbel moved back and forth between the two courts. In October he was back at the Texas legation at 3 Saint James Street in London, and in December he was again in Paris. As the year drew to a close, he became homesick. Since his arrival in Europe the only members of his family he had heard from were Curtis and Caroline. He wrote Moses that he was "pained by the idea that no one of you will take the trouble to write." He begged George to join him so that he could introduce his younger brother to "good society" in France and England, but mainly so that George could have the advantage of studying medicine in Paris, where "the facilities of acquiring anatomical and surgical knowledge are *immeasurably* greater than at any school in America." For the same reason Ashbel urged Caroline's husband, Dr. Kittredge, to "come to Paris and stay with me for a few months." He told Caroline that she could not know how often and how affectionately he thought of her and pleaded for more letters.[30]

---

[27] Ashbel Smith to General Sancho, September 7, 1842; Ashbel Smith to Anson Jones, September 8, 1842.

[28] Ashbel Smith to Washington Irving, September, 1842.

[29] Ashbel Smith to M. Guizot, August 15, 1842, in Garrison, ed., *Diplomatic Correspondence*, pp. 1137–38; Ashbel Smith to Lord Aberdeen, August 19, 1842.

[30] Ashbel Smith to Caroline Kittredge, November 12, 1842.

About this time Ashbel received word that Antoinette Huie had married an old acquaintance. His own thoughts were very much on matrimony. He declared to Caroline his intention to marry on his return to America. "I have lived single long enough," he said, and asked her what she thought of his proposing to Maria Hudson. His diplomatic training was an excellent preparation for matrimony, he felt, for it had given him "a cool temper and a wary tongue."

Early in December, Ashbel received a long letter from his friend W. D. Miller, who was acting as Houston's private secretary. The letter was a litany of woes concerning the Republic. Miller characterized Texas as without strength and without confidence, in a state of collapse, prostrate and powerless. He warned Ashbel that he did not expect Texans to pay their taxes and that Congress would probably abolish or reduce the tariff; consequently, the chargé could not depend upon receiving his salary and might soon be forced to rely upon his own independent means.[31]

The new year 1843 began for Ashbel on a more cheerful note as he attended the traditional New Year's reception held by the French royal family for the diplomatic corps. The Texas minister was impressed by "decrepitude and simplicity" of the king. His Majesty's stocky build and coarse features seemed to Ashbel more appropriate for a "sturdy grazier" than for a "decendent [sic] of royal blood for a thousand years." The physician noticed that the king's face looked "heavy" in repose, though the hazel eyes often had a "waggish expression when relating some anecdote or eyeing some newly presented person bedizened with finery." Over the next few weeks, as Ashbel came to know the king, he developed a respect for the monarch's "powerful intellect" and decided that the queen, who was more patrician and regal in appearance than the king, had "not a tithe" of his intellect.[32]

While the decorations of the hall and the rich dresses of the aristocrats entertained the eye, the ceremony inevitably was stiff, for conversation was confined to a "few good natured inquiries and commonplace compliments." Ashbel was swept by a feeling that it was an idle ritual, and yet he considered that "no wise man underrates forms," and he understood the diplomatic importance of calling formally on the

---

[31] W. D. Miller to Ashbel Smith December 8, 1842.
[32] Ashbel Smith, "Description of Louis Philippe," April 11, 1848, Ashbel Smith Papers.

king to make the compliments of the New Year.[33] For Caroline's amusement Ashbel made note of the dress and manners of the aristocratic ladies. He himself dressed in the fashion of upper-class gentlemen of the day: black dress coat, black trousers, plain waistcoat and stock, varnished boots, and white gloves.

For diplomatic purposes Ashbel took full advantage of his access to royalty on social occasions. One such opportunity occurred after a dinner given in honor of the Duchess of Kent by the King of France. After the meal, as Ashbel strolled in the salon of the Tuileries with the duchess, she commented that she took a great interest in Texas, for her son had invested in a plan to introduce into the Republic large numbers of immigrants. Pretending to be aware of the scheme, Ashbel drew from her the information that the prospective immigrants were indoctrinated in the "principles of abolition"—which meant they would vote down slavery at the polls. He learned further from the garrulous duchess that the "first chapter" was to introduce 15,000 immigrants in eighteen months. This kind of information was helpful to the chargé in deciding whether or not to grant permits to would-be colonizers.[34]

To enlarge his sources of political information, Ashbel became a member of the Circle Aquiole, composed chiefly of the noblesse, who many afternoons played cards from two until six. Although he privately condemned their style of life as "an idle and unprofitable existence," it was at these informal gatherings that he saw dukes, marquises, and counts. Such topics as slavery, finances, and the personalities of political leaders were discussed at the meetings, and he had a chance to spread propaganda about the desirability of Texas for French immigrants and to appraise the attitudes of the members toward the Republic.

In the 1840s there were many misconceptions about Texas and Texans. People who knew little about it wrote wildly exaggerated and lurid accounts of life in Texas. Ashbel assumed that one of his duties was to keep up with what was being written about his adopted country. He encouraged knowledgeable friends and men like William Kennedy and Henry Stuart Foote to put their talents to work to give true descriptions of the Republic and its people.

When an Englishman named Captain William Houstoun and his

[33] Ashbel Smith Journal, January 1, 1843.
[34] Ibid.

family prepared to sail for Texas in their 219-ton yacht, Ashbel wrote to Texas friends asking them to welcome the Houstouns. Matilda Houstoun, the captain's wife, later wrote *Texas and the Gulf of Mexico*, which was printed in two small volumes. The book was favorable to the Republic and encouraged immigration. When Ashbel read her book, he found it "spritely and entertaining" and recommended it highly. There were, however, other words about Texas by visitors that incensed him. Two books especially provoked his anger and disgust. The first, *The History of the Republic of Texas, from the discovery of the Country to the Present Time and the Cause of her Separation from the Republic of Mexico*, by Nicholas Doran P. Maillard, was published in London in 1842. Picturing Texas as an unhealthy, savage country, it warned Britons against emigration and also against recognizing Texas as an independent nation, claiming that it had acted in a "treasonable" manner toward Mexico.[35] Ashbel informed Anson Jones that Maillard had also written a letter to Lord Aberdeen trying to prejudice him against the Republic but added that he did not think the letter produced "the slightest effect."[36]

The second objectionable book about Texas, the one that enraged Ashbel, was *Narrative of the Travels and Adventures of Monsieur Violet, in California, Sonora, and Western Texas*, by Captain Frederick Marryat, also published in London. The book, which claimed to be a true account, pictured Texans as murderous, brawling, rude, cowardly, lazy, and drunken. Ashbel recognized in Monsieur Violet the notorious Count de Narbonne, a swindler and talented confidence man who had completely fooled some Texas leaders and whom he had met shortly before he left for Europe. Ashbel denounced the book in the London press, pointing out many errors and extensive borrowings from previously published works. In one of his letters, published in the *London Herald*, he railed against the book's "silly absurdities" and "monstrous falsehoods." Narbonne was thoroughly discredited, and subsequently the *Matagorda Weekly Dispatch* published a parody of the book called *Journal of the Seeings, Sayings, and Doings of the Count de Gnaw-Bone in the Prairies and Bottoms of Texas . . . Being a Sequel to "Monsieur Violet."*[37]

[35] Walter Prescott Webb, ed., *The Handbook of Texas*, 2:132.
[36] Ashbel Smith to Anson Jones, May 17, 1842, in Garrison, ed., *Diplomatic Correspondence*, pp. 955–58.
[37] Ashbel Smith to L. M. Rate, March 24, 1843; Ashbel Smith to Sam Houston,

Chargé d'Affaires to Saint James and Saint-Cloud 85

Ashbel was bitterly disappointed when it became apparent that his brother George was not going to be able to raise enough money to join him. The chargé's own financial situation was shaky. As Miller had predicted, his salary had been delayed, and Ashbel asked George to go to Austin to see Houston or Jones and try to obtain part of his salary for him. If that was impossible, George was to try to arrange a leave for Ashbel. "Write to me immediately," he told George. *"Remember I cannot remain in Europe without money, nor return without leave."*[38]

Early in March, Ashbel contracted an illness which he diagnosed as "a severe attack of modified small pox." He was confined to his bed for two weeks and to his flat for another week. Although he wrote to Caroline that he did not believe the attack would leave any scars, it did leave two or three deep pits on his face.

When he recovered from his illness, Ashbel made a trip to Brussels to try to secure Belgian recognition of Texas and to negotiate trade and emigration agreements between the two countries. He had met Leopold I, a son-in-law of Louis Philippe, in Paris at court entertainments. Now the king invited the chargé to dine and introduced him to leading politicians and industrialists, as well as to his own family. In later years Ashbel still remembered meeting Leopold's daughter, the doomed Carlota, who was then a "playful, cheery little girl." During several interviews Leopold told Ashbel that he was prepared to establish treaty relations with Texas on the usual grounds of the most-favored nation. He assured the chargé that the Belgians *were* interested in Texas from a commercial viewpoint but had to be concerned about their relationships with the United States and Mexico and could not afford to risk offending either power, especially since rumors of annexation were becoming more insistent. As a result Belgium did not at this time—or at any time—sign a treaty with the Republic.

Ashbel took advantage of his trip to Belgium to visit Antwerp, Amsterdam, The Hague, and Waterloo. These historic places stirred him: "My blood was often elevated within me, and I felt my dignity as a man increased while standing on ground where so much had been suffered and accomplished," he wrote Maria Hudson. He found Holland "fancifully pretty," saying that it "pleases and amuses," but

October 30, 1843; Ashbel Smith to Robert Walsh, November 27, 1843; William R. Hogan, *The Texas Republic*, p. 179.

[38] Ashbel Smith to George Smith, March 1, 1843.

he thought Dutch women "not as graceful as the French nor thoroughbred as the English."[39]

When Ashbel again tested the Spanish attitude toward the Republic, he found it similar to Belgium's. Washington Irving told Ashbel that "all parties in Spain are determined to maintain slavery in Cuba."[40] Irving and Ashbel kept in touch and developed a personal friendship as well as a friendly diplomatic relationship. They attended social functions together in Paris and were in agreement in their indignation at the "violent and indecent" language used in some of the European papers in articles about Texas and the United States. The sixty-year-old Irving suffered from poor health; Ashbel considered his symptoms and prescribed medicines and a diet for him.

After he was presented to Queen Victoria, Ashbel found himself a member of the highest social circle in London. He was invited to all the levees at Saint James's Palace and attended balls, galas, and dinners at Buckingham Palace. Lord Aberdeen invited him to a dinner to celebrate the queen's twenty-fourth birthday. Ashbel enjoyed finding himself in such company, and yet he had a strong sense of the artificiality of some of the entertainments.

Describing an "evening party" at Buckingham Palace, which included the emperor of Russia and the king of Saxony, as well as Queen Victoria and Prince Albert, Ashbel noted that the refreshments of "wines, tea, ices, jellies, etc.," were agreeable, as was the music. It was also pleasant to "converse with one's acquaintances," but as far as the illustrious personages were concerned, he found the occasion "stupid enough": "The high born mob were kept at a respectful distance from majesty, at which they gazed as any other multitude would stare at great folks."[41]

For his own enlightenment Ashbel regularly visited the Houses of Parliament to hear the great debates and to become familiar with their methods of carrying on business. He kept a list of words used by the best English speakers in ways different from the ways they were used by the best speakers in the United States. He thought that the Duke of Wellington had "strong practical good sense" but was "no orator."

During a debate over sugar duties in which Gladstone, Joseph

---

[39] Ashbel Smith to Maria Hudson, July 27, 1843.
[40] Ashbel Smith Journal, December 6, 1843.
[41] Ibid., June 8, 1844.

Chargé d'Affaires to Saint James and Saint-Cloud 87

Hume, and Hampton participated, he found it impossible to hear because of the noises made by the members—"roaring, shouting, and crowing—*crowing*"—he repeated in his journal. Nevertheless, he found greatness in the character of the English people and admired their honesty and sincerity.[42] In passing, however, he did not fail to notice their eccentricities and mused in his diary whether the English "patent double candle extinguisher, which put out the candle after one got into bed, was as ridiculous as the French spring hat that opened by "merely placing it on the head."

Ashbel's curiosity led him to visit Newgate and other prisons in and near London, and he also made trips to the Stock Exchange, the docks, the Chiswick Gardens, and the National Gallery. He met outstanding literary people, such as Edward Trelawny, and one morning at a breakfast given by Lord Monckton, he found Charles Dickens and William Makepeace Thackeray among the guests. As impressive as the company was the menu, which included such exotic delicacies as Russian sardines and reindeer tongues.[43]

Ashbel stayed in London longer than he had intended, because he wanted to keep an eye on the abolitionists. They were being stirred up by a man named J. P. Andrews, who, although he was acting on his own initiative, had access to some of the British leaders and was causing much excitement among antislavery groups. In an interview Lord Aberdeen and Ashbel Smith frankly expressed their opposing views about abolition, but Ashbel was satisfied that he had made the foreign secretary aware that Andrews had no official connection with the Republic.[44] So far Ashbel was pleased with the way he had done his job. "I have established in London a very fair reputation as a man of good sense and ability," he told George.

Leaving L. M. Rate in charge of Texas affairs at the London legation, Ashbel set out again for France, where he took "permanent" lodgings in Paris at 1, place Vendôme. Almost immediately he met with William Henry Daingerfield, who brought greetings from Sam Houston and the news that Ashbel was now Sir Ashbel Smith, a Knight of the Order of San Jacinto.

[42] Ibid., June 15, 1844.
[43] Ibid., June 21, 1844.
[44] Ashbel Smith to Anson Jones, July 31, 1843, in Garrison, ed., *Diplomatic Correspondence*, pp. 1116–19.

The Knights of San Jacinto had been created by Sam Houston so that the diplomats of the Republic would not have to appear titleless and ribbonless among the aristocratic diplomats of Europe. The ensign of the order, as decreed by Houston, was a green ribbon, to be worn in the buttonhole of the coat "opposite the heart." The president had not asked the Texas Congress to approve the order but had declared, ". . . as I am a friend to 'Order,' I would surely have a right to start an order, and then to create some reward for the *worthy*, as we have no cash, to encourage Gentlemen in preserving order."[45] Another honor that Houston bestowed on Ashbel at about this time was the title "Volunteer Aid to the President, with the rank and grade of Colonel in the staff."[46]

When Ashbel received word that Sam Houston had declared a truce with Mexico pending the signing of an armistice agreement, he wrote the Old Chief that the proclamation was "most glorious and important news" and congratulated him on "this signal triumph of your policy."[47]

The chargé spent his thirty-eighth birthday, August 13, 1843, writing official dispatches. The following week he went to Neuilly to call on Louis Philippe and present his compliments on the occasion of the birth of a daughter to the princess royal. He had a long conversation with the king about Texas during this visit. They discussed the question of annexation in detail, and Ashbel found the king knowledgeable about the Republic and its problems. To Ashbel's trained eye the king appeared to be "thoughtful, careworn, dissatisfied, *preoccupé*."[48]

When the king, the French foreign minister, and other court officials went on vacation in the late summer, Ashbel did likewise, staying at the country home of a friend who had been a fellow student some twelve years before in Paris. Life in rural Soisy-sous-Étoilles on the Seine was simple and regular. Between eight and nine in the morning he had a bowl of milk and bread and then spent two or three hours copying his old dispatches into the legation register. After that he read the paper and some pages in Rousseau's *Confessions* and strolled about

---

[45] Sam Houston to William Henry Daingerfield, January 28, 1843, in Houston, *Writings*, 3:310.
[46] Ashbel Smith to Sam Houston, August 1, 1843.
[47] Ibid.
[48] Ashbel Smith Journal, August 19, 1843.

the village. At six o'clock he dined and chatted; at nine he went to bed. The life was a contrast to the social whirlwind of the big cities, and he took advantage of the opportunity to get to know the countrypeople, attending the funeral of his washerwoman, watching the local guards review, and visiting a gypsy camp. He noted that the gypsies reminded him of the Comanche Indians in Texas.[49]

That fall Ashbel made several other excursions to different parts of France. In the wine-making country by "inquiry and observation" he learned about champagne making and was inspired to write for the National Institute in Washington an article on the cultivation of grapes and the preparation of the famous wine. Touring the chateau country, Ashbel met some "lively and entertaining" French girls, but he decided that they were too "frisky" for a grave man to think of with serious intentions.

In the latter part of 1843, Ashbel was thinking often about romance and about religion, especially Roman Catholicism. He was filled with awe when he visited the great Gothic cathedrals in Europe, but he disliked the ritual and the dogmatic beliefs of the Catholic church. He preferred the "good sense" of the Episcopal church or "old-fashioned Presbyterianism with the security of its rigid doctrine of duty."[50] The reason for Ashbel's renewed interest in Catholicism that fall was that he was "half in love" with one of the daughters of General Winfield Scott. She had visited Europe with her mother and other family members, and Ashbel had been introduced to the group in Paris. The Scotts had entertained him there, and he had traveled with their party to Rouen. Before the romance became full blown, however, Miss Scott had returned to the States, and Ashbel was left with his memories. To Caroline, who had heard that he was engaged to Miss Scott, he wrote denying the rumor, adding, "She is R.C.—noble-minded and highly gifted." He told Daniel: "I have been and still am considerably in love. . . . There are no dangerous symptoms except that I have taken a fresh impulse toward Catholicism." To Miss Scott he wrote, "I watch the winds daily during your voyage over the water."[51]

Before long Miss Scott was replaced in his thoughts and affections

---

[49] Ibid., August 23, 1843; October 1, 1843.
[50] Ibid., January 15, 1843.
[51] Ashbel Smith to Caroline Kittredge, May 1, 1844; Ashbel Smith to Daniel Seymour, October, 1843; Ashbel Smith to Miss Scott, October 17, 1843.

by another young visiting American named Margaret Johnston. Her family was not as prominent as General Scott's, and Ashbel's friends apparently were not as aware of this romance, but Margaret's image was deeply etched in Ashbel Smith's memory.

Occasionally Ashbel, along with the other foreign ministers, was invited to dine with the French royal family. He found the royal food good, but not as good as that served in other French homes. He liked the "quiet and pleasant manner" of the French ruler. From time to time Ashbel called on the royal family at Neuilly. These informal visits had a set pattern: the queen and others played whist in a corner of the room, the king's sister and several ladies sat at a center table embroidering and talking, and eight or ten gentlemen stood around the room. Neither the king nor they sat down. Tea and ices were offered by servants. Visitors left when they pleased without formal leavetaking, and by ten the salon was deserted.[52]

"The Texas Question"—whether or not Texas would or should be annexed to the United States—was a topic of discussion at most of the social gatherings Ashbel attended that winter. When asked about it, his invariable answer was that the numerical majorities of the northern states in both houses of the United States Congress rendered annexation so improbable—or, rather, "politically impossible"—that Texans need not consider the question. Privately Ashbel wrote to Daingerfield, "I regard the union of Texas to the U.S. as impracticable and the agitation of this subject therefore as injudicious as far as concerns Texas."[53] In January, 1844, he told Rate, "The incorporation of Texas into the American Union is utterly out of the question; and no proposition to this effect will be made by Texas."[54]

When he was proved wrong by both houses of the Texas Congress, which passed resolutions in favor of annexation by nearly unanimous votes, Ashbel fumed, "I think I know the motives of this act of folly: annexation however is *wholly out of the question.*"[55]

During the intermissions of the annexation drama Ashbel prepared a paper on the history and geography of Texas to be presented to the Royal Geographical Society in Paris. The group had elected him to

[52] Ashbel Smith Journal, December 30, 1843.
[53] Ashbel Smith to William Daingerfield, December 21, 1843.
[54] Ashbel Smith to L. M. Rate, January 10, 1844.
[55] Ashbel Smith to L. M. Rate, March 2, 1844.

Chargé d'Affaires to Saint James and Saint-Cloud

membership the previous fall, and he had promised to make a report on the Republic. Besides being a medical mecca, Paris was a center for geographical scientists, and one of the distinguished men in this field whom Ashbel met was Baron Alexander von Humboldt. The two men exchanged books and visits, and the chargé discovered that, even though the seventy-five-year-old baron was showing his age, his mind was still keen.

Ashbel had to postpone reading his paper until the summer meeting of the society, for that spring he decided to fulfill his long-held dream of a visit to Italy. Although he had not heard from George in months and his finances were "pretty slender," he decided to take what might be his only opportunity to gratify his longing to see Rome.

Traveling by steamer and diligence through Avignon and Genoa, he reached Rome in time for Holy Week. Archbishop Giuseppe Garibaldi, whom Ashbel knew as a fellow diplomat in Paris, arranged for him to be under the special care of the commandant of the Swiss Guard, who saw that he had the best seats for the various ceremonies of the Easter season. Ashbel was deeply moved by the solemnity of the vespers in the Sistine Chapel, with the gradual extinguishing of the lights as the day faded and the "peculiar quality" of the vocal music. The next day he attended a mass conducted by the pope, who was clothed in "white wrought with gold" and surrounded by cardinals in scarlet. For another ceremony, the ritual representation of the Last Supper, Ashbel was one of the half-dozen visitors assigned a place on the platform.[56]

Archbishop Garibaldi presented Ashbel to the pope for a private audience, and the chargé found the pope affable and good-tempered but "possessed neither of vigorous nor subtle understanding." During the interview, which lasted almost an hour, the topic of discussion was mainly the religious condition of Texas. "I dare say the Pope expects to pen us all in his fold eventually," Ashbel wrote Sam Houston.[57]

Before he returned to France, Ashbel visited Herculaneum, Pompeii, Naples, and Florence. He was enchanted by the beauty and fertility of the land and by the richness of Italy's art treasures. "I revelled in statuary," he wrote Daniel. But however much he appreciated the beauty of the scenery and the art, he came away from Italy with a low

---

[56] Ashbel Smith to Maria Hudson, March, 1844.
[57] Ashbel Smith to Sam Houston, June 2, 1844.

opinion of its inhabitants. "The citizens appear to be in a state of moral abandonment far below that of our slaves." he commented.[58] The trip proved more expensive than he had expected, and he arrived back in France with ten francs in his pocket.

He learned that while he was in Italy a treaty for annexation had been signed by James Pinckney Henderson and Isaac Van Zandt for Texas and John C. Calhoun for the United States. Ashbel's cousin Melancton Seymour wrote prophesying that the United States Senate would reject the treaty. "Your Texas folks should have held off until after the Presidential election. Why didn't your natives wait awhile?" he asked. Ashbel wondered the same thing. The United States Senate concurred with Melancton and rejected the treaty on June 8.

Privately Ashbel wrote to Rate, "The sooner we are thoroughly convinced we must go alone, the better for us."[59] The chargé told Anson Jones that at first England and France were "extremely dissatisfied" over the annexation threat but that he had "wholly" removed this feeling from Lord Aberdeen's mind by explaining that Texans had embraced the idea of annexation because they were weary of war and threats of war and that if England and France would act to force Mexico to peace annexation would not take place.[60]

When he went to the palace to discuss the situation, Ashbel was warmly greeted by the king, who took him into a private chamber and served him "iced chocolate." Louis Philippe told Ashbel that he believed Mexico would make peace if it was offered enough money—the king, as he talked, "making a gesture with his fingers as if offering and taking a bribe." Ashbel replied that Texas had no ready money but that it would enter into an agreement to pay in the future a reasonable sum for Mexico's relinquishment of any disputed territory. Ashbel's impression from their conversation was that France was opposed to annexation, but not as strongly as England was. As he was leaving, Ashbel was flattered that the king told him he was always "especially welcome."[61]

Back in England, June 24, Ashbel had another interview with

---

[58] Ashbel Smith to Daniel Seymour, April 30, 1844.
[59] Ashbel Smith to L. M. Rate, May 8, 1844.
[60] Ashbel Smith to Anson Jones, July 1, 1844.
[61] Ashbel Smith to L. M. Rate, July 9, 1844; Ashbel Smith Journal, July 19, 1844; Ashbel Smith to Anson Jones, July 31, 1844, in Garrison, ed., *Diplomatic Correspondence*, p. 1159.

Chargé d'Affaires to Saint James and Saint-Cloud 93

Lord Aberdeen, during which his lordship suggested that the British and French governments unite with Texas in a "Diplomatic Act" that would ensure peace and settle boundaries between Texas and Mexico and guarantee the separate independence of Texas. The United States was to be invited to participate in the act, and so was Mexico, which, in the event of its refusal, would be forced to submit to the act's provisions.

In relaying this offer to the Texas leaders, Ashbel warned that such an act might give the European nations the power to interfere in Texas affairs and suggested that there might be a ten-year limit on the "no annexation" provision, though he was aware that Lord Aberdeen considered Texas's independence as of paramount importance, since the earl did not want England to be in the position of "beating the bushes for the United States to catch the bird."[62]

Ashbel found Lord Aberdeen's attitude toward Texas more friendly than ever before, and he believed the foreign secretary sincere in his desire to aid Texas *if* it remained independent. Lord Aberdeen several times told Ashbel that he regretted the agitation for the abolition of slavery in Texas, which had created "so much dissatisfaction" in England, and assured him that in the future the British Foreign Office would have nothing to say or to do with regard to this issue.[63]

President Houston ordered Anson Jones to send Ashbel Smith instructions to conclude the "Diplomatic Act" with England and France. Jones, however, now president-elect of Texas, did not obey Houston's orders. Instead he sent the chargé the leave of absence that Ashbel had requested back in the spring and told him, "It is the desire of the President that all future negotiations . . . should be conducted at the seat of government of Texas."[64]

Ashbel was pleased to have the leave and also that Jones was to succeed Houston. He liked Jones and his wife, Mary, and respected him for his "comprehensive understanding and judgment" and for his "great stores of acquired knowledge." In his letter of congratulation to Jones on his election, Ashbel summed up his opinion of his *own* repu-

---

[62] Ashbel Smith to Anson Jones, June 24, 1844, in Garrison, ed., *Diplomatic Correspondence*, pp. 1153–56.
[63] Ashbel Smith to Sam Houston, June 2, 1844.
[64] Anson Jones to Ashbel Smith, August 1, 1844.

tation: "I leave behind me at the courts to which I have been accredited a reputation for capacity and conduct of which I am not ashamed."[65]

After two and a half years in Europe, Ashbel had cause to be concerned about his personal affairs. George was he knew not where and apparently was neglecting to take adequate care of his brother's affairs. Dr. Bowers had quit as overseer at Headquarters to go into full-time practice. The main house was boarded up, and Old Peter was left as caretaker. Ashbel's cousin Henry Gillette had taken Ashbel's other slaves to Houston, where Gillette had opened a school.

Brother Henry, who had written only one letter to Ashbel in all the time he had been gone, now wrote depicting their parents' condition as distressing. He reported that Phoebe had had only one new dress in five years, "and that a calico," and that Moses was equally destitute of clothing. Both had to work too hard at their ages and, though Caroline's husband was kind to them, he was not able to help them financially. Henry admonished Ashbel: "Come back to the United States to quit pursuing the little honors of life. . . . Squander no longer in the worthless foolishness of ambition for public life the extraordinary talents you possess."[66] As always, Henry was able to prick Ashbel's conscience. He replied, defending himself, saying that, rather than squandering time, in addition to carrying out his offficial duties he was acquiring knowledge. Furthermore, he had expected to have George come to Paris to study medicine under his guidance. Ashbel told Henry that if their parents and the Kittredges could be persuaded to move to Tennessee near Henry he would seriously consider moving there also.

In the midst of his preparations to leave Europe, Ashbel took time to write to Samuel F. B. Morse to alert him that the French government had appointed a commission to report on the *télégraphe électrique*. Ashbel thought his friend's device superior to any other experimental models he had seen, and he suggested that Morse present it to the commission. Ashbel also reported to Morse on his efforts to find out about English progress on the telegraph: "I saw Prof. Wheatstone's apparatus at King's College in London. . . . The names of Wheatstone, Faraday and others are often mentioned in connection with this sub-

---

[65] Ashbel Smith to Anson Jones, November 14, 1844.
[66] Henry Smith to Ashbel Smith, August 1, 1844.

Ashbel Smith's commission as surgeon general of the Republic of Texas Army, June 5, 1837. *Courtesy Barker Texas History Center, University of Texas at Austin*

Sam Houston's residence in Houston, 1837, which he shared with Ashbel Smith. *Courtesy Southwest Collection, Texas Tech University*

Building at 103 Jermyn Street in London, where Ashbel lived during his mission as chargé d'affaires to the Court of St. James, 1842.

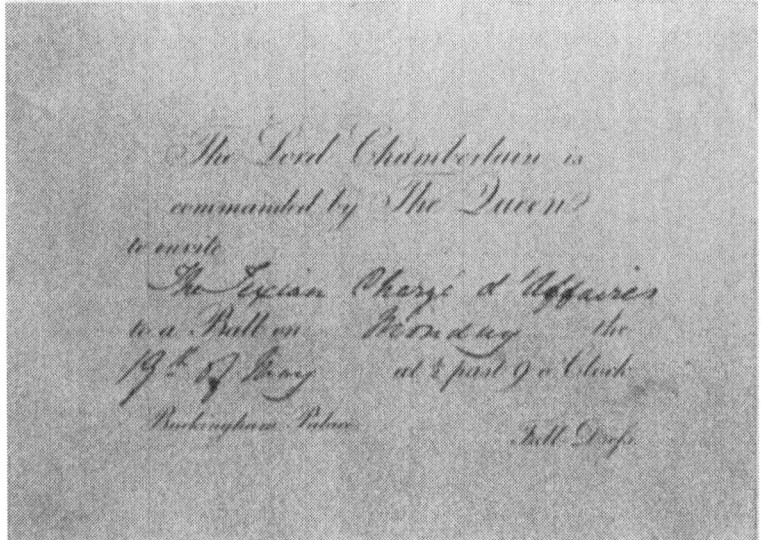

Ashbel's invitation to a ball at Buckingham Palace, London, 1845. *Courtesy San Jacinto Museum of History Association*

Evergreen, Ashbel Smith's home from late 1847 until his death, at Evergreen Point near present-day Baytown. *Courtesy Texas State Archives*

Portrait of Ashbel Smith in Confederate uniform by S. Salomon, probably painted in Memphis in 1862 after the Battle of Shiloh. *Courtesy Barker Texas History Center, University of Texas at Austin*

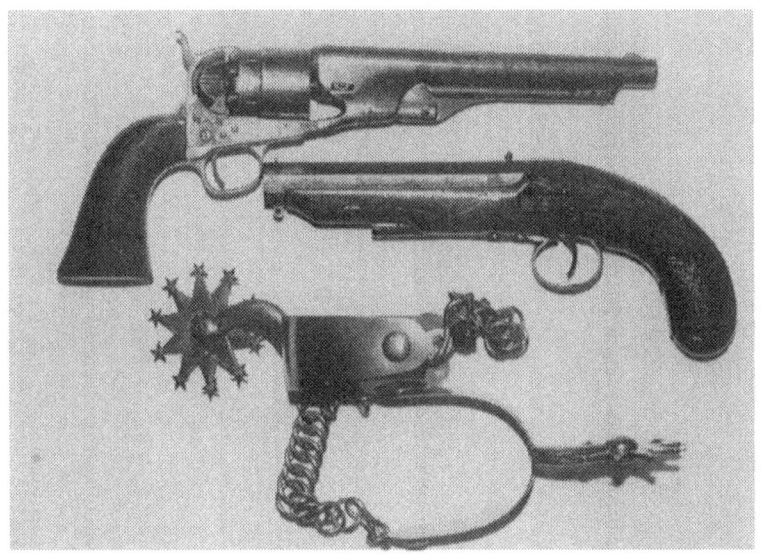

Revolver, pistol, and spurs of Ashbel Smith. *Courtesy San Jacinto Museum of History Association*

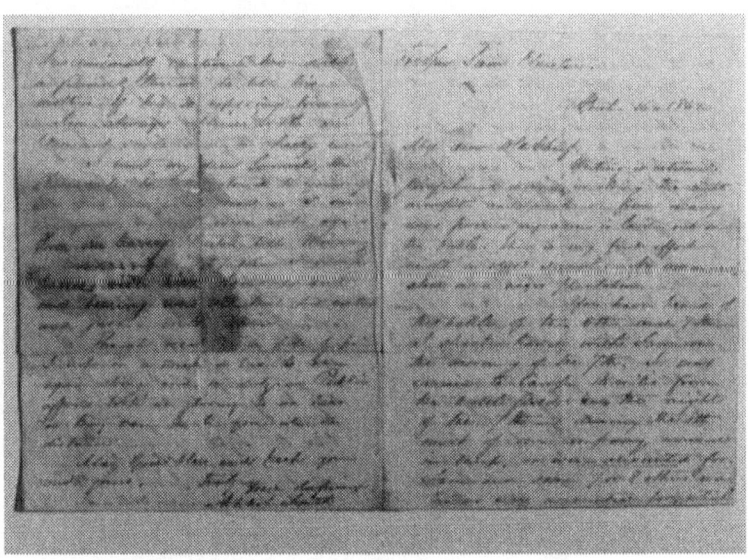

Letter from Ashbel to Sam Houston written after the Battle of Shiloh. *Courtesy San Jacinto Museum of History Association*

Portrait of Ashbel made in Paris in 1878 while he attended the international exposition there. *Courtesy Texas State Archives*

Ashbel's foster daughter, Anna Allen Wright. *Courtesy Barker Texas History Center, University of Texas at Austin*

Desk of Ashbel Smith, now owned by Larry J. Enderli, Baytown, Texas.

Left: Certificate from the first Houston State Fair to Ashbel for the best still-wine made of Texas grapes, May 23, 1870. *Courtesy Barker Texas History Center, University of Texas at Austin*. *Right*: Ashbel's perpetual calendar shelf clock, made by B. B. Lewis in Bristol, Connecticut, and patented in 1862. *Courtesy San Jacinto Museum of History Association*

Chargé d'Affaires to Saint James and Saint-Cloud 95

ject. I once spoke of your telegraph to Mr. Wheatstone but my remarks resulted in no conversation."[67]

When Ashbel's belongings were packed for shipment back to Texas, they filled three trunks and four cases. One trunk contained his personal letters and his clothes, plus a sword and a cane that Houston had given him. The other two trunks and the four cases were filled with books and pamphlets of all sorts. Ashbel made a list of every title—it filled nine pages and included everything from Aesop's *Fables* to Humboldt's *Travels*, plus many of the Greek and Roman classics, six volumes of Shakespeare, and many medical books in different languages.

Before he left England, Ashbel had a long interview with Lord Aberdeen. They discussed the possibility of war between Texas and Mexico, and the British foreign minister told the chargé that his government had "enjoined on Mexico in the most earnest and explicit terms to abstain from any attempt to invade Texas." Ashbel left the interview—and England—satisfied that he had had no small part in changing the atttude of the English toward Texas from distrust and disfavor to "thoroughly good and friendly confidence."[68]

Ashbel took the mail train from London to Liverpool on December 3, 1844, and the next day sailed for the United States on the *Arcadia*. After a tempestuous crossing he arrived in Boston on December 21. That same day Eben Allen, acting secretary of state of Texas, wrote a letter to him offering him the position of secretary of state of the Republic of Texas in the administration of President Anson Jones.

[67] Ashbel Smith to Samuel F. B. Morse, November 12, 1844.
[68] Ashbel Smith to Anson Jones, December 24, 1844.

CHAPTER SIX

The Final Act in This Great Drama (1845–1847)

AFTER spending a few days in Boston recovering from seasickness, Ashbel went on to Hartford and stayed with his parents for a week. George had part of Ashbel's salary to give him, and Ashbel gave Moses some of it to pay off debts. When George confessed to squandering a large sum of Ashbel's money, Ashbel, touched by George's poor physical condition and contriteness, only talked with him "earnestly" about his future. Then Ashbel took George to New York, enrolled him in the medical school of New York University, got him a job in the office of a doctor friend, and deposited five hundred dollars with the Seymours to cover his expenses.[1]

From his next stop, Washington, D.C., Ashbel wrote to Anson Jones that "public sentiment in the northern cities and in Congress is more favorable to annexation than I expected to find it."[2] He visited President John Tyler one evening "en famille without ceremony" and "rattled" sculpture and Italy with Tyler's young bride. The president, he found, was sanguine about the eventual success of annexation.

Ashbel also had a long interview with John C. Calhoun. Despite the twenty years' difference in their ages, the two men had much in common. Both were bookish, intelligent, indefatigable talkers, and graduates of Yale. They discussed soils and agriculture, as well as politics, especially annexation, which Calhoun did not believe would pass

---

[1] George eventually settled in Memphis, where he became noted for his gambling skill. He practiced medicine there and in later years acquired a farm.
[2] Ashbel Smith to Anson Jones, January 11, 1845.

The Final Act in This Great Drama

during the current session of Congress. Ashbel's high opinion of Calhoun was reaffirmed: the statesman was "lofty and generous, incapable of a mean, sordid thought." Writing to Maria of the visit, Ashbel included Calhoun's autograph for her collection.[3]

Continuing his journey to Texas, Ashbel stopped in Memphis, where he found his brother Henry away at Somerville court. In Memphis, Ashbel received an urgent request from Anson Jones to take charge of the Department of State of the Republic at his "earliest convenience." Hurrying on to New Orleans, he was delayed there waiting for the next ship to Texas. During the stopover he had a private meeting with J. de Arrangoiz, the Mexican consul general, who assured him that Mexico would make peace with Texas—on the condition that Texas remain an independent country.

Ashbel's reception in Texas was mixed. Editorials expressed concern about his activities abroad and his attitude toward annexation. His friends greeted him warmly, however. Arriving at Washington-on-the-Brazos on February 7, 1845, Ashbel accepted the thanks of President Jones for a job well done and the position of secretary of state at a salary of $1,500 a year. He was pleased to find that Lord Aberdeen had indeed sent a strong dispatch to Mexico warning against aggression and happily noted that the document's tone was "not merely decided—it was imperative."[4]

After taking care of the most pressing paper work connected with his new position, Ashbel took a few days' furlough to hurry to Galveston Bay. He found Headquarters in better shape than he had expected. In fact, Old Peter had managed to make a better crop than anyone else on the bay and had two hundred dollars' worth of corn for sale, as well as potatoes and other produce. There was plenty of meat, with a good stock of hogs and cattle, which Ashbel's neighbors had cared for on shares.[5]

While he was on the bay, Ashbel suffered from his old familiar complaint, malaria. When, however, news reached him that on February 28 the United States Congress had passed a joint resolution for annexation, he forgot his health and rushed back to Washington-on-the-Brazos. The Texas capital was a hornet's nest of activity and intrigue.

[3] Ashbel Smith to Maria Hudson, January 12, 1845.
[4] Ashbel Smith Journal, March 6, 1845.
[5] Ashbel Smith to George Smith, February 27, 1845.

Texans in general were hell-bent for annexation, but some of the persons Ashbel felt closest to did not share the general enthusiasm for becoming a part of the United States. Lamar was opposed to the idea, and Ashbel believed that Anson Jones also preferred independence, though he found the president determined to show no bias and to present the citizens of Texas with a choice. In later years Ashbel praised Jones's "sublime calmness" amid the clamor and the lies, threats, and denunciations against him and his cabinet. Sam Houston's stand was characteristically enigmatic, though his mentor, Andrew Jackson, sent letters and messages urging annexation through Jackson's nephew Andrew Jackson Donelson, the United States chargé d'affaires to the Republic.

Nothing Jones or his secretary of state said could penetrate the sentimentality and emotionalism that surrounded the issue. Ashbel believed that much of the fuel that fed the flames could be traced to Washington, D.C., and President Polk's emissaries, such as Archibald Yell, former governor of Arkansas, who held pep rallies and made lavish promises about what the federal government would do for Texas and also made offers of offices to aspiring Texas politicians in return for working to achieve annexation. Many unkind cuts were taken at Jones and his secretary of state as they stoically continued to work to give the Texans a rational choice. Perhaps the unkindest cut, as far as Ashbel was concerned, came from Memucan Hunt, who told him that he would not try to prevent the people from "tarring and feathering President Jones nor his cabinet members," if they did not move quickly toward annexation.

On March 29, Ashbel had a conference at Washington-on-the-Brazos with Saligny and Captain Charles Elliot, the chargés d'affaires of their majesties the king of France and the queen of England. These representatives officially invited Texas to accept the good offices of France and England for an "early and honorable settlement of their difficulties with Mexico upon the basis of the acknowledgment of the Independence of Texas by that Republic." Acting under instructions from Anson Jones, Secretary of State Smith accepted the offer and drew up a preliminary treaty, which provided that Texas would not accept any proposal or enter into any negotiations to annex itself to any other country for a period of ninety days from the date of the conference.[6]

[6]"Memorandum of a Conference held at the State Department at Washington-on-the-Brassos on the 29th March 1845," Ashbel Smith Papers.

The Final Act in This Great Drama 99

This treaty, to be known as the Smith-Cuevas Treaty, was carried to Mexico by the British minister, Captain Elliot, to be signed by the Mexican secretary of state, Luis G. Cuevas.

In the meantime, as news of the United States' offer of statehood spread throughout Texas, wild celebrations were accompanied by the booming of cannons to spread the news to rural dwellers. Henderson wrote Ashbel that when the news reached San Augustine the expression of universal joy was beyond anything he had ever seen "on any occasion." Ashbel did not share the spirit of jubilation. He believed that, once Mexico acknowledged the independence of Texas, the Republic's "pecuniary and material interests" and "the convenience of the people" would be better served by remaining independent. His public posture was to "cheerfully abide by the decisions of my fellow citizens."[7] Until annexation was definitely accomplished, however, it was his duty to promote Texas's interests as an independent country.

With his strong sense of duty he could not refuse when President Jones, prompted by Saligny and Elliot, asked him to return to Europe to make the seemingly inevitable annexation as palatable as possible to foreign leaders. On his way to Galveston, where he would embark for Europe, Ashbel kept silent about his purpose, letting it be rumored that he was going to Washington, D.C., to talk over terms of statehood with American leaders. He wrote back to President Jones from Galveston: "I am forced to believe that an immense majority of citizens are in favor of annexation . . . and that they will continue to be so in preference to Independence though recognized in the most liberal manner by Mexico. . . . When it is known that I am going to Europe, . . . *I feel convinced that public opinion will be inflamed beyond control.*"[8] He planned to delay his departure, remaining in Memphis long enough for Jones to send a message overland by John Bowers if the president decided to cancel the mission. Jones did try to send a recall notice to his secretary of state, but the country was flooded by heavy rains and Bowers could not get to Memphis in time to reach Ashbel before he left.[9]

Ashbel's prediction about public reaction to his trip was fully realized. He along with Jones was accused of selling Texas for "British gold." The *Galveston News* fretted: "We should like to know what he

[7] Ashbel Smith to Sam Houston, April 7, 1845.
[8] Ashbel Smith to Anson Jones, April 9, 1845.
[9] John H. Bowers to Ashbel Smith, April 20, 1845.

went for, what he has done, how much money he has pocketed, . . . what plan will next be fallen upon to disburse our public funds."[10] The *New Orleans Commercial Bulletin* speculated on the motive that had led the secretary of state to "desert his post at the capital of Texas at this important juncture in the affairs of his country."[11] The *New York Morning News* said: "It is difficult to imagine any other than one object of such a post-haste speed on the part of this functionary on the way to London—namely to ascertain from England what terms they can get, in the way of money, for their debt, as the condition of refusing annexation to the United States."[12] Bowers wrote Ashbel, "The Telegraph man embraces every opportunity to slander you. I hope you will stop his mouth on your return."[13] One evening soon after Ashbel's departure, while respectable citizens of Galveston were assembled at the Tremont House to discuss annexation, a mob of about fifty rowdies gathered near the market and hanged and burned an effigy of him. There were reports that he had also been burned in effigy at San Felipe.

On his journey, mindful that history was in the making and wanting the record to read correctly, Ashbel wrote letters marked "private" to Sam Houston, Anson Jones, Moseley Baker, Barnard Bee, and John Bowers in which he stated that upon his return he would work for annexation, if it had not already been accomplished. Later he asked his friends to produce these letters and have them published as proof of his goodwill toward annexation. In the letters he also pointed out that he was leaving Texas with extreme reluctance and at great personal sacrifice. To his cousin Henry Gillette he expressed the opinion that the wild speculation in the United States about his purpose in going to Europe might be all to the good: "A little alarm would do the American people no injury. Their politicians would not come up to the sticking place as regards Texas but from the apprehension that our country should conclude to get along without them."[14]

Ashbel reached London on May 14 and called at the Foreign Office the same day. After interviews with Lord Aberdeen and the under-

[10] *Galveston News*, April 22, 1845.
[11] *New Orleans Commercial Bulletin*, April 17, 1845.
[12] *New York Morning News*, quoted in *Journal of Commerce*, April 30, 1845.
[13] John H. Bowers to Ashbel Smith, April 20, 1845.
[14] Ashbel Smith to Henry Gillette, June 3, 1845.

The Final Act in This Great Drama 101

secretary of state, Ashbel reported, "I think I may safely assert that this Government regards annexation as certain, that they will not use any efforts to prevent its consummation, nor take any exception to it afterward"—all of which did not mean that the British *liked* the idea of annexation.[15]

In addition to holding meetings with members of the Foreign Office staff, Ashbel found time to promenade in Hyde Park, observe Derby Day at Epsom, and attend a dinner of the Committee of the Royal Society, at which "animal magnetism" was the chief topic. He saw the American actress Charlotte Cushman on stage and also socially. He admired her talent and wrote letters of introduction for her to influential friends in Paris. He also found time to buy books and a fine barometer.

In mid-June, Ashbel went to France, where he paid a visit to Louis Philippe and the royal family. The king spoke at length about his opposition to annexation and told Ashbel that he believed the American government was tending toward ultrademocracy and lawlessness. He cited as a curious example observations that he had made in Ohio on a trip some years earlier. Nevertheless, Ashbel concluded that the French government, like the English, would take no public exception to the annexation of Texas by the United States.

Ashbel worried over being in a "false position" at home. His letters were guarded, for he did not trust the English, French, American, or Texas post offices and thought that his mail might be spied on. As soon as he received notice of his formal recall, he began packing, and by August 1 he had reached New York.[16]

One of the old friends he saw there was Samuel Morse, who several years before had gratuitously granted the Republic of Texas the right to use his magnetic telegraph. At this meeting he assured Ashbel that when Texas became a state it would have the same right.

Ashbel visited his Seymour relatives in New York City, where he was detained by an attack of fever. When he had recovered somewhat, he went to Hartford, where he found Caroline in the ninth month of another pregnancy. Continuing on to Ohio to visit Curtis, Ashbel was forced to prolong his stay there by a severe chest cold. His brief stop-

---

[15] Ashbel Smith to Texas Secretary of State, June 3, 1845, in Garrison, ed., *Diplomatic Correspondence*, p. 1199.

[16] Ashbel Smith Journal, n.d. (ca. August 5, 1845).

over in Memphis was not a happy one. The brothers quarreled over Henry's management of Ashbel's real estate in Tennessee and of Ashbel's slaves. Ashbel had a long talk with his slave Albert, who chose to stay in Memphis for another seven months, since he was making good wages at the job he was hired out to do. In a matter of weeks, however, Albert wrote to Ashbel to say that he was sorry he had not gone with him, adding, ". . . if you had the good thoughts for me that I have for you nowing how bad I wants to bee at home you wold make them seven months role round like seven minits."[17]

Ashbel left Memphis abruptly while Henry was away from the house. Henry was remorseful and wrote Ashbel an affectionate letter, apologizing for any wrong he had done his brother and asking Ashbel to return soon so that he could "repair the unkindness." "Let us try hereafter," said Henry, "to be as brothers ought to be the best of friends."[18]

One of Ashbel's first actions upon his arrival in Texas was to send a long letter to the editor of the *Galveston Civilian* explaining and justifying his behavior during the annexation dispute.[19] In a letter to Henderson he stoutly defended the Smith-Cuevas treaty:

So far from regretting that I signed it I rejoice in having done so. Texas enters the Union with brighter mien than she would have done without an acknowledgment of our independence by Mexico. But for the treaty with Cuevas, history would have remained that having wrested Texas from Mexico, we were forced to throw ourselves into the arms of the U.S. for our feebleness.[20]

Ashbel believed that in some ways he had been made the scapegoat in the controversy. Although he told Henderson that "I came back as quickly as possible to show my teeth to my enemies," under his façade of scorn he was deeply hurt. He congratulated Henderson on being the candidate for the first governor of the state of Texas and mentioned that, although he would like to stand for the United States Congress, he was afraid that he was "still too unpopular" to be elected.

President Jones welcomed Ashbel back to the capital and gave his wholehearted approval to Ashbel's performance as secretary of state "in all particulars." He also gave Ashbel permission to publish any documents in the Texas State Department files as he thought necessary or

---

[17] Albert Smith to Ashbel Smith, August 29, 1845.
[18] Henry Smith to Ashbel Smith, August 21, 1845.
[19] Ashbel Smith to H. Stuart, editor of *Galveston Civilian*, August 7, 1845.
[20] Ashbel Smith to J. P. Henderson, September 22, 1845.

The Final Act in This Great Drama   103

proper. Last but not least the president authorized Ashbel to make out an account of his expenses for audit.

During the fall of 1845, Ashbel worked with Jones and other cabinet officials to wind up the affairs of the Republic. On October 13, the date for the vote on the annexation proposal and the state constitution, Ashbel acknowledged that annexation was "in the hearts of the people" and voted yes. On December 29, 1845, when President Polk signed the Act of Annexation, Ashbel Smith and his fellow Texans became citizens of the twenty-eighth state.

In his own mind, however, Ashbel was never convinced that they had made the right decision. Increasingly, as the years passed, he took opportunities to point out the failure of the federal government to fulfill many of the promises it had made when it was courting Texas in 1844 and 1845. Thirty years after annexation Ashbel told an audience that the people of Texas, "relying on the promises made by the federal officials, and animated by affection for the country of their birth, . . . sacrificed as on an altar their independent autonomy."[21]

As the curtain descended on the Republic and the year, Ashbel considered what he should do next. He wrote to Maria Hudson, "You occupy more of my thoughts than any other human being." He mentioned that he was still "hunted in the newspapers as a wild beast" and that he had been standing "sullenly at bay" and almost scorned human sympathy, for his enemies were not "worthy of my disdain."[22] When Caroline wrote to announce that he had a new niece, he responded, "I love it already very much. I feel quite alone in the world. I hope your children will be some company for me, especially the little girl."[23]

During January, 1846, Ashbel twice entertained a visiting German naturalist, Ferdinand Roemer, and supplied him with information about Texas. Roemer was surprised by the austere living quarters of the former Texas minister—both in Galveston and at Headquarters, on the bay. Roemer commented that his host's tiny one-room house in Galveston appeared to be built of boards loosely thrown together. The only furnishings were a bed, a small table, two broken chairs, and a chest full of papers and books. Paying a call one day, he found Colonel Bee lying on the bed and Ashbel seated on the chest in the middle of

---

[21] Ashbel Smith, *Reminiscences of the Texas Republic: Annual Address Delivered Before the Historical Society of Galveston, December 15, 1875.*

[22] Ashbel Smith to Maria Hudson, January 2, 1846.

[23] Ashbel Smith to Caroline Kittredge, December, 1845.

the floor, which was strewn with papers in "wild disorder." The German scientist soon found, however, that the simple surroundings "did not preclude a many-sided, thorough knowledge and a finished urbanity of manner."

Two weeks later Ashbel happened to embark on the same steamer on which Roemer and Mr. and Mrs. Houstoun were traveling, bound for a few days' visit at Colonel Morgan's home. Ashbel invited them all to visit Headquarters. Again Roemer marveled at the rough accommodations of this accomplished gentleman:

> The manor house was a common two roomed log cabin, built of partly hewn logs. The simple furniture consisted of a bed, a table and a few chairs, the seats of which were made by stretching a calfskin tight over them. On the wall near a huge fireplace, in which logs four to five feet in length could be placed, hung an American rifle with a long, heavy barrel, and a shot gun.
>
> In the corner of the room stood a tall cabinet, whose contents contrasted sharply with the surroundings. It contained chiefly books which formed a small but carefully selected library. Not only were the Greek and Roman classics represented, but also the best and choicest selections of English and French literature.[24]

Roemer noticed several other log houses for guests and for slaves and log structures serving as stables and a corncrib. At the back of the farm was level prairie, and on one side was a forest. As they rode about the plantation, the visitors and their host twice startled herds of deer, and Roemer saw his first flock of wild turkeys.[25]

On February 19, 1846, Ashbel was in Austin to witness the "death of the Republic and the birth of the state" in a ceremony in which President Anson Jones turned the leadership of Texas over to Governor James Pinckney Henderson. As he watched the Texas flag lowered and the United States flag raised in front of the capitol, Ashbel heard Anson Jones say, "The final act in this great drama is now performed; the Republic of Texas is no more." Jones was wrong. There would be one more act—or at least an epilogue—including violent and bloody scenes, before the drama was finally ended.

Throughout the early spring of 1846, Ashbel busied himself overseeing the crops and animals at Headquarters. For the moment he had no official duties, and he had not yet returned to the practice of medi-

---

[24] Dr. Ferdinand Roemer, *Texas*, trans. Oswald Mueller.
[25] Ibid.

cine. Watching with great interest Houston's performance as a United States senator, Ashbel read with care the copies of his speeches his old friend sent him.

He was also involved in public education in the new state. "We are trying to do something in relation to common schools in Texas," Ashbel wrote to Henry Barnard, adding, "If hereafter I have any other pursuit than the strenuous practice of medicine, I shall devote myself to that of education." In January the Convention of the Friends of Education met in Houston to talk about some of the problems connected with education in Texas, including selecting textbooks, establishing a college to train teachers, and improving the "mode" of instruction. The convention formed an organization called the Texas Literary Institute. Chauncey Richardson was named president, and Ashbel Smith vice-president.[26]

No matter what activities occupied Texans that spring, their attention was never completely diverted from Mexico and its deteriorating relationship with the United States. In his campaign for the presidency Polk had followed Andrew Jackson's advice to promise the country "All of Oregon, All of Texas." When his efforts to negotiate with Mexico for disputed land in Texas and elsewhere failed, the United States prepared for war.

When the formal declaration of war came in May, 1846, Ashbel Smith immediately joined the Texas Volunteers. At first he was stationed at a camp near Point Isabel, close to the mouth of the Rio Grande, in low, flat wet prairie land covered with mesquite and prickly pear. He observed that the health of the men was generally good in spite of certain hazards of the region, such as centipedes, millipedes, tarantulas, and rattlesnakes.[27]

Tents were in short supply, and the Texans suffered greatly from exposure during the wet spring and early summer. It rained incessantly during the last three weeks of June, and for one three-day period Ashbel and the men in his company stayed wet to the skin night and day. Every blanket was soaked, and even the clothes in their packs were sodden. As the prairie became a lake, the men cut green grass to make themselves raised pallets to avoid lying in water. Cooking was impossible, and Ashbel described their dry bread as turning into the

---

[26] James D. Carter, *Education and Masonry in Texas, 1846 to 1861.*
[27] Ashbel Smith to George Smith, July 12, 1846.

consistency of a poultice. His squad subsisted for a time chiefly on raw pickled pork.[28]

The joy of the soldiers when the sun appeared soon turned to misery, for with the sunshine came swarms of insects. The most troublesome were the large blowflies. Blankets that had been spread out to dry were covered with masses of larvae, which in a matter of hours became creeping maggots, crawling over and into everything. Ashbel removed four of the loathsome vermin from the ear of a Mexican servant. Gulf breezes were of some help in controlling the mosquitoes, but at times the creatures were maddening to both men and horses. Although he did not connect the mosquitoes with malaria, Smith noted that the brisk breezes that accompanied stormy weather seemed to prevent its occurrence. He concluded that exposure to extremely wet or hot weather was not harmful to the men but that when the rains slackened and left pools of stagnant water the "miasma" somehow increased the cases of fever. The main complaint that he treated was diarrhea.[29]

Soon after he arrived at the camp, Ashbel rode out to the field where the battle of Palo Alto had taken place. He observed that many bodies of Mexicans killed in the battle were still lying where they had fallen. The rains had not begun, and the temperature ranged from 80 degrees at night to 95 degrees in the shade during the day. The bodies had dried up and become almost mummified. After the rains began a few days afterward, he discovered that the bones of the bodies had been macerated and cleaned by the downpour. He went on to Matamoros, where he obtained permission to visit the Mexican hospitals and observe the treatment of the wounded, taking notes on the kinds of wounds and the patients' responses to various treatments.[30]

On the Fourth of July the men of all the companies in the area gathered for a celebration. Ashbel was asked to give the principal address. He invoked the spirits of James Bowie, William B. Travis, James Fannin, Benjamin Milam, and Davy Crockett, vowing, "You have not shed your blood in vain," and exhorting the soldiers to follow the examples of these heroes.

Early in July, Ashbel was transferred to Matamoros, where Lamar and Henderson were stationed. Camp life there was as monotonous as

[28] Ibid.
[29] "Report on the War with Mexico," Ashbel Smith Papers.
[30] Ibid.

the food, which was invariably coffee, boiled rice, bread, and fried bacon, occasionally with fresh beef or game. To break the routine, Ashbel and Lamar planned a big game hunt. One morning after an early breakfast they mounted their horses and, accompanied by three Mexican servants, struck off into the desolate country east of the camp. Their "game" were the domestic creatures that had strayed from farms and become wild. During the day the Mexicans lassoed four wild asses, and Ashbel shot an old bull and a sow. The wounded sow turned on him but fell dead of her wound before she could reach him. The men spent almost the entire day in the saddle, much of it riding at a gallop. As a welcome relief to their usual diet they ate "excessively" of the prickly-pear fruit and were made half sick by their greed. In describing the day, Ashbel did not complain of the heat or of fatigue but instead imagined that he could understand the enjoyment of tiger hunting from the "pleasure" this experience had brought him.[31]

As July dragged on, Ashbel became discouraged about the chances that the Texas Volunteers would get into a "fight." After a talk with General Zachary Taylor, he was even more pessimistic: the general believed strongly that Mexico should be invaded from the Gulf, not overland from Matamoros.

One hot summer day Ashbel was seized by the sensation of "a great rush of blood" to his head. The seizure, which he termed "apoplectic," was followed by a general weakness. He asked for a leave of absence and returned to Headquarters, where he treated himself mostly by sleeping, eating no meat, and drinking only water. By the last week of August he was feeling well enough to make his long-planned trip North.

Ascending the Mississippi River on the way to New York, his steamer, the *Josephine*, stopped to assist a Louisiana steamer that had run aground. On board the Louisiana ship were Sam Houston and Thomas Rusk, Texas's senators, who were on their way home after the closing session of Congress. The three Texans enjoyed a long political discussion while the senators' ship was being pulled off the bank. Houston expressed some dissatisfaction with Polk, whom he had supported. He also told Ashbel that he had not drunk any "spirituous or vinous beverage" since he left Texas. Rusk verified Houston's good behavior and suggested that Houston might find himself a candidate for

---

[31] Ashbel Smith to George Smith, July 12, 1846.

the White House if he continued his model behavior. Ashbel pondered this idea as he proceeded on his way. He considered the propriety of writing a letter to the editor of some northern paper supporting Houston for the presidency but put the idea aside for the time being.[32]

Detouring to Washington, Ashbel visited President Polk to give a firsthand account of the activities of the Texans in the Mexican War. The former secretary of state for the Republic still smarted from the treatment he and other Texas officials had received from Polk during the annexation negotiations, but Ashbel felt an obligation to report to Polk directly. It was also good politics.

Reaching Hartford, Ashbel spent several weeks with his parents on their farm and then moved into town to stay with the Kittredges. The "old bachelor," as he called himself, delighted in romping with his two nephews, Ashbel Smith and Henry Grattan, and getting to know his dark-haired, bright-eyed little niece, Jessie. The Kittredges' older daughter had died while Ashbel was in Europe. Ashbel told Caroline that "like most bachelors" he knew a great deal about rearing children. Two of his rules were that children should always be told the truth and that they should never be struck.

In New York, Ashbel visited his relatives and friends and spent hours in political talk. General Taylor was much discussed as a presidential possibility. Reporting his findings to Houston, Ashbel wrote: "If General Taylor should be the candidate of the Whigs, we shall want a candidate who can overmatch him in military renown. . . . Your friends are well aware you can give Gen. Taylor long odds and beat him."[33]

One chore that Ashbel performed on this trip was to examine texts and lists of books offered by publishing houses so that he could suggest suitable books for Texas schools to the Texas Literary Institute. For the first time in fifteen years he visited New Haven, where he attended the ordination of Theodore Dwight Woolsey, president-elect of Yale. Looking up his old professors, Ashbel found great enjoyment in "talking" Latin, Greek, philosophy, metaphysics, and travel with them.

When he first planned this trip to the North, Ashbel had told Caroline that he really had no definite reason for coming, but that was

[32] Ashbel Smith Journal, August 29, 1846.
[33] Ashbel Smith to Sam Houston, fall, 1846.

The Final Act in This Great Drama

hardly the whole truth. Apparently Margaret Johnston was in his thoughts, although her name does not appear in his diary or in his letters since his first meeting with her. On October 13 he wrote a letter to her asking her to be his wife, telling her that he had loved her from the moment he met her in Paris with "all the vast and profound devotion of which my strong and violent nature is capable." Time and distance, he told her, had only increased his love, and he had used the name Margaret as a talisman "in presence of fierce political opponents . . . in difficulty and in danger, in the desert and on the campaign." He promised her a devotion "more intense and profound" than that any other man could give her and asked to be allowed to devote the rest of his life to her. He delivered the letter to Margaret in person. The next day he noted cryptically in his journal: "Answer from Miss M. J.—The poetry of life is gone."[34]

On the return trip to Texas, Curtis accompanied Ashbel as far as Memphis. Also along was Curtis's oldest son, Ashbel Grattan, who was to accompany his Uncle Ashbel home to Texas for a long visit. During the two-week stopover in Memphis, Ashbel and Henry reconciled their differences and resumed their affectionate if sometimes abrasive relationship. One of the services Henry performed for Ashbel was to act as go-between in an "affair of the heart." The forty-one-year-old bachelor was seriously wife hunting. During this visit he explored the possibility of marrying a Judith Pope, who had attracted him on previous visits to Memphis. Afraid of another rejection, he sent his tentative proposal to her in a roundabout way through Henry and her father. Her answer was no, though she expressed high regard for her cautious suitor. Ashbel was dejected over this second refusal in a few weeks, and, with perhaps a taste of sour grapes, he told Henry that he had wanted to marry not "for the woman, but to have children."

While he was in Memphis, Ashbel visited the new medical college there. He was offered a professorship but did not give a definite answer. He longed to live near his close relatives but told Henry Gillette, "Such reputation as I have is identified with Texas, and I am unwilling to dissever myself from the state."[35]

When he reached Headquarters late in December, his health seemed improved, but his gloomy feelings matched the dreariness of

[34] Ashbel Smith Journal, October, 1846.
[35] Ashbel Smith to Henry Gillette, December 28, 1846.

the weather. Uncertainty about his future filled him with an "unreasoning discontent." He knew that he needed "occupation" but was unsure where to find it. He had brought the rest of his slaves with him from Memphis, since the only immediate prospect he saw was to become a sugarcane grower. He realized, however, that plantation life would not satisfy his restlessness. He wrote to medical friends, sounding them out on the possibility of obtaining a chair in one of the New York schools of medicine but received no encouragement, for the competition for such positions was great, and many distinguished medical men had claims on each place.

On the night of January 1, 1847, Ashbel went to bed as usual after a quiet and "abstemious" day. He slept well but awoke in the morning with an attack similar to the one he had suffered on the Río Grande the previous summer. He thought he detected some symptoms of incipient paralysis and noted that mental activity of any duration brought on alarming recurrences of the "fullness" in the head and severe headaches. He reluctantly decided that he must stop all mental labor for several months. His illness made him long more than ever to be closer to his family. He was still thinking about moving to Memphis. "Father and Mother could live with me," he told Henry. "If my health fail utterly I want some attention more than that of negroes—mother alone could give it to me, and I might be company for her and father." He admitted miserably, "I have of late suspected that my affliction of the head may arise from a 'mind diseased'—if so, I must try to live with mother and father."[36]

Although he did not suffer another acute attack, his symptoms bothered him for months. In the mornings he could perform a little mental activity, but by afternoon he felt "dull and stupid." He was depressed and melancholy. Sam Houston and Daniel Seymour prescribed matrimony to cure his depression and physical ailments. Houston told him:

... if I can have the pleasure to see you, I am sure, I can devise some plan, by which, you will be restored to health. You know that my treatment is partly depletive, & partly, translative! ... I really do think, if I could see you, and thereby induce you, to court, and marry some fine woman, that you would recover by a most rational treatment![37]

[36] Ashbel Smith to Henry Smith, January 8, 1847.
[37] Sam Houston to Ashbel Smith, April 12, 1847, in Houston, *Writings*, 5:10.

The Final Act in This Great Drama 111

In February, Ashbel was called from his convalescence to attend Margaret Houston. He traveled to Grand Cane, on the Trinity River, where she had moved to be with her brother and mother after Sam Houston returned to his senatorial duties in Washington. Margaret was suffering from a painful lump on her right breast, but Ashbel did not want to attempt its removal for she still had milk in the breast following the birth of her last child. After treating the breast and giving instructions for her care, he returned home. But the tumor grew rapidly and broke, and Margaret sent for him in alarm. When he saw her condition, Ashbel was afraid to delay the operation any longer, though he hated to perform such serious surgery with Houston so far away. The amputation was carried out successfully—without an anesthetic, for the pious Margaret would not touch whiskey, the only one available. The wound healed nicely, and Sam Houston had another reason to feel "a deep and abiding sense of obligation" toward his old roommate. A few weeks later he presented Ashbel with a fine stallion named Arabian John.

In May, Ashbel successfully operated on another distinguished patient, performing surgery for hemorrhoids on John Hemphill, chief justice of the Texas Supreme Court. Ashbel tried to limit his practice to surgery, for which he was well trained, but he could not refuse his services to friends who came to him with other problems, even though there was little money to be made from general practice, for most of his patients simply did not have cash to pay his fees.

Ashbel considered going to Veracruz and joining the United States Army, which was on the move toward Mexico City. His health was still uncertain, however; intermittently he suffered from malaria, digestive upsets, and severe headaches. Since he could not join the action, he contented himself with writing an article for the *Galveston News*, expressing confidence that Mexico would soon be conquered and outlining an elaborate plan to answer the question: What shall be done with Mexico? His plan was modeled on the governance of the East Indies by the East India Company, a system which he pointed out had worked for two hundred years.[38]

When yellow fever returned to Galveston in the fall of 1847, Ashbel Smith was one of its early victims. He diagnosed his case as "se-

---

[38] Ashbel Smith scrapbook, May 18, 1847, Ashbel Smith Papers.

vere"; for eleven days he could not sit up in bed. One night about midnight he vomited some brownish fluid, which made him suspect the beginning of black vomit, a fatal symptom. His ideas became "singularly" cool and collected as he faced what he supposed was certain death. In this case his prognosis happily proved erroneous, and he made a good recovery. In fact, he found that his head was decidedly better than it had been for months, and he rejoiced that he could again exert himself mentally without strain. During his convalescence Plato was "an infinite delight" to him.[39]

As soon as he was strong enough, he began treating other victims of the epidemic. He made dissections and took notes with the view of adding additional cases to the second edition of his pamphlet on yellow fever. Using a mild treatment, which involved minimum medication and maximum nursing care, Ashbel lost only one patient during the siege.

In the late fall Ashbel was offered an opportunity to buy a number of acres adjoining his plantation by his neighbor, Moseley Baker. Although he had no ready cash, it was too good a chance to let pass, and Ashbel agreed to buy the land for $5,000. He paid $3,000 by exchanging some of his other property and also raised $300 in cash for a down payment, which left him with a debt of $1,700. To help pay off the debt and to allow himself more freedom, Ashbel entered into a partnership with a Dr. John C. Taylor, an Englishman, who had the "best practice in Galveston."

Baker's farm had been called Evergreen, and Ashbel kept the name for his own plantation. He hired Wager Smith as his overseer for the combined Headquarters and Evergreen estate. Ashbel proposed that the two men work on shares, Wager taking one-third of the profits of the plantation and one-fourth of the increase in the stock on their final division. Of his sixteen slaves—eight adults, four teenagers, four children—Ashbel planned to use two or three to wait on him as he traveled between the plantation and his medical practice in Galveston.

Ashbel wrote to Kincaid that he now had "one of the best places in this part of the world—1600 acres situated on the water and steamboats passing daily and all seasons of the year." Although he did not realize it at the time, in purchasing Evergreen, Ashbel Smith had ac-

---

[39] Ashbel Smith to Daniel Seymour, November 11, 1847.

quired the house and land that he would call home for the rest of his life. He did realize what was lacking to make his house a home. When Daniel Seymour reported that Henry Barnard had married, Ashbel wished his friend well and sighed, "This marriage revives in me an intense sense of my own desolateness."

CHAPTER SEVEN

To Enter Battle
(1848–1855)

DISTRESSED by an increase in medical quackery in Texas, Ashbel Smith and his partner, John Taylor, met with nine other Galveston physicians on January 17, 1848, to form an organization called the Medical and Surgical Society of Galveston. Its purpose was to create higher standards for the profession by promoting training and sharing knowledge, establishing a medical library, and appointing a board of censors to control licensing of doctors in Texas. The society voted to send Ashbel as a delegate to the third annual meeting of the new American Medical Association, to be held in Baltimore, Maryland, that spring.[1]

Ashbel wrote to his state representative, Charles Keenan, a fellow physician, urging him to help bring about the establishment of a state medical society and suggesting that he appoint delegates to the AMA meeting. Since Ashbel would be there anyway to represent the Galveston medical group, he volunteered to represent the state also.[2] But the legislature failed to act, and the state society was not approved.

Another controversy was beginning to occupy Texans' attention: the issue of slavery. Many years before, as a newspaper editor in North Carolina, and later as minister to England and France for the Texas Republic, Ashbel had formulated and articulated his ideas about slavery. When a county convention met at Galveston on January 31 to elect delegates to the state convention, Ashbel was there, emphatically expressing his opinion that the United States Congress had no authority to establish *or* to abolish slavery.[3]

[1] Nixon, *The Medical Story of Early Texas*, pp. 467–71.
[2] Ashbel Smith to Dr. Charles Keenan, February 5, 1848.
[3] Anna Irene Sandbo, "Beginning of Secession Movement in Texas," *Southwestern Historical Quarterly* 18 (July, 1914): 44–45.

To Enter Battle 115

The first anniversary of the Battle of Buena Vista coincided with the celebration of George Washington's birthday on February 22, 1848. Ashbel was called upon for a speech honoring both events, which he delivered in the Methodist Church in Galveston. Tracing the state's history, he vindicated its rights to the soil of Texas, justified its claim to the Río Grande as a boundary, and asserted the righteousness of the role of the United States in the war with Mexico. He shared the general euphoria over the idea of manifest destiny. "It is our destiny, our mission to civilize, to Americanize this continent," he told his audience.[4] The speech was received enthusiastically, though one reporter heard political overtones and suggested that "the hero of San Jacinto" so floated before Ashbel Smith's vision that he could not see General Taylor clearly.[5] In a letter to Sam Houston, written soon after the Washington Day speech, Ashbel again encouraged Houston to oppose Taylor in the coming presidential election.

In the same letter Ashbel suggested that his friend might use his influence to help establish a federal marine hospital at Galveston—with Dr. Ashbel Smith as hospital surgeon.[6] The federal hospital was not forthcoming, but Houston did use his senatorial influence to have Ashbel appointed to the West Point Board of Visitors for the June, 1848, examinations at the academy.

Leaving Galveston on April 30, Ashbel went to Baltimore, where he attended the AMA convention and also the stormy Democratic Convention that nominated Lewis Cass, whom Ashbel had known in Paris, as its presidential candidate. The conservative Cass, who had been United States Minister to France, governor of Michigan Territory, secretary of war, and a United States senator, was the father of the idea of "popular sovereignty." His willingness to allow the expansion of slavery into newly acquired territories made him acceptable to southern representatives like Ashbel, when it became clear that the convention was adamant that the nominee must be a northerner.

After the convention Ashbel went on to West Point to meet the other members of the board of visitors, who elected him president at their first meeting. Under his direction the board did a thorough job of inspecting the academy and the 272 cadets enrolled in it. The tone of

---

[4] Ashbel Smith, *An Address Delivered in the City of Galveston on the 22d of February, 1848, the Anniversary of the Birthday of Washington, and of the Battle of Buena Vista*.

[5] Ashbel Smith to Sam Houston, March 25, 1848.

[6] Ibid.

the detailed report clearly shows Ashbel's style. It manages to combine patriotic sentiments with praise for the things the academy was doing well and explicit suggestions for correcting its deficiencies. The buildings, the uniforms, the water supply, the hospital facilities, the mineralogical collection, and the cadets' physical and mental abilities were all looked into.[7] After the examinations Ashbel made a speech to the graduating class. He reminded the cadets of the "weighty and solemn" obligation they now had to repay their country for the years they had been maintained at public expense. The end of his speech was calculated to inspire in the young men some sober thoughts about what that debt might be: "Your bones may whiten on a foreign strand. They may moulder in Mexico or other lands, or happily be brought home to be entombed in your native soil, . . . but your true sepulchres will be in the undying gratitude, the eternal remembrance of your country."[8]

When the business of the board was completed, Ashbel went on to Harvard and Yale to attend their commencement ceremonies. At Yale he was invited to give a speech before a meeting of the Yale alumni. After being introduced by Silliman, Ashbel gave them some "plain facts about Texas." He told them that Texas had laid the foundation for a system of common schools and that in Galveston there were 400 pupils in the schools, which were open to every child. He described the rapid population growth in Texas, pointing out that when the Texas Revolution commenced fifteen years earlier the population of Texas had been "not 15,000 [but] within twelve years . . . [had] increased to 153,000."[9]

Ashbel was invited to give a paper on "yellow and bilious fevers" before the New York Academy of Medicines. The paper was well received, and the academy sent him a diploma signifying his election as a corresponding fellow of that organization. Late in the fall he addressed a mass meeting of Democrats in Newark, New Jersey. After the meeting he was asked to speak at Tammany Hall, in New York City. This speech, supporting General Cass and discussing the free-soil issue, was reported in the *New York Herald*.[10]

[7] "Report on the Board of Visiters [*sic*], West Point Military Academy, June, 1848," Ashbel Smith Papers.

[8] Ashbel Smith, "Address before the Officers and Cadets of the United States Military Academy," June 18, 1848, Ashbel Smith Papers.

[9] Ashbel Smith speech, 148th commencement of Yale, August 16, 1848.

[10] *New York Herald*, November 5, 1848.

To Enter Battle

At last, on December 1, Ashbel turned his face toward the South. He passed the long hours of the journey reading a life of Louis Philippe, which he dismissed as a "mere compilation from works within the reach of everybody," and the New Testament in Greek. To read the New Testament in translation, he commented, was the equivalent of viewing Caesar in "modern pantaloons and a beaver hat" instead of a toga and laurel crown. When he came to the story of the miracle of Christ's restoring the man's withered hand, he commented in his journal: "The man was directed to stretch forth his hand—what is the cure for the withered heart? Is it not to stretch *it* forth also; but whereunto or to what? Aye to what—in this world?"[11]

In Memphis, Ashbel found the inhabitants in a state of panic because of an outbreak of cholera. His acquaintances begged him to stay with them while the disease raged. Consequently, he spent almost six weeks in Memphis, serving as an active member of the board of health, using the treatment he had found most effective in managing the disease, and taking notes of his observations of his own and other doctors' patients.

The trustees of the Memphis Medical College, who were reorganizing that institution, invited him to accept a chair in the new school and also to help organize it. Ashbel responded wih a long letter drawing up a plan for the establishment of a "first class" university in Memphis. He believed that the time and the place were right for the establishment of a university with a superior medical school to serve the great Mississippi Valley. Among his suggestions were plans for keeping the university free of religious or sectarian influences, means of raising funds, courses of study, ideas for recruiting faculty, and a description of necessary buildings.[12] Ashbel indicated that he would be willing to accept the chair of surgery but made it clear that he was not interested in teaching medicine or anatomy.[13] He did not propose to sever his connection with his plantation but planned to live there when the university was not in session.

When the cholera epidemic abated, Ashbel returned to Galveston Bay after an absence of nine months. He found himself pressed for money, since Moseley Baker had died of yellow fever during his ab-

---

[11] Ashbel Smith Journal, January 9, 1849.
[12] "Letter from Doctor Ashbel Smith to the Trustees of the Memphis University, 1/25/1849," Ashbel Smith Papers.
[13] Ashbel Smith to Dr. Lewis Shanks, March 4, 1849.

sence, and Ashbel owed Baker's estate about $600 on the Evergreen purchase. He set about the disagreeable task of writing dunning letters to friends and patients who were in debt to him and also undertook to enlarge his property. He already had title to the lower half of an island called Hog Island or Goat Island, next to Evergreen. Now he made application to have his bounty claim of 1,280 acres located there also. That was accomplished, and he used the entire island to raise hogs and later to run cattle.

That spring Sam Houston wrote to Ashbel from Huntsville inviting him to spend some time there. "I want to see you, if possible as much, or more than I ever did," the Old Chief said.[14] By then, however, Ashbel was preparing for yet another trip. He was to deliver an address to the Yale chapter of Phi Beta Kappa. Rufus Choate had originally been designated speaker for 1849 and Ashbel Smith for 1850, but when Choate was unable to fulfill his engagement, Ashbel was called on to substitute in August, 1849.

Ashbel had other business to take care of along the way. One of the exciting topics in Texas circles was the coming of the railroad. No longer would Texans be restricted to traveling overland only as fast as a horse's legs could be made to move. Competition for railway routes was keen, and the governor appointed Ashbel one of the Texas delegates to a convention to be held in Memphis on July 4, for the purpose of gathering information about several proposed routes for a great "national road from the waters of the Gulf of Mexico to the Pacific Ocean." The Texas delegates were to present to the convention the advantages of the southern route through Texas. Writing to a friend about the importance of the railroad to Texas commerce, Ashbel remarked that he was "determined to enter battle on the great, agitating questions of the day."

When he arrived in Memphis, he learned that the railroad convention had been postponed until October. He did not mind, for he had business to take care of in connection with the medical school of the proposed university. He wrote to distinguished medical colleagues in various states, urging them to become members of the faculty. Although he could not know it, all of this activity was a dress rehearsal for similar activities that would occupy him during the last years of his life.

After several weeks in Memphis, Ashbel continued northward, at-

---

[14] Sam Houston to Ashbel Smith, May 31, 1849, in Houston, *Writings*, 5:94.

tending the National Educational Convention in Baltimore and then going on to New Haven to address the Phi Beta Kappa chapter.

The topic that Ashbel chose to present to that elite group was "The Permanent and Unchangeable Identity of the Human Race." Although the fossil remains of Neanderthal man would not be identified for another seven years and Darwin would not drop his bomb for another decade, the theory of evolution was very much in the air in the late 1840s. A developmental view of the universe had appeared in Robert Chambers's *Vestiges of the Natural History of Creation*, published anonymously in 1844. Although *Vestiges* specifically allowed God a role in creation, its ideas were considered so shocking that it was condemned by most religious leaders and by many men of science, including Thomas Huxley. This notorious work was the inspiration for Ashbel's speech. He undertook to show that man had undergone no change in his physical, mental, or moral nature since earliest recorded times and therefore by logical inference to prove the "unchangeable sameness of our race in all ages of the world past and to come."

Ashbel used his extensive study of ancient statuary in the Louvre, the British Museum, the Vatican, and Florence to demonstrate that men had not changed physically over the years. In considering the mental caliber of ancient and modern man, Ashbel coupled Homer with Shakespeare, Euclid with Sir Isaac Newton, Socrates with John Locke, and the building of the pyramids with the invention of the telegraph by Morse. Men of genius have always existed and always will exist, he concluded.

The speech ended with an appeal for unity between the North and the South. "Woe to the man or party which through mad ambition or pharisaical fanaticism, would rend asunder the union," he warned. Apparently this group of intellectuals approved the ideas in his speech, for they praised it and published it in booklet form.[15]

Passing through Washington, D.C., on his way home, Ashbel spent some hours visiting with John C. Calhoun, for whom time was running out. Ashbel found his old friend gloomy about the condition of the South and the state of the Union in general. One of the points on which they strongly agreed was their dislike of presidential conventions and the evils they believed attended them.

---

[15] Ashbel Smith, "An Oration Pronounced Before the Phi Beta Kappa Society of Yale College," August 15, 1849.

One of the questions the two friends probably discussed was the burning issue whether or not the United States should annex Cuba. Ashbel argued strenuously against annexation privately and in a letter to the editor of the *New York Journal of Commerce*.[16] He thought that the annexation of Cuba would be fatal to the interests of slaveholding states, bringing disaster to both masters and slaves. He particularly feared that the annexation of Cuba would ruin the sugar planters in Louisiana and Texas—himself included—for he had decided that sugarcane would be a more profitable crop than cotton for Evergreen, and he was determined to become a serious sugar producer. Accordingly, on his return to the bay, he occupied himself with planting cane, buying kettles, building sugarhouses, and planning a mule-driven operation.

Early in 1850, Ashbel became involved in a partnership in which he would expend much time and energy in the next few years. Over the past decade he and Gail Borden had come to know and like each other. Both men were restless, curious, energetic, interested in new ideas. In contrast to Ashbel, with his slight build, Borden had a Lincolnesque stature. His homely, honest face inspired trust, and his letters reveal an open, earnest, deeply religious nature. On January 21, Borden wrote to Ashbel describing an invention that he hoped his scientific friend would help introduce and promote among his learned acquaintances. The product Borden described as a "portable desiccated soup bread," made by combining a meat extract with flour and baking it. By this process eleven pounds of meat could be reduced to one, and one ounce of the resulting meat biscuit could easily be reconstituted into a pint of rich soup in minutes.[17]

Ashbel tried the biscuit and found it good. He forwarded samples of it to the American Association for the Advancement of Science with a letter pointing out the great advantage of the cheap, nutritious, easily transported biscuit over many other kinds of food. He promised Borden that he would send samples to the American Medical Association when it met in Cincinnati later in the year. The two men had at least a verbal understanding by which Ashbel would share in the profits from the meat biscuit in return for promoting it in various ways.

When critics pointed out that the idea of the meat biscuit was not

---

[16] Ashbel Smith to Editor of the *New York Journal of Commerce*, September 21, 1849.

[17] Gail Borden to Ashbel Smith, January 21, 1850.

new, Ashbel angrily answered that Borden's product not only was different from any previous dried-meat product but also possessed superior nutritive and practical virtues, which he enumerated at length.[18] One service Ashbel did for Borden was to give him a letter of introduction to John H. Brower, former Texas consul to New York from the Republic and now a well-to-do New York merchant. This connection was to be of considerable aid to Borden in his efforts to obtain funds to manufacture the biscuit.

After Borden began operating his biscuit factory in Galveston (at Strand and Rosenberg streets), he urged Ashbel to bring Sam Houston to visit so that the senator could carry word back to Washington that the machinery and apparatus were "clean and nice—fit for the most delicate."[19] Ashbel helped Borden obtain cattle for his operation and helped advertise the product. When the meat biscuit received good reports from several military officers, the United States secretary of war ordered that it be given a "fair trial," and the partners were very optimistic.

As 1851 began, Ashbel was busy setting up the sugar mill at Evergreen, but he took time to write a report entitled "On the Climate, Etc. of a Portion of Texas" for *Southern Medical Reports*, edited by his friend Dr. E. D. Fenner, of New Orleans. Dr. Fenner, irritated that no other Texas doctor had sent in a report, printed the article with the disgruntled comment, "We had expected something more than a brief general communication from a retired practitioner."[20]

The springtime of the year rekindled smoldering feelings in Ashbel when he met by chance a cousin of an old friend, Dr. Gibson, of Salisbury, North Carolina. Ashbel wrote to Dr. Gibson renewing their friendship and asking certain questions that he wished to be answered by Dr. Gibson's wife, who had been Mary Phifer's confidante in the days when that lady had "occupied all" his thoughts. He revealed to the Gibsons that he had heard from a reliable source that Mary was married. Now he wrote: "Is she happy? Does she ever cast a thought on him who once lived only for her? I am not a desponding sentimentalist, but I need not be ashamed to feel an abiding interest in her who held the spell of my life."[21] Obviously the passage of fourteen years

---

[18] Ashbel Smith to Gerard Hallock, Editor, *Journal of Commerce*, April, 1850.
[19] Gail Borden to Ashbel Smith, October 30, 1850.
[20] *Southern Medical Reports* [New Orleans] 2 (1851): 458.
[21] Ashbel Smith to Dr. Gibson, February 22, 1851.

since their affair had not banished Mary from his thoughts or from his emotions, which is perhaps the main reason why a man so warm-hearted, home-loving, and sincerely fond of children had never managed to find the right woman to give him the family he longed for.

Ashbel kept an eye on the meat-biscuit industry, which was now well under way—or was it? Gail Borden believed that he had to commence business "on a large scale" even if it broke him, and it nearly did. After turning 190 cattle into 16,000 meat biscuits, the inventor was heavily in debt. In addition, the cattle delivered in the winter were poor, and so were sales. It became necessary to suspend operations temporarily.[22]

When friends suggested to Borden that he attend the Great Exhibition at the Crystal Palace in London to display and promote his product among the industrial leaders of the world, Borden turned to Ashbel for counsel and urged his friend to go with him. Ashbel, who was becoming bored with farm life, jumped at the chance to go to Europe again. It was decided that Ashbel would go ahead so that he could visit relatives along the way. Borden would follow, and they would leave for London together from New York. Borden was delayed in Galveston, however, and Ashbel, who had been designated by Governor Peter H. Bell a Texas delegate to the exhibition, could not wait for his friend if he was to be in London in time for the opening of the exhibition on May 1.

As it was, Ashbel with a couple of barrels of meat biscuit in tow, barely managed to get passage on the *Baltic*, which made a rough but fairly quick voyage of twelve days from New York to Liverpool. When Borden reached New York, instead of following Ashbel's injunction to "sail by the next steamer," he delayed, scurrying around ordering parts for the factory machinery, talking with Brower about funding, and setting up advertising projects. He drew "heavily" upon Ashbel's letters in writing advertisements but longed for his friend's presence: "Oh for two hours of your head and mind to assist in this matter." Some of Borden's advisers thought he should stay in America and develop that market first, but Ashbel's cheering, "spirited" letters settled Borden's mind about going to Europe—the lure was irresistible. He told Ashbel ". . . your great experience and knowledge of facts . . . have acted on me all the while like the pole star on the *magnet*."[23] In the meantime

---

[22] Gail Borden to Ashbel Smith, January 31, 1851.
[23] Gail Borden to Ashbel Smith, April 22, 1851.

Ashbel made the most of his opportunities to display to advantage the meat-biscuit barrels in the meager array of products from America.

Before he left New York, Ashbel had arranged to send reports on the exhibition to the editor of the *New York Journal of Commerce*, and he fulfilled this promise with several long descriptions of the affair. He was named a judge on one of the juries, and he had inside knowledge of much that went on.

Opening day was a typical London day—cloudy with occasional gleams of sunshine. The queen was to arrive at the Crystal Palace at twelve noon. At nine Ashbel and two other commissioners set out in a hackney cab, which dashed and rattled in and out of the stately parade of fine carriages bearing the nobility to the palace. It had been six years since Ashbel had seen Queen Victoria. Her homeliness was no longer compensated for by youth, and he found her "very plain indeed." His trained eye observed her clinically:

She is very short and inclining to be dumpy, light chestnut hair, light gray eyes and very prominent nose large pinched and red at the tip; skin very coarse and irregularly spotted with red, mouth large and heavy with white strong good teeth; her bust from the neck down is good. Taken simply and physically nothing can be imagined more coarse and plebian than her person, yet her movements are so graceful and dignified that you soon forget she is dumpy.[24]

The queen led by the hand the young Prince of Wales, who Ashbel observed had not inherited the regular handsome features of his father but resembled the queen's family.

More romantic to Ashbel than the members of the royal family was the aging Duke of Wellington. Shrunken and hard of hearing, the old hero took no notice of the cheers which greeted his unsteady progress down the long aisles, even though he drew more applause from the crowd than did the queen.

In his capacity as a United States delegate Ashbel was invited to attend the lord mayor's ball at Guildhall. He was impressed anew by the reverence of the British people for aristocracy as he observed the dense crowds that waited through most of the night for the pleasure of seeing their queen dash by in a closed carriage and beholding their betters pass "in the obscurity of the night." Inside, the great hall was also crowded. At one end was a raised platform with a throne for the queen. On the platform there was room for the diplomatic corps and

[24] Ashbel Smith to Editor, *Journal of Commerce*, May 1, 1851.

other distinguished persons, including Dr. Ashbel Smith. Presentations were made to the queen as the company filed silently past her majesty.[25]

Ashbel was assigned to serve on a jury that included Horace Greeley, founder and editor of the *New York Tribune*, whose antislavery and Republican attitudes were "obnoxious" to many southerners, including Ashbel. He made a speech urging the committee to elect the "strongest man" as their chairman—meaning himself. When Greeley was appointed chairman, Ashbel sharply criticized the "injudicious" choice and later complained to Dr. Lyon Playfair, the fortuitously named special commissioner of juries, that Greeley was absent from London during an important part of the jury's deliberations.[26]

In the early days of the exhibition the London *Times* and other English papers sneered at the American offerings, and Ashbel felt "mortified" that the United States had not bothered to give Europe "ocular proof" of the "variety and extent of its resources, or of the inventive skill and enterprise of its citizens." By mid-July, when the juries had finished their work and the medals had been awarded to the exhibitors, Ashbel was both pleased and displeased with the honors given to American entries. He protested the "bad taste and perverse judgment" of the council of chairmen for not awarding the American sculptor Hiram Powers a more important medal for his famous statue *The Greek Slave*, which caused a sensation at the Crystal Palace. Ashbel also scolded the council for giving only a small medal to Mr. Samuel Colt for his revolver, which Ashbel called "the most efficient weapon of all known small arms."[27]

On the other hand, Ashbel rejoiced that the *America* beat the British *Titania* in the yachting regatta, a feat that showed America to be the superior ship builder. He also crowed that reporters who had ridiculed Cyrus Hall McCormick's Virginia reaper as awkward had to admit its excellence in performance, and so did the judges, who gave it the only gold medal awarded to an agricultural implement. Also, Ashbel boasted, an American named Hobbs had picked the finest English locks and displayed an unpickable lock of his own. He was proud of the showing of several American products: Virginia tobacco was called un-

---

[25] Ashbel Smith, "Loose Memoranda, London, 1851," Ashbel Smith Papers.

[26] Ashbel Smith to Editor, *Journal of Commerce*, July 25, 1851; Ashbel Smith to Dr. Lyon Playfair, Commissioner of Juries, August 25, 1851.

[27] Ashbel Smith to Dr. Lyon Playfair, Commissioner of Juries, August 25, 1851.

rivaled, American cotton was judged superior, and Kentucky ham was voted best in flavor.[28]

Perhaps the most satisfying awards ceremony to Ashbel was the bestowing of a gold medal on Borden's meat biscuit. The product was analyzed in the laboratory of Mr. Playfair and found to be "highly nutritive and having good preservative qualities." Ashbel reported, "Among the various preparations of food presented in the Exhibition, no one was deemed worthy of the same high approbation as the meat biscuit."[29] Borden was present to demonstrate the preparation of the biscuit, and the future of their venture looked rosy to the partners.

They drew up a series of contracts, which were witnessed by Abbott Laurence, the American ambassador to England. Ashbel's share was to be 10 percent of Borden's United States patent, one-half of all profits from sales to any foreign government, and the right to apply to the emperor of Russia for a patent to manufacture and sell meat biscuits in that country.[30] When he went to Paris in September to attend the fetes given by that city in honor of the exhibition, Ashbel made a speech about the meat biscuit before the French Agricultural Society. The French papers gave good notices both to the invention and to the Texan's excellent French.

Ashbel found France in a "singular" condition. Louis Philippe, the "Citizen King," had gone into exile, and Louis Napoleon ruled as president of the Second Republic. Plots, state trials, and espionage were the order of the day, and yet Paris was as "lively, gay, holiday-like and overflowing as ever." Ashbel was presented to the president at the Élysée. His impression of the French leader was that he had great "aplomb" and that he spoke in a "grave and sensible manner."[31]

When he returned to London in late September, Ashbel found the absorbing topic to be Cuba and America's filibustering expeditions on the island. In lead articles English papers stereotyped Americans as lawless, aggressive, and lax in political morality. In letters to the London *Times* and other papers Ashbel took it upon himself to explain the "true cause and origin of the whole movement in Cuba." He informed the British people that the creole population of Cuba had begun the revolutionary effort because of the insecurity in their lives re-

---

[28] Ashbel Smith to Editor, *Journal of Commerce*, August 29, 1851.
[29] Ibid.
[30] Contract between Gail Borden, Jr., and Ashbel Smith, London, July 17, 1851.
[31] Ashbel Smith Journal, September 5, 1851.

sulting from the meddling of British abolitionists with the slavery institutions of the island. This meddling, along with apprehension about their fate following the European war, had led Cubans to look to America for protection and had aroused American sympathy for them. Cubans generally disliked Americans, Ashbel admitted, but they feared British protection more. Like "most" other Americans, he avowed, he did not want to possess Cuba, but he also did not want to see her destroyed by the greed of other powers.[32]

Punch magazine quoted from Ashbel's letter in an article ridiculing the ambivalent American attitude toward Cuba and referred to him as the "doughty" Ashbel Smith. Doughty or not, he seems to have been pleased by the mention in *Punch*, for he acquired several copies of the article.[33]

Returning to the United States in October 1851, Ashbel made a long stopover in New York to spend some time with Borden, whom he prodded to "*advertise, manufacture, and sell.*" Borden needed encouragement, for the United States Army had returned a negative report on the meat biscuit after new trials. Not only did they find it unpalatable and lacking in nourishment, but they also claimed that it sometimes had disagreeable side effects, such as headaches, nausea, and diarrhea. Sales were lagging, and Borden's debts were pressing; he begged Ashbel to help him stave off his creditors.[34] "It was by your advice and encouragement that I have been induced to expend so much," the besieged inventor reminded his partner. Ashbel's grandiose schemes for promoting the biscuit to the ends of the earth—Russia, Algiers, Turkey—were enticing but impractical: ". . . if I had the means I would follow precisely your advice," Borden wrote sadly.[35]

Back at Evergreen the day after Christmas, Ashbel turned his thoughts to a subject that would increasingly occupy his time and attention for the rest of his life—education. He sat down to prepare a memorial to the members of the Texas legislature suggesting that they should appoint a state school commission for the common schools of Texas. His twelve-page memorial was full of practical details on setting up a workable, fair, and adequate system of free education for all Texas

---

[32] Ashbel Smith, "Memorandum Concerning Cuba," *Galveston News*, January 20, 1852; Ashbel Smith to London *Times*, September 5, 1851.
[33] *Punch*, vol. 21, Ashbel Smith Papers.
[34] Gail Borden to Ashbel Smith, December 23, 1851.
[35] Ibid.

children guided by a competent commissioner.[36] No doubt he envisioned himself in such a role, which would be similar to that of his friend Henry Barnard in Connecticut.

Education in Texas badly needed champions. From firsthand experience Ashbel knew how bad the school system was, especially in remote places like Galveston Bay. When his nephew Ashbel Grattan Smith had visited him a few years earlier, the boy had been taught by a local schoolmaster for two weeks and then "graduated" because the teacher, who could barely read and write, had taught him all he knew.

Texans urgently wanted better schools so that they need not send their children north to get a decent education. The growing bitterness between the North and the South made this an increasingly important issue.

In the spring of 1852, Colonel H. L. Kinney, a promoter from Corpus Christi, was planning the first state fair of Texas. It was to be a grand fair—partly commercial and partly agricultural. The colonel confidently expected to draw thousands of people from other states and foreign countries, including Mexico. He needed a dynamic superintendent for the fair and could think of no better person than the distinguished Texas statesman who had participated in the Great Exhibition in London.

Kinney was gratified by the energy and enthusiasm with which Ashbel Smith undertook the job. The fair, held during the first two weeks of May, had something for everyone. Entertainment was plentiful, including bullfighting, a circus, opera performances, concerts, horse racing, rodeo events, and, to the chagrin of the superintendent, some informal sports, cockfighting and gambling. In between the entertainments were brisk buying and selling of livestock, blankets, bridles, saddles, and foodstuffs. Ashbel had, of course, brought along a supply of meat biscuit, which won an award. Colonel Kinney was selling town lots at $100 each, and Ashbel took advantage of the opportunity to purchase two choice lots on the beach in the town area.[37]

The fair also had a taste of politics. Ashbel introduced to the fair visitors General José María Jesús Carbajal of the Liberating Army of

---

[36] Ashbel Smith to the Legislature of the State of Texas, December 26, 1851.

[37] Ashbel Smith to Editor, *Journal of Commerce*, April 30, 1852; Hortense W. Ward, "The First State Fair of Texas," *Southwestern Historical Quarterly* 57 (October, 1953): 163–74; Ashbel Smith, "Report on Corpus Christi Fair," *New Orleans Daily Picayune*, May 13, 1852.

Mexico.[38] The fair failed to attract the large numbers Kinney had anticipated, and it was not an unequivocal success, but Ashbel Smith considered that it had made a "highly respectable" showing for Texas.

Soon after the fair closed, Ashbel set out for the North to attend to politics and business, as well as visit family and friends. June 1 found him in Baltimore, where he was elected a vice-president of the Committee on Organization for the Democratic National Convention. After a long deadlock between Lewis Cass and James Buchanan the convention compromised by nominating Franklin Pierce of New Hampshire, who had shown sympathy with southern interests in the past. While the convention was in session, Ashbel and Senator Houston kept in close contact; the trains between Baltimore and Washington, D.C., made it convenient for them to meet frequently.

After the convention Ashbel hurried on to New York City, where a desperate Gail Borden was impatiently waiting for him. The meat biscuit was receiving a great deal of negative reaction, and the unhappy inventor was sure that much of the problem was caused by improper preparation of the product. He had nearly driven himself into a nervous collapse trying to demonstrate to every foreign-bound ship's steward and every army and navy cook in New York the correct procedure for turning the dry biscuit into a delectable soup. The pressures of mounting debts, equipment purchases, paperwork, and advertising had become unbearable.[39]

Borden particularly wanted Ashbel to work on publicity in the United States and Europe so that they could begin to realize a profit from the money and time already invested. Ashbel was able to soothe Borden, though he did him little practical good. In fact, by encouraging the inventor to promote the meat biscuits in hospitals and giving him introductions to doctor friends, he started his embattled friend on another hopeless round of activity.

Telling Borden that it was financially impossible for him to go to Europe to promote their interests, Ashbel suggested that he cancel his interests in the European patent so that Borden could get someone else to sponsor the product abroad. Borden agreed, and after he re-

---

[38] Ernest C. Shearer, "The Carvajal Disturbances," *Southwestern Historical Quarterly* 55 (October, 1951): 223ff.

[39] Gail Borden to Ashbel Smith, March 3, 1852; March 11, 1852; October 14, 1852; Ashbel Smith to Gail Borden, May 28, 1853.

turned to Texas, Ashbel wrote to Borden officially relinquishing his interest in the European patent for the invention. Borden continued to seek Ashbel's advice and sympathy, however, as he struggled to produce and sell his product, and Ashbel continued to promote it where he could.

In the mid-nineteenth century cholera was even more dreaded than yellow fever. In 1852 another cholera epidemic appeared imminent, and Dr. Ashbel Smith, who rightly considered that his experience with the disease had made him an authority on it, wrote a paper intended to dispel some of the fears and misconceptions about it. He began by admitting that the medical profession was still "wholly in the dark" about its cause and mode of communication. Citing the contradictory and confused directions for treatment prescribed by his colleagues, Ashbel called its treatment "the reproach of the healing art."

He described the common symptoms of cholera as an insidious diarrhea with no pain and no fever, a rapidly progressing weakness, and a gradual "refrigeration" of the body surface leading to collapse. He stressed the importance of arresting the disease early, before the symptoms became acute. His recommended treatment in the early stages was complete bed rest, a hot mustard footbath, brandy, peppermint, laudanum, paregoric and camphorated spirits, calomel, and opium. Cholera in its early stage was easily managed, he suggested, and might yield to "quack nostrums" if they contained warming stimulants and opiates and were combined with good nursing. In the intermediate stage the skill and judicious treatment of a physician could save lives. Finally he emphasized that there was a connection between the disease and lack of cleanliness and sanitation.[40]

Along with other Texans, Ashbel Smith dreamed of railroad lines linking all the major towns of the state and the rest of the United States. He had seen firsthand in Europe and in the eastern United States their efficiency in transporting freight, mail, and passengers. As usual, he did more than merely dream about the possibility. When a convention met in Houston in October, 1852, to consider the construction of a railroad from Galveston Bay to the interior of the state, Ashbel was elected its vice-president. He was also named chairman of a committee to draft resolutions expressing the purposes of the convention.

---

[40] Ashbel Smith, "Cholera," n.d., Ashbel Smith Papers.

The *Galveston News* reported that Dr. Ashbel Smith addressed the group, urging them to encourage railroad enterprise "in his usual happy and eloquent style."[41]

In the Methodist Church in Austin in January 17, 1853, Ashbel met with a small group of physicians who would make medical history in Texas. They had come to the capital to organize a state medical association. For years Ashbel had been pleading with medical friends in the Texas legislature to use their influence to set up a state association. In an article published in *Southern Medical Reports* in 1851, he had written that Texas had no medical organization and little prospect of one, "each doctor acting independently and sometimes adopting a sort of armed neutrality system." Considering the fact that only eighty doctors met in 1848 at the organizational meeting of the American Medical Association in New York, thirty-five was a respectable showing for the first meeting of the Texas association.

At the first session Ashbel was appointed to a committee of four to draft a constitution and bylaws.[42] At two o'clock the next afternoon the committee submitted its recommendations, which were adopted with very few changes. Pat Ireland Nixon says that "Dr. Ashbel Smith was . . . without doubt the author of the committee report."

The constitution provided that the second meeting of the association was to be held the same year on November 16. The highlight of the second meeting was the presidential address by Dr. George Cupples, who singled out Ashbel Smith as "a distinguished ornament of our profession" and praised him for his efforts to establish the association.[43]

After such an enthusiastic beginning and the prompt granting of its charter by the Texas legislature, it is puzzling that the Texas Medical Association became dormant and did not meet again for sixteen years. Many reasons have been given: difficulty of transportation, strong feelings of independence among Texas doctors, schisms within the group, the extreme poverty of some members, and finally the Civil War and the difficult time of Reconstruction. Whatever the reasons, the infant association, which seemed to have such promise, was inactive for many years.

[41] *Galveston News*, October 4, 1852.
[42] "Proceedings of the Texas Medical Convention," Texas Medical Association, January, 1853.
[43] Nixon, *The Medical Story of Early Texas*, pp. 472–73.

To Enter Battle   131

After the first meeting Ashbel had remained in Austin to attend another organizational meeting in February. This group was concerned with another of his great interests, agriculture. When a group of Texas farmers and stockmen gathered to organize the Texas State Agricultural Society, they elected Ashbel Smith president. In his inaugural address he stressed the importance of regular meetings of planters to share knowledge, which he equated with power and wealth. He spoke at length on the importance of cotton growing in Texas and assured his fellow farmers that the cotton worm and other blights could be scientifically studied and conquered. He recommended the cultivation of wheat in Texas to diversify the "too great sameness of cotton and cane culture." He suggested to the stockmen that the shorthorn Durhams of England and the northern United States, which fattened easily, might be bred with the tough longhorn Texas steers to produce a highly desirable animal. "We can *bread* and *clothe* Christendom," he declared, "and make a significant contribution to Texas by adding the . . . dignity of science to the eminent respectability of practical agriculture."[44]

In April, Ashbel delivered a speech on his third great interest, education, at the commencement of Austin College, situated at that time in Huntsville. He told his listeners that a liberal education was the key to enable one to think clearly on all subjects. In college we should learn how to learn, he said, and warned against being "one-sided" by studying any one subject too exclusively. "Our education should never cease—no more in knowledge than in virtue. Our heads should become stronger as well as our hearts purer."[45]

The remaining months of 1853 he divided between practicing medicine and managing his plantation. In late summer an outbreak of yellow fever in Galveston and Houston took all of his time. Sometime during this siege he took up residence in Houston with the intention of continuing his practice there indefinitely. In Houston he found considerable excitement over the American, or Know-Nothing, party, whose aim was to suppress further immigration and to prevent foreigners from having political power. Strongly opposed to the party and all that it stood for, he made a speech fiercely denouncing it to a large crowd in Houston. It was the first public speech in the city openly condemning

---

[44] Ashbel Smith, "Address to Texas State Agricultural Society," Austin, February 5, 1853.

[45] Ashbel Smith, "Address to First Commencement of Austin College," Huntsville, April, 1853.

the Know-Nothing party, and it caused so much resentment that Ashbel was again burned in effigy, this time in front of the old capitol.[46]

In August, 1854, Ashbel wrote a newsletter for the *Journal of Commerce*. He reported that the early cotton crop was good and the sugarcane well matured but that the price of sugar was so ruinously low that for some planters producing molasses did not cover the costs of cooperage and shipment. He rejoiced that the law forbidding the sale of spiritous liquors in a quantity less than a quart had been adopted by every county in the state. This act was expected to close most of the tippling shops, called "groceries," which were regarded as breeding places of crime. "It is hoped," wrote Ashbel, "that the closing of these miserable resorts will diminish somewhat the numerous assassinations, which are now so frequent in Texas as to be appalling. The estimate of one every other day is probably below the mark."[47] Toward the end of the letter he mentioned that there had been six to ten deaths from yellow fever in Galveston.

By September 12 there were a few cases of the dread yellow jack in Houston, two of which were fatal. It soon became obvious that the fall of 1854 would see another epidemic of the disease in the coastal area. To combat exaggerated rumors and horror stories connected with the epidemic, Ashbel undertook to furnish twice-weekly reports to the *Houston Star and Telegraph*. As the disease spread, he gave accurate accounts of the numbers of deaths, and he gave the people commonsense advice about how to take care of themselves during the siege—there were no hospitals, public or private, in Houston. Possibly the most valuable advice he offered was the caution that many died of the fever because of ignorance of its insidious nature. Relapse during convalescence was common and often fatal and could be caused by "an error of diet or exposure." The real period of danger, he warned, was when the patient appeared to an inexperienced nurse to be out of danger.[48]

Perhaps to prove his contention that wheat could be grown anywhere in inhabited areas, Ashbel had a bushel of seed wheat and one of rye planted at Evergreen in the spring of 1855 on a dry, sandy sassafras ridge. Both crops matured perfectly, giving good yields of sound grain.

---

[46] Editorial, *Texas Medical Record*, 1880, p. 196.
[47] Ashbel Smith to Editor, *Journal of Commerce*, August 18, 1854.
[48] Ashbel Smith to *Houston Star and Telegraph*, September 12, 1854.

To Enter Battle

At that time, however, cotton was more profitable, and Ashbel did not repeat the experiment.

In the midst of his other activities he did not forget "Uncle Gail." Borden, in Galveston to look over the "wreck" of his business and hard-pressed by creditors, turned to Ashbel for help. Should he send a "ton or two" of the meat biscuit to hospitals in the Crimea? Would Ashbel give him the names of influential people who might act as proxies in Europe? And would Ashbel write letters to those people? Finally, would Ashbel help him sell portions of his Texas lands to enable him to pay off some of his debts? After all this Borden told his partner that he was about to begin work on a new invention—the concentrating and preserving of milk—just as soon as he could find "parties to advance the means."

Ashbel did supply names and write letters to acquaintances who might be able to help Borden with his European sales of the meat biscuit. Whether or not he helped with the land sales is not recorded. Nor is Ashbel's reaction to the news that Borden was off again chasing another dream. "Stick your memory," Borden told him, "with the idea that milk will be as common on ship board as sugar."[49] Even if Ashbel had wanted to pursue this dream with his friend, he had no funds to invest in it. Thus he did not become involved in the development of condensed milk and missed the opportunity to share in that dream as it became a lucrative reality.

In the spring Ashbel was called on for a number of speeches to different groups. His favorite topic was the Crimean War. In talks to Andrew Female College in Huntsville and to the Houston Lyceum he pointed out that many Europeans had at first thought of the war as a holiday excursion. He dismissed the "magisterial" arguments of the London *Times* that the war was "internecine," using the history of Christianity to prove his point. Then he got into the "real" reasons that England and France entered the war. "Russia," he said "has become too great, too powerful. She endangers the balance of power."[50]

---

[49] Gail Borden to Ashbel Smith, December 19, 1853; January 11, 1854; December 5, 1854; September 22, 1855.

[50] Ashbel Smith speeches folder, n.d., Ashbel Smith Papers.

CHAPTER EIGHT

The Connecticut Rebel
(1855–1863)

IN the summer of 1855, Ashbel's friends suggested that he stand for election as one of the two Harris County representatives to the Texas legislature. Knowing that it would be a way to gain a larger audience for his views on such issues as railroads, education, and finances, he accepted the challenge and won the seat. When the legislature convened, he was appointed to four important committees: education, public debt, slaves and slavery, and internal improvements. The Sixth Legislature was a contentious group, and Ashbel Smith was in his element.

A hint of abolitionist sentiment was a red flag to make him paw the floor and bellow. A few days after the session opened, he thought he heard this dangerous subject espoused in a speech by a colleague. Jumping to his feet, he demanded the floor, and made an impromptu speech in which he eloquently and categorically denied the right of the United States Congress to control slavery. To prove his point, he read from the American Constitution every passage relevant to slavery. He went on to argue that slavery was a practical good and therefore could not be a moral evil, since the "creator himself . . . cannot make the same thing both right and wrong." He declared that not only does the Bible *not* condemn slavery, it commands it, adding, "That which is once right in the eyes of God is always right."[1]

In 1855 know-nothingism occupied much newspaper space. Writing from the East, friends like Henry Barnard and Gail Borden asked Ashbel about the "dark lantern order" in Texas. "Is it the same old Whig coon with three additional stripes or rings around his tail?" asked

[1] "Legislative Proceedings," *State Gazette Appendix*, November 16, 1855.

The Connecticut Rebel 135

Borden. Ashbel Smith Kittredge wrote his uncle, "I suppose you are attacking and overthrowing the Know Nothings. I hope you are, for I detest them." One of Ashbel's friends, however, was on the opposite side of the fence. Sam Houston's support of the Know-Nothing party, added to his unpopular vote on the Kansas-Nebraska bill, caused some members of the Texas legislature to urge the group to censure him.

For the first time Ashbel Smith and Sam Houston were openly at odds politically. The gentleman from Harris made his feelings clear to the members of the house and to his fellow Texans. He did not approve of Houston's vote against the Kansas-Nebraska bill and agreed that it was "unwise." He repudiated and condemned the doctrines of the Know-Nothing party and was sorry that Houston was involved with it, but he reminded his fellow legislators of their debt to the old warrior:

... Gen. Houston is ... part and parcel of the history of the Old Republic and the present great State of Texas. Flings have been made on this floor at his personal courage, and the charge of treason reiterated to satiety. He bears 3 wounds in front received in fighting the battles of his country. Let those jest at scars who never felt a wound; the charge of cowardice comes with an ill grace from those who never faced an enemy. And as for treason ... the charge is an outrage.[2]

A few days later Ashbel received a note from Houston assuring him, "I write this to say that whatever our political [differences] may be, they will not with me disturb our personal regards," and asking Ashbel to meet with him at Halls House in Austin when Houston arrived there the following week.[3]

Houston's arrival in the capital was the occasion for various Know-Nothing celebrations, including a parade and a barbecue. The legislature voted to extend him the customary courtesy due a former official of the Texas government, inviting him to sit within the bar of the house. Some disgruntled members tried to prevent his appearance by passing resolutions and amendments until Ashbel accused them of trying to circumvent the will of the house by "gagging" it with "much speaking."[4] After cooling his heels on the porch of the capitol for three hours, Houston was finally admitted to the house chamber. A few days later, Smith of Harris voted with the majority of his fellow legislators

[2] Ibid., p. 35.
[3] Sam Houston to Ashbel Smith, November 20, 1855, in Houston, *Writings*, 6: 207–208.
[4] "Legislative Proceedings," *State Gazette Appendix*, November 26, 1855.

in approving a resolution that stated, "the Legislature approves the course of Thomas J. Rusk in voting for the Kansas-Nebraska Act and disapproves the course of Sam Houston, in voting against it."

As chairman of the Committee on the Public Debt of Texas, Ashbel had a stormy time, both within his own committee and with the house members during his defense of the public-debt bill on the floor. He considered the paying of war debts incurred during the Texas Revolution to be a matter involving the honor of Texas. Other legislators did not agree with him, and some members of his committee issued a minority report complaining of his high-handedness in managing committee meetings. On the floor W. R. Poag from Panola baited the chairman about several points in the majority report, which Poag accurately described as "long, laborious, able, ingenious and learned." After long debate the measure passed, and it turned out to be one of the few important pieces of legislation passed during the regular session of the Sixth Legislature.

In mid-January the Democratic State Convention met in Austin for four days. Ashbel was appointed to the committee to draft a platform, which was adopted without a dissenting voice "amidst shouts and cheers." The platform included a warning: ". . . all efforts of the abolitionists or others made to induce Congress to interfere with questions of slavery . . . are calculated to lead to the most alarming and dangerous consequences . . . including endangering the stability and permanency of the union."[5] Before the convention adjourned, Ashbel Smith was appointed to a committee to draft a report on the proceedings to the state's Democrats.

Back in the legislature, Representative Smith defended the rights of the "preemptioner who has settled upon a little tract of land, cultivates it, and makes the wilderness blossom like the rose" over those of the "big-bellied" land speculators.[6] He also introduced resolutions for the establishment of a state bureau of agriculture and for the appointment of a state geologist.[7]

Other measures that occupied his time during the winter session he labeled "internal improvements." He was in favor of allowing Texas railroads to be built through private enterprise rather than by the

[5] "Official Proceedings of the Democratic State Convention," January 16–19, 1856.
[6] "Legislative Proceedings," *State Gazette Appendix*, December 8, 1855.
[7] "Legislative Proceedings," ibid., November 12, 1855.

state. In December he introduced a bill asking for an extension of time to be granted to the Galveston-Houston Railroad, and he also argued for a railway-loan bill, which would provide building funds for private entrepreneurs.

Mr. Smith of Harris had decided opinions on other issues. In commenting on a resolution on amending the law regulating appeals in criminal cases, he said: "I am not tender-footed on this subject. My sympathies are not in favor of the criminal; they are in favor of the law-abiding members of society. Let the murderer be hung; the public good requires it. I go, sir, for the good, honest wholesome hanging. If the murderer is good for nothing else, he is good for an example."[8] He joined James W. Throckmorton and others in protesting a bill passed by the house relinquishing state tax revenues to the counties for two years, overriding the veto of Governor Elisha M. Pease. Ashbel agreed with his friend Pease that the measure would create a dependence on the state treasury and would favor large, rich counties while oppressing poor, weak ones.

On one occasion when a bill pertaining to wills was under discussion, Ashbel became so incensed with the "sneer, threat and bluster" tactics of the professional lawyers in the group that he rose to attack them:

In my opinion, a country gentleman is as competent to understand the objects of the law, to appreciate the workings of the laws which are in force, and to form a judgment of what the public good requires as if he had been trained and practiced in all the chicanery and technicalities of magistrates and district courts; and when such matters are discussed I shall not be deterred from expending any opinion I may entertain from the slightest apprehension of sneers and bluster.

He pointed out to the lawyers that while such behavior might serve to intimidate witnesses it was hardly calculated to win friends for the causes they advocated in the legislature.[9]

With Henry Barnard's prompting, Ashbel was continuing his efforts to set up a system for organizing the common schools of Texas. During a special session he introduced a resolution to establish a board of education, whose members would serve for two years without compensation. The secretary of the board, he proposed, would perform

[8] "Legislative Proceedings," ibid., July 14, 1856.
[9] "Legislative Proceedings," ibid., July 9, 1856.

the duties of superintendent of common schools. The act did not make it through the house.[10]

When the legislature adjourned for the last time, Ashbel returned to Evergreen and was a gentleman farmer for the remaining months of the year, making good harvests of cotton, cane, and corn. He was troubled by the letters that came from Phoebe, Caroline, and Ashbel Smith Kittredge telling of his father's poor health, the feebleness of both his parents, and their intense eagerness to see him. He became afraid that he might not see his father again and set out for Hartford during the first week of January, 1857. Again he had had difficulty finding a suitable overseer. He finally left the plantation in charge of L. D. Page, who wrote cheerful letters saying that all was well but was reported by Ashbel's neighbors to be spending most of his time comfortably ensconced in the house, waited on by Ashbel's slaves, and to be absent from Evergreen from Thursday through Monday.

While waiting in Galveston for a ship to New Orleans, Ashbel passed the day with an old friend, Colonel Ebenezer Allen, who urged him to run for the United States Senate. The idea pleased Ashbel, but he told Allen that he was afraid that the stand he had taken on some of the bills in the last session of the Texas legislature would hurt his chances for election. Also, whether or not he discussed it with Colonel Allen, he was thinking seriously about another political position.

In Hartford, Ashbel found his father better than he had feared, though feeble in body and mind. It was apparent that neither Moses nor Phoebe could continue farming, and the family discussed plans for their future. Henry Barnard, a regular visitor to the aged couple, promised Ashbel that he would continue to watch over them and do what he could for their comfort. Barnard himself was in an almost desperate financial plight—in need of every dollar he could get. He asked Ashbel to solicit subscriptions to his educational journal in Texas.

Either during his stay at the North or on his way home Ashbel made his way to Salisbury. Mary Phifer was now a widow, and perhaps he wanted to test his feelings. Whatever passed between them he did not record, and nothing serious came of their meeting. While he was in North Carolina, Ashbel did, however, meet another young woman named Christina with whom he exchanged promises to write. She was

---

[10] *Journal of the House of Representatives, 6th Legislature,* July 23, 1856.

a Roman Catholic and gave him some Catholic literature, which he promised to read carefully.

During the months of his northern visit Ashbel made several trips to Washington, D.C., where he talked politics with Senator Houston. He told Houston that the people of Texas were disappointed that Houston had not been nominated for president instead of Franklin Pierce. "I'm sure the people at large would greatly prefer yourself.... you are by long odds the strongest man in the nation," he assured his friend.[11] After Houston declared that he had no intention of running for governor during the upcoming campaign, Ashbel confided that he expected to be a candidate for the governorship himself.

This plan, however, did not work out. When the state Democratic convention met at Waco on May 4, 1857, the delegates nominated Hardin R. Runnels for governor and F. R. Lubbock for lieutenant governor. Less than two weeks after the Waco convention Houston announced his candidacy for governor as an independent. He explained to Ashbel his change of mind, saying that he felt that the main issue at the regular convention had been "Houston and anti-Houston" and that he had decided to accept the challenge. "The riders are all up and the drum tapped," he told his old friend. Ashbel replied that he had not expected his Old Chief to run and indicated that, although he himself had withdrawn from the race, he could not disown the obligation he had undertaken: to support the party nominee.[12]

When a group of maverick Democrats held a meeting in Houston and put Ashbel's name in nomination for the Texas legislature, he refused the honor, for he did not think it was a legitimate group representing the Democrats of the county. He was a true party man and would vote for the rightful nominees of the party.[13]

The race between Houston and Runnels for the governorship was as fierce and bombastic as the race of 1841 between Houston and Burnet for the presidency. E. H. Cushing, editor of the *Telegraph and Texas Register*, and other friends pressed Ashbel to write and speak on Runnel's behalf. Ashbel refused to be one of the "dogs" Houston said were "barking" at him. The hounders included Henderson, who, since he could not draw Houston into a debate, followed him from town to

---

[11] Ashbel Smith to Sam Houston, June 28, 1857.
[12] Ashbel Smith to Sam Houston, July 25, 1857.
[13] Ashbel Smith to C. F. Duer, July 5, 1857.

town, answering his arguments point by point.[14] Diplomatically Ashbel retired to Evergreen, where his worst enemy was the cotton worm, and spent the summer reading and writing. It was, however, a temporary retirement. He told Houston, "My present quiet is like the yankee's getting off his horse to get on better again."

When the election was over and Runnels had won, Houston, now at Huntsville, wrote inviting Ashbel to come for a visit:

The fuss is over. The sun shines as ever. What next? . . . There are matters of vast import now on hand, and I would like to see you in relation to them. . . . Is there any way we can contrive a pow-wow, that we may unite in trying to draw the veil partially aside, and take a peep into coming events? I want to talk grave as well as laugh with you. . . . Oh, I do want someone who has seen other days in Texas to talk with! If you come to see me, I bind myself to make you laugh.[15]

Ashbel replied, "I have many things to say which cannot be easily expressed in writing," but he was unable to go to Huntsville before Houston had to return to his senatorial duties in Washington.

When the Texas legislative session opened in November, Ashbel was eager to know what was going on, even though he was not officially part of it. He kept up a lively correspondence with friends in the legislature, such as Throckmorton, sending them his opinions on various issues. He was particularly concerned about the bill to establish a state college, over which the legislators were split into "one-university," "two-universities," and "no university" factions.[16] Ashbel urged his friend P. W. Kittrell, chairman of the House Committee on Education, to support the one-university plan. Kittrell did so but told Ashbel that much debate over the location of the school had "hung up" the measure and that he trembled for its success.[17] His fears were confirmed when the lawmakers managed to talk the issue to death for the time being. Ashbel again tasted the bittersweet fruit of party loyalty when Kittrell informed him that Governor Runnels "has vetoed your railroad."

In 1858 three of Ashbel's close friends died, and each death brought him new obligations. The first death occurred in Houston on

---

[14] J. P. Henderson to Ashbel Smith, June 21, 1857.

[15] Sam Houston to Ashbel Smith, August 22, 1857.

[16] "Kittrell, Pleasant Williams," in Walter Prescott Webb and H. Bailey Carroll, eds., *Handbook of Texas*, 3:479.

[17] P. W. Kittrell to Ashbel Smith, December 3, 1857.

January 9, when Anson Jones raised a pistol to his head and ended his life in the Old Capitol hotel, the same building where he had begun his public career. In the days of the Republic, Anson and Ashbel had been fellow pioneers, fellow physicians, fellow planters, and fellow politicians and statesmen. The abuse and misunderstanding that they had suffered in connection with annexation had strengthened the bond between them. When Jones became disenchanted with Sam Houston and bitter about the ingratitude of Texans, who had failed to send him to the United States Senate, Ashbel had remained his friend.

Ten years earlier, when Jones had asked for Ashbel's permission to use some personal documents in a history of annexation that Jones proposed to publish, Ashbel had encouraged him to give the world the "solemn truth, fearlessly." After the suicide of Thomas J. Rusk in July, 1857, Jones began thinking that he might at last become a United States senator. He wrote to Ashbel, "I have always regarded you among my best, most trusted and ablest friends," and asked for his opinion and his support.[18] When Ashbel wrote back encouragingly, Jones began a covert campaign to remind influential Texans of his past services and sacrifices for the state—since it was not considered proper to seek the appointment overtly. Convinced that he would at last receive the recognition he deserved, Jones went to Austin in November to be conveniently on hand when the Seventh Legislature met and offered him the senatorship. When the vote was taken, however, James Pinckney Henderson was chosen, and Anson Jones received not one vote. That was the final blow. Jones' despair and bitterness became unbearable, and a few weeks later he committed suicide.

Old friends Ebenezer Allen and Ashbel Smith came to the aid of Mary Jones and her four children. A strong, capable woman, Mary believed that farming was what she knew best. She had the proceeds from the sale of Barrington, the Joneses' home near Washington-on-the-Brazos, and Ashbel sold her about 425 acres of his old Headquarters land on easy terms.[19] There she settled and became an active member of the community, using the nursing skills she had acquired and working to obtain capable teachers for the small private schools in the area.[20]

One of Mary Jones's first concerns was to have published her hus-

---

[18] Anson Jones to Ashbel Smith, July 24, 1857; September 25, 1857.
[19] Agreement between Ashbel Smith and Mary Jones, Anson Jones Papers.
[20] Mary D. Farrell and Elizabeth Silverthorne, *First Ladies of Texas*, pp. 59–63.

band's bulky manuscript that he had labored on during the last decade of his life. Not knowing how to find a reputable publisher, Mary Jones turned to Eben Allen and Ashbel Smith. When Ashbel went to New York in the fall of 1858, he took the manuscript along and asked the editors of D. Appleton and Company to make an estimate of the cost of printing the book. Their estimate was accepted. When the book turned out to be longer than originally planned and some editorial changes were made in it, Eben Allen advised Mary Jones not to accept it. The publisher appealed to Ashbel Smith, and eventually, after he had reconciled Mrs. Jones and the publisher, the books were printed, bound, shipped, and paid for.[21]

In the spring of 1858, Ashbel Smith, now fifty-two, was still romantically inclined and involved. His correspondence with Maria Hudson continued, and she gave him every opportunity to think that he could successfully press his suit with her. She wrote: "Why do we live so far apart? Why am I so isolated in soul, while there is one person on the earth to whom I can so truly and fully express myself?"[22] He was having an even more passionate exchange with the young woman named Christina whom he had met in Salisbury. She insisted that he burn her letters, and he told her that he carried them constantly on his person until he reluctantly "committed them to the flame." Her letters must have repeated some of the Salisbury gossip that she had heard about Ashbel and Mary Phifer, for he wrote Christina with seeming indifference: "For aught I know, she may be again married," revealing, however, his vacillation about Mary by adding, ". . . had I been sure of my own wishes, that is, had I been clear that I wished to marry her . . . it would be more easy to carry her by storm than by cautious wooing." He begged Christina to write often and to allow him to keep her letters.[23]

In June, 1858, for the second time that year, news of the untimely death of a close friend reached Ashbel. James Pinckney Henderson

---

[21] D. Appleton & Co. to Ashbel Smith, November 9, 1859. The manuscript was published under the title *Memoranda and Official Correspondence Relating to the Republic of Texas*. The finished copies reached Texas about the time the Civil War began. Except for the few that were sold and the many that were pilfered, the books were stored in boxes at Houston and Galveston for almost seventy years, until they were discovered and rescued from obscurity by Herbert Fletcher. Rio Grande Press (Glorieta, N. Mex.) reissued the book in 1966.
[22] Maria Hudson to Ashbel Smith, March 28, 1858.
[23] Ashbel Smith to Christina, January 3, 1858.

had died at the age of fifty in Washington, D.C. Ironically, Henderson, who would have preferred to stay in Marshall practicing law, had been elected to the United States Senate by the same Texas legislature that had ignored Anson Jones's desperate desire for that position.

In spite of chronic poor health caused by tuberculosis, Henderson had always led an active life, physically and mentally. His influence and enthusiasm had brought Ashbel to Texas, and he had sold Ashbel the land for his plantation on Galveston Bay. From time to time Ashbel had acted as Henderson's physician, and the two had been together frequently on social, business, and political occasions. Even after Henderson settled in east Texas, they kept in close touch. Henderson still owned heavily timbered land on the bay, which increased in value as construction began on the railroad, which developed an enormous appetite for cedar ties and logs for bridges. In Henderson's absence Ashbel had looked after his friend's property.

When Henderson married Frances Cox, of Philadelphia, Ashbel became her trusted friend also. After Henderson's death Frances wrote to Ashbel that her husband had "had no friend for whom his own feelings were stronger or upon whose friendship he would have relied more implicitly." She added, "I think if you had been with him in his last illness his life *might* have been prolonged a few months."[24] A goodly portion of Henderson's estate consisted of his land on the bay, and his widow turned to her husband's old friend for help in arranging to sell part of it and have the timber on the rest cut and sold. Ashbel advised her to sell it piece by piece as good opportunities arose, and he spent much time and effort managing the property to her best advantage.

In 1861, fearful that communications between them would be cut off because of the war and that she might die before they were restored, Frances, then living in Philadelphia, added a codicil to her will making Ashbel Smith her executor and guardian of her children's interests in Texas, calling him her husband's "best and oldest friend." Long after the Civil War, Ashbel continued to exchange letters concerning the Henderson land with Frances and her brother James Cox.

In the summer of 1858, Ashbel was invited to become the superintendent of Houston Academy. Henry F. Gillette had called the school he opened in 1844 the Houston Academy. This academy was a

[24] Francis Cox Henderson to Ashbel Smith, October 6, 1859.

new school that had been built through the efforts of private citizens of Houston and the generous donation of $5,000 by Mason J. H. Stevens. It was a two-story brick building with a cupola supported by Ionic columns and topped by a gilded globe. Ashbel wrote to Henry Barnard:

> We have built a school house in the city of Houston. It is an excellent building; large, substantial . . . being fashioned in a measure after some of your model schoolhouses. By estimate it will seat between 300 and 400 pupils, and is provided with the necessary additional rooms. It is indeed a noble structure. . . . I have given the Trustees your School Architecture and some nos. of your Journal of Education.[25]

Ashbel agreed to take the position of superintendent temporarily, while the school was being organized. He helped plan the curriculum and select the faculty of five teachers. The academy opened with between 140 and 150 students. In 1864 it was commandeered by the Confederate Army for a soldiers' hospital, and later it became part of the Houston public school system.[26]

The third death in 1858 that affected Ashbel profoundly was that of his father on December 1. Ashbel went north in the early fall of 1858 and remained there until the early spring of 1859, so it is probable that he was with his father during his last days. There is practically no record of these months in Ashbel's papers, but the very fact that there were no family letters seems to indicate that all the members were gathered together at this time. Moses had been feeble and mentally deranged much of the time since his severe illness in 1854, and his death at the age of eighty-three was not unexpected.

Ashbel always had a close relationship with his father. Moses's letters to Ashbel reveal a sly sense of humor and loving concern for this son who had far surpassed him in education but not in pride or integrity. Ashbel's letters to his parents show a respect that was more than a sense of duty, and also a deep appreciation for what they gave him. In his own life-threatening illness soon after he reached Texas the first time, Ashbel had wanted to see his father more than any other person.

Ashbel and his brother Henry were named the executors of Moses's will, in which he left his estate to Phoebe during her lifetime and then to the five children share and share alike. A codicil, however,

---

[25] Ashbel Smith to Henry Barnard, July 6, 1858.
[26] James David Carter, *Education and Masonry in Texas to 1846*, pp. 271–73; Ashbel Smith was also a Mason, a member of Caledonia Lodge No. 68.

added to the will in 1854 stated: "My sons Ashbel and Henry being men of wealth and willing thereto, so far change this will as to direct that the shares of my estate which it gives to them, be given to my daughter Caroline and to my son George."[27]

The year 1859 was tense and ominous for Texans, especially for those who involved themselves deeply in politics. Sam Houston's chances for the governorship were at the center of stormy debates over the secession issue. Charles Power, Houston's brother-in-law, wrote to Ashbel, "I think if the old Dragon will run again, that he can make the race this time, the reaction in his favor is wonderful." The delegates to the Democratic convention held at Houston on May 2 renominated Runnels, but a gathering of party bolters calling themselves "National Democrats" met in Austin and nominated Houston as their candidate.

G. W. Paschal, editor of the *Southern Intelligencer*, in a letter to Ashbel begged him to "throw off any chains which you may feel at that abortion of a convention [the regular one] and advise General Houston to run. Help us, Ashbel. The people will elect Houston whether he will or not."[28] And the people did elect their old hero, giving him a much greater margin over Runnels than they had given Runnels over Houston two years earlier. Whether or not Houston got Ashbel Smith's vote is a mystery. Like many other Texans, Ashbel considered himself bound to vote for the party's nominee or not to vote at all. Years later Ashbel would claim that he never voted other than a straight party ticket, so he may have been one of the abstainers.

At any rate Ashbel spent most of the campaign on Galveston Bay, tending his crops and his stock. The previous fall Ashbel had received a letter from Sam Houston informing him that Houston intended to engage seriously in the "shepherdizing" business at Cedar Point and offering Ashbel $4 a head for his sheep. Houston particularly wanted Ashbel's sheep, for they were used to salt water and acclimated to the coastal area. "I admit your universal intelligence, and ability in general matters," Houston said, "but you would not do, *personally* as a sheep man!"[29] Ashbel may not have appreciated Houston's disparaging remarks about his sheep husbandry, for he took great interest and pride in his sheep. "I was among the first to catch the sheep mania in Texas,"

[27] Will of Moses Smith, July 18, 1854.
[28] George W. Paschal to Ashbel Smith, May 27, 1859.
[29] Sam Houston to Ashbel Smith, October 29, 1858.

he told a friend. In the mid-1850s he had paid $200 for a fine Merino ram, which he had bred to his twenty Mexican ewes. His flock had grown to more than 100 in four years, and the quality of the wool had greatly improved. He ordered more Merino rams and ewes in the summer of 1859. He discovered that the worst enemies of his flock were his own hogs, especially the sows, which "waited for the lambing of the ewe as patiently as an animal of prey." Buzzards also destroyed many winter-dropped lambs, as did the neighbors' dogs. "I scarcely ever knew a man who had a dog which would molest sheep," Ashbel wryly commented, "but all the dogs of his neighbors are chartered sheep-killers!"[30]

As the decade of the sixties opened, there were more pressing things to think about than sheep. Ashbel Smith had become prosperous during the fifties, thanks to his agricultural and stock activities, his medical practice, and his land speculation. A census compiled in 1860 included him among the "wealthy" Texans of Harris County. He was listed as a fifty-year-old planter with $100,000 of real property, $35,000 of personal property, and twenty-seven slaves.[31] The listing was correct except for the age; that was four years short of the fact. Apparently, as he grew older, Ashbel considered his birthday a movable feast, for it appears as different dates in different documents and was even at first incorrectly engraved on his tombstone.

In July, 1860, Sam Houston wrote Ashbel a friendly letter, asking him to look over Houston's property at Cedar Point and send him a report. A postscript to the letter warned, "Beware of the Fire eating Disunionists, no matter in what clothing they may be presented."[32] Over the past decade Ashbel also had urged the necessity of preserving the Union in speeches, letters to newspapers, and private correspondence. But when he spoke to one of the last graduating classes of Rutersville College, near La Grange, although he still stressed the value of the American Union, he denounced northern "insults" to southern states and told the graduates:

I can readily conceive of invasions of our rights by the Northern States and moreover I greatly fear them, when this Union would lose all value in my eyes.

[30] Ashbel Smith to Col. B. P. Johnson, July 26, 1859; Ashbel Smith to *Galveston News*, December 30, 1874.

[31] Ralph W. Wooster, "Wealthy Texans 1860," *Southwestern Historical Quarterly* 71 (October, 1967): 176.

[32] Sam Houston to Ashbel Smith, July 25, 1860.

Whenever its forms shall serve to cloak aggressions and to give impunity to wrong, then its disbandonment and disruption will become our solemn duty.[33]

His idealistic view of slavery did not waver. He declared that no "right thinking" person would condone the African slave trade, but he believed that freeing the slaves in the South would cause chaos and misery for them and for their masters. He cited the New Testament as teaching the proper relationship: "Upon the Master an enjoined humanity and kindness; upon the servant obedience and honest service."

During the state Democratic convention, held in April, the states'-rights leaders gained control and, abandoning caution, declared Texas's right to withdraw from the Union and become again a "sovereign and independent nation." After Lincoln's election a group of Democrats met in Harris County and chose Ashbel Smith and two others to go to Austin to try to persuade Governor Houston to convene the legislature or call a convention to take up the matter of secession. Houston did not respond to this request, or to many similar ones, until states'-rights leaders set up a convention in defiance of his refusal to act.

When the convention submitted the question of secession to the voters, the conclusion was foregone. On February 24, 1861, Ashbel wrote to his nephew Ashbel Smith Kittredge, telling him that, as of March 2, "Texas will be no longer one of the United States. The madness of Black Republicanism has destroyed the best government ever devised by man." He feared that communication between Texas and Connecticut would be broken and told his namesake: "When I think of . . . my dear old mother, from whom I am separated, my heart seems ready to break. Tell her that time and distance only increase my affection for her."[34]

As soon as secession was approved, Ashbel began preparing for the war. By the time the guns were fired at Fort Sumter, he had gathered together a company of friends and neighbors and, having been elected their captain, had drilled and trained them in martial arts. The company, called the Bayland Guards, included two of Anson Jones's sons and Sam Houston's oldest son, Sam, Jr.

By April 27 the company had its required complement: one captain, three lieutenants, four sergeants, four corporals, two musicians,

---

[33] Ashbel Smith speech folder, n.d. (ca. June, 1859).
[34] Ashbel Smith to Ashbel Smith Kittredge, February 24, 1861.

and between sixty-four and one hundred privates, and Captain Smith offered its services to the governor.[35] There was a delay in orders for their induction, and the men became impatient. Equally impatient, their captain obtained a copy of the prescribed oath, and after he was himself sworn into the Army of the Confederate States of America, he administered the oath to the men of the Bayland Guards. The ceremony took place on August 13, 1861, Ashbel's fifty-sixth birthday.[36]

In true bureaucratic style the oath was readministered by an approved army agent toward the end of August. This repetition later led to confusion about the date the Bayland Guards were officially mustered into service. Ashbel, adamantly and loquaciously holding out for the earlier date, eventually persuaded the authorities to enter the earlier date in the records and to begin the pay period from that time.

At first the Bayland Guards were designated Company C, First Regiment, Texas Infantry. When it was discovered that a Texas regiment in the brigade of John Bell Hood, which had been formed at Dumfries, Virginia, in September, 1861, was also called the First Texas Infantry, the designation of Ashbel's group was changed to Second Texas Infantry. Ashbel was disappointed that his regiment was not number one, and whenever he got the chance, he pointed out that the Bayland Guards were part of the first regiment actually formed in Texas.

When Ashbel asked for guns for his company, he received praise from the adjutant general: "Your communication . . . breathes that patriotism which I would expect from one who has performed so prominent a part in the past history of Texas." The adjutant general added, however, "His excellency regrets that he unable at present to furnish [guns] to your company."[37] Shortage of arms and ammunition was to be a chronic problem for the company.

When his old friend Francis R. Lubbock became governor, Ashbel wrote to him suggesting that "every man able to bear arms should be a trained, drilled disciplined soldier." The theme of his long letter was that Texans must "become a warlike people." He suggested that the slaves should be organized as a labor force to produce food and clothing for home use and export and free white men to take up their "warlike duties." He reported to Lubbock that, although he worked his men

---

[35] W. J. Mills to Ashbel Smith, November 7, 1861.
[36] Military Order Book, p. 32, Ashbel Smith Papers.
[37] Adj. Gen. Byrd to Ashbel Smith, July 12, 1861.

hard, he believed that his relationship with most of them was "affectionate" and with all of them "very friendly." As always he drew inspiration from history and measured himself against his ancient heroes: "In ancient Greece and in ancient Rome, in the periods of their power and glory, their citizens were men both of thought and action. Their statesmen were soldiers, scholars, and philosophers."[38]

For six months the Bayland Guards remained in Texas, drilling, practicing with arms, and working on fortifications. As time passed, the men became impatient for "real" action. At last marching orders arrived, and under the command of Colonel John C. Moore the Second Texas moved out of camp at 6:00 A.M. on March 12, 1862. Traveling by railroad to Beaumont, the group boarded a steamboat bound for Weiss's Bluff, on the Neches River. Following an overland march to Alexandria, Louisiana, they took another steamboat to Helena, Arkansas. The last leg of the journey was an exhausting march to Corinth, Mississippi. They arrived on April 1 and joined the forces under Ashbel's old friend General Albert Sidney Johnston.

On Wednesday, April 3, after only one day of rest, the regiment marched out of Corinth headed for Pittsburg Landing, Tennessee, and a battle that would satisfy the most fireeating among them—a battle that would be called Shiloh, after the little meetinghouse standing on the battlefield. There were, however, more hardships to endure before the battle began. Provisions ordered for the regiment did not arrive, and the men ran out of food, their shoes were already well worn, and many of them were soon marching over the rough terrain on bare feet. Nevertheless, they were eager and excited as they approached the site where they would have their first taste of battle.

Early on Sunday, April 6, the regiment moved onto the battlefield in support of General William Joseph Hardee's division. In the preliminary fighting they lost one man, and two or three were wounded. At 8:30 A.M. they moved to the right and took up positions in the front line near a small stream called Lick Creek. All the streams in the area were full, and the Union troops were deployed so that the streams protected their flanks. Captain Smith was ordered to send out his men to cover the regiment's front and to determine the exact position of the enemy. Then the regiment was to advance double-quick and fight its way to the Union camp.

---

[38] Ashbel Smith to F. R. Lubbock, February 1, 1862.

The space between the lines was so narrow that Colonel Moore could order only three companies to advance. Company C was one of these. After a brief, furious conflict the men opened a path for the regiment, which charged the enemy camp with rebel yells. As senior captain of the left battalion, Ashbel led it in the charge. The fighting on both sides was determined and fierce. Half of Ashbel's men were severely wounded or killed, and he himself was shot in the arm. According to an eyewitness account by one of his men, when he felt the bullet sear his arm, Ashbel exclaimed, "God damn it!" A moment later he recovered himself and prayed, "Lord forgive me!"

In spite of its heavy losses the regiment completed the attack successfully, demolishing the fearsome "hornet's nest" of Union gunners, forcing the surrender of several Union regiments under General Benjamin C. Prentiss, and capturing several pieces of enemy artillery. But the Texans' elation at success on the first day of fighting was quenched when they learned that the Confederate commander, General Johnston, had been killed in the action.

Among the seriously wounded in Ashbel's company was young Charles Elliot Jones, who later died of his wounds. Sam Houston, Jr., was reported missing. Also injured in the battle was Ashbel Smith Kittredge, who was fighting with a Tennessee regiment. The Second Texas Infantry Regiment was instructed to inscribe "Shiloh" on its battle flag, and in his official report of the battle Colonel John C. Moore mentioned Ashbel Smith's "severe wound" and commented, "He had borne himself with great gallantry during the day, and we thus lost for the present the services of a brave and excellent officer."[39] While convalescent, Ashbel was promoted to lieutenant colonel.

Ashbel was sent first to a hospital in Memphis, where his brothers, Henry and George, were working as civilians in the supply service. Then he was moved to a plantation to continue his recuperation. He was feverish for many days, and his wound, which involved his right armpit, made writing extremely painful. As soon as he could prop his arm on a table and manage a pen, he wrote to the Houstons to offer

---

[39] Ashbel Smith Journal, (ca. 1862); orders and reports concerning the Battle of Shiloh in *The War of the Rebellion; Official Records of the Union and Confederate Armies*, X, pt. 1, pp. 560–64; Allan C. Ashcraft, *Texas in the Civil War: A Résumé History*; James Lee McDonough, *Shiloh; Pioneer Sketches, Cedar Bayou to San Jacinto*; Military Order Book, Ashbel Smith Papers; Confederate Records, U.S. Archives, Washington, D.C.

what information and comfort he could about Sam, Jr., who was still missing. Ashbel praised Sam's behavior, telling the Old Chief that his son was "conspicuous in his fighting like a hero and with the coolness of a veteran." Ashbel begged the Houstons not to despair, assuring them that many men who were reported missing were later found to have been accidently separated from their companies or to be in enemy hospitals recovering from wounds. Ashbel added, "Though weak and full of pain, I hope in a week or two to be again strong and on duty."[40]

It was two months before Ashbel could use his arm, and it would continue to bother him for years. Nevertheless, he was back in action by the first week in May. He was able to take part in the Battle of Farmington, which took place a few miles from Corinth. During the action Union soldiers fired at the Confederates from the front, but the southerners kept up a return fire without breaking their line as they moved forward, driving the enemy before them from one point to another until they reached a swamp, where further pursuit was useless. The troops returned to camp in high spirits. The report of the commanding officer stated, "The Second Texas, commanded by Lt. Col. Smith behaved well, officers and men keeping at all times in good order, though marching rapidly and under fire."[41]

On May 16, Ashbel was appointed acting inspector general of the brigade of General D. H. Maury, at Priceville, Mississippi. His duties included seeing that proper discipline and drill were carried out, that paperwork was done according to prescribed forms, that each regiment provided itself with "sinks in the proper places according to regulations," and that men were not allowed "to commit nuisances elsewhere."[42]

In late May the Second Texas Infantry was proud to be designated the sharpshooters for Moore's Brigade. Ashbel boasted to John Bowers: "The Second Texas is the bully regiment of this army—it is acknowledged to have . . . no equal. It is recently uniformed anew; and its stately tramp and arms glittering in the sun as they move to the stir-

---

[40] Ashbel Smith to Sam Houston, April 16, 1862, San Jacinto Museum of History Association.

[41] Report of Col. John F. Fagan, May 11, 1862, *The War of the Rebellion*, X, pt. 1, pp. 829–30.

[42] General Order 1, May 16, 1862, Military Order Book, Ashbel Smith Papers; General Order 64, June 5, 1862, ibid.

ring music of our new band, are a display full of glory." He also told Bowers to tell a "dear friend . . . who lives on Main Street . . . that I am shortly coming."[43]

The purpose of Ashbel's return to Texas was to recruit men to fill the vacancies left in the ranks of his regiment by the devastation at Shiloh. Back home, he became concerned with the defense of his state, as one traumatic event after another shook Texas. The United States Navy bombarded Corpus Christi and Lavaca and captured Sabine Pass and Galveston, and he began to feel that he should be recruiting for Texas. With this idea Sam Houston agreed. "Another man ought not to leave Texas," he wrote his old roommate. The letter, which may have been the last Ashbel received from Houston, closed with "affectionate regards" and as always with a postscript: "See the Governor if you can!!!"[44]

Despite his reservations about the wisdom of his mission, Ashbel energetically proceeded with his recruiting efforts. He was helped by the enactment of a new conscription law that raised the age limit to include males from eighteen to forty-five. In December he finally began the long trip back to Mississippi with almost 200 recruits.

While he was in Texas, Ashbel was promoted to full colonel and named the commander of the Second Texas Infantry to replace Colonel William Rogers, who had been killed at Corinth. Soon after his return to Mississippi, Ashbel's faith in the excellence of his regiment was confirmed by a letter from Major General Maury, who said: "The regiment has served with me since the evacuation of Corinth, and I have no hesitation in stating that in camp, on the march, on the field of action, it was always one of the very best and staunchest regiments in my command."[45] Another piece of news that pleased Colonel Smith was that Ashbel Smith Kittredge, who had recovered from the wound he had received at Shiloh, had requested and received a transfer to his uncle's company.

In the prelude to the Seige of Vicksburg in the early months of 1863, the Second Texas Infantry was transferred from Yazoo City to Fort Pemberton, on the Yazoo River, where it took part in the Battle of

[43] Ashbel Smith to John H. Bowers, July 31, 1862.
[44] Sam Houston to Ashbel Smith, November 18, 1862, Houston, 8:323.
[45] Gen. Dabney H. Maury to Ashbel Smith, January 14, 1863, *The War of the Rebellion*, LII, pt. 2, p. 409.

The Connecticut Rebel 153

Tallahatchee. Near the fort the men threw up a line of cotton bales and earth extending from the Yazoo to the Tallahatchee River and swung a raft out across the Tallahatchee to obstruct the passage of the enemy.

On the morning of March 11 Union forces arrived with nine gunboats, twenty-four transports, and a land force of 7,000 infantry and artillery. Two of the gunboats were the ironclads *Chillicothe* and *De Kalb*. The fighting lasted for six days, and although the Confederate troops had to conserve ammunition, they drove the Federal soldiers up the river. In his report of the battle the commanding general included a commendation: "Col. Ashbel Smith, commanding Second Texas, in charge of the right of our defenses, with great gallantry and skill prevented the enemy turning that flank."[46]

After the battle Ashbel sat down to write to a young woman friend in Houston. She may have been the same friend he had mentioned to Bowers, perhaps Eva Harris, who, according to one of Ashbel's contemporaries, was engaged to Ashbel during the Civil War.[47]

With his customary romantic coloring Ashbel described the action for her:

The cannonading . . . was glorious. The day was a very bright one, except so far as the whole sky was obscured by the vast volume of smoke vomited from the guns. The roll of cannon from both sides for nearly all day was incessant. Many of the pieces were of the largest calibre; the reverberation from the tall timber skirting the river increased and prolonged the roar, producing the effect as if of a furious, mad, unappeasable thunderstorm in a cloudless sky.

He mentioned to her with joy a treasure he had found in an abandoned farmhouse, a copy of Horace in Latin. Since he read Latin with about as much ease as he read English, he enjoyed the songs of the " Old Roman" in the long hours between battles. Far from depressed by his war experiences, he described his health as "iron," his spirits as "bounding," and his heart as "resolute."[48]

In the latter part of April the Second Texas was moved to a bivouac on Chickasaw Bayou, nine miles above Vicksburg. When General William Tecumseh Sherman began bombarding Synder's Bluff in a feint designed to cover General Ulysses S. Grant's actual crossing of the Mis-

[46] Report of Gen. W. W. Loring, March 22, 1863, *The War of the Rebellion*, XXIV, pt. 1, pp. 415–17.
[47] Dr. Samuel Clark Red, *Biographical Sketch of Ashbel Smith*, pp. 23–24.
[48] Ashbel Smith letter, Fort Pemberton, April 8, 1863.

sissippi about fifty miles southwest, the Second Texas was transferred to that area. After Sherman's expedition was recalled, Smith's men marched back to their old base at Chickasaw Bayou.[49]

Three days later Confederate leaders realized that the immediate danger was *south* of Vicksburg, and the Second Texas was ordered to Warrenton, an abandoned town about eight miles below Vicksburg. When they left the Chickasaw camp, the men were allowed to take only the clothes they wore plus one extra shirt and one blanket. Only ammunition and a few indispensable cooking utensils were allowed to be taken from the camp; most of the men's personal effects were left behind and later fell into enemy hands.

In Warrenton the Second Texas took its turn manning a redoubt and patrolling the banks of the river above and below the town. The redoubt was cannonaded regularly every evening by a Union gunboat, but no one was seriously wounded.[50]

When Confederate forces suffered defeats at Champion Hill and other eastern sites, it became necessary for General John Clifford Pemberton's men to fall back upon Vicksburg, and the Second Texas was also moved back into the city. After some shuffling about of regiments, the Second Texas was assigned to the fort commanding Baldwin's Ferry Road at the most advanced point of the Confederate lines. Colonel Smith described their position with relish: "This was the assailable point of our lines, the place of danger, the post of honor, the key of this portion of our works of defense."[51]

In accordance with his belief that "the spade is a military weapon," he set his men to work improving the fort and the surrounding area. He had them dig a ditch two feet deep inside the parapet where the men could stand without being exposed to enemy fire. They constructed a line of rifle pits across the gorge of the fort, and they added two feet to the parapet to strengthen it. They also cleared the view by burning intervening houses and cutting down trees.

On the evening of May 18 outposts reported Union troops on Baldwin Ferry Road. From behind irregular crests of small hills facing the fort Union soldiers began a steady bombardment with canon and rifles. As more enemy troops came into position, the firing within and

[49] Ashbel Smith, "Second Regiment Texas Volunteer Infantry," report, n.d. (ca. July 8, 1863), Ashbel Smith Papers.
[50] Ibid.
[51] Ibid.

outside the fort became deafening. Colonel Smith reported, ". . . the uproar and rattle was incessant and very grand." The enemy's Minié balls swept within two feet of the ground in the fort, forcing the Texans to lie flat on the ground at night and to seek the protection of the ditches next to the parapet and traverse by day.

Early on the morning of the twenty-second, Union forces began a fierce cannonading, which they kept up until 10:00 A.M., the hour that Grant had set for an all-out attack on Vicksburg. At the appointed hour swarms of Union soldiers hurled themselves at the fort's breastworks. The Texans welcomed the first wave of the enemy with murderous fire, standing in exposed positions on the banquettes. As the ground became covered with enemy dead, the Confederates broke into wild yells. The Union soldiers, however, outnumbered the Confederates ten to one, and even though one of their regiments had been thrown into confusion, they continued to attack. None of them managed to scale the wall, but some found temporary protection in the ditches at the foot of the fort's lunette, forcing the Confederates to expose themselves dangerously to fire at them.[52]

Inside the fort Colonel Smith positioned his men in three ranks. The front rank, next to the parapet, was to maintain fire; the second rank waited on bended knee with guns loaded and bayonets fixed. These two positions alternated as the guns of the front rank became heated. The third rank, four paces to the rear, lay on the ground (to avoid the Minié balls) with guns loaded and bayonets fixed, ready to replace any of their fallen comrades. The plan worked. The enemy made three determined attempts to scale the top of the works but each time was thoroughly repulsed.

Early in the fighting enemy fire caused some of the protective cotton bales to break open, and the cotton was thickly scattered. When some of it ignited, the third rank of men had to brush it away with their hands to prevent it from carrying the fire to the ammunition boxes. When burning clouds of smoke nearly blinded the men in one angle of the fort, Colonel Smith called, "Volunteers to clear that embrasure!" Four men, including his nephew, sprang forward and fired their guns within five paces of the muzzles of their opponents, hurling them back-

[52] Ashbel Smith Journal, 1863; reports concerning the siege of Vicksburg, *The War of the Rebellion*, XXIV, pt. 2, pp. 326–95; Peter F. Walker, *Vicksburg: A People at War, 1860–65*; A. A. Hoehling et al., *Vicksburg—47 Days of Siege*; Edwin C. Bearss, *Texas at Vicksburg*; Ashbel Smith, report to Captain James M. Loughborough, July 8, 1863.

ward into the ditch. One of the four volunteers fell to the platform dead, and another was mortally wounded. Kittredge was spared, and throughout the duration of the siege Ashbel kept him busy carrying messages across the field to other commanders in the city—an extremely perilous undertaking. For his gallantry Ashbel recommended his nephew for promotion to lieutenant, and the request was granted.

To clear the ditches in front of the fort, Ashbel had his men use spherical cannon shells as hand grenades. The effect was "good," and there was a slackening of enemy fire. As night fell, the firing gradually ceased, and the Union soldiers returned to their covers in the woods and hollows.[53]

After dark Ashbel examined the area in front of the fort and discovered the ground thickly strewn with bodies of the enemy dead—sometimes piled two or three deep. He reported, "Along the road for 200 yards the bodies lay so thick that one might have walked the whole distance on them without touching the ground." He also discovered that the Union soldiers for their protection had dug many holes in the ground. He ordered them filled with "yankee carcasses" and earth so that they could not be used again.[54]

Cannonading and bombardment continued on May 23 and 24, but on the twenty-fifth there was a truce to allow the Federal troops to bury their dead. On the day of truce Ashbel had an interview with some Union officers. They told him that the reason the Union troops attacked with such recklessness was that they were confident of a quick victory after the relative ease with which they had defeated the Confederate troops at Baker Creek and Champion Hill. They admitted to astonishment at finding themselves still outside the fort after the first day of fighting.[55]

Also on this day of truce Ashbel had a meeting with a young Union soldier—a meeting filled with the pathos of a war that made enemies of those who normally would have been close, even intimate, friends.

---

[53] Ashbel Smith, "Second Regiment Texas Volunteer Infantry," report, n.d. (ca. July 8, 1863), Ashbel Smith Papers.

[54] Reports on this day's casualties at Vicksburg differ. After the surrender of Vicksburg a Union report listed 600 killed and 1,200 wounded. The Second Texas Infantry reported 53 killed, 73 wounded, and 15 missing of the 468 men engaged in the action.

[55] Ashbel Smith, "Second Regiment Texas Volunteer Infantry," report, n.d. (ca. July 8, 1863), Ashbel Smith Papers.

The soldier was the son of Hannah Burnet's sister, Mary Clopper, of Ohio.[56]

Having failed to take the city of Vicksburg by assault, the Union army prepared to take it by siege. Soon cannons and rifle pits with breastworks bristled from every eminence facing the fort. For the next six weeks the Texans endured a fierce cannonade one to four times every twenty-four hours, and an incessant stream of Minié balls swept just above the upper slope of their parapet. The Texans urgently asked permission to return "shot for shot with interest," but Colonel Smith daily received orders and admonitions to husband his small supply of ammunition, and he could not permit them to do so. All the men "slept on their arms" and suffered from fatigue, but they did not despair. In fact, Ashbel reported to his superiors that the Second Texas soldiers did their duty "without a murmur" and even with "gaiety."

From about the middle of June to the end of the siege on July 4 the contest became almost hand to hand. Having completed parallel trenches near the fort, the northern troops tried to undermine it by pushing forward three saps. Large sap rollers were moved along the head of each sap for the protection of the sappers. These sap rollers, cylinders seven to eight feet long and four and a half feet in diameter, had cotton cores surrounded by cane and covered with wire matting. As the saps approached to within eighteen to twenty feet of their ditch, the Texans tried every means they could devise to stop them, using shells as hand grenades and even throwing dirt clods. For a time they tried in vain to burn the sap rollers wtih fireballs of cotton soaked in turpentine, but these were drawn into the saps and extinguished. Then they bowled an eighteen-pound shell wrapped in the soaked cotton against one of the sap rollers. The fireball exploded and ignited the sap roller, which was consumed. The cotton core of the second sap roller was ignited by a fuse fired from a smoothbore musket, and it, too, was consumed by flames.[57]

Conditions were as desperate within the fort as they were in the city itself. Having left Chickasaw Bayou without extra clothing and with only a single blanket each, the men were soon ragged and dirty. During the early days of the siege drenching rain turned the ground

---

[56] Mary Clopper to Ashbel Smith, October 17, 1880.
[57] Ashbel Smith, report of Texas Second Infantry at Vicksburg, n.d., Military Order Book, Ashbel Smith Papers.

into ankle-deep mire. In addition to making for miserable conditions, the rains caused Colonel Smith great concern that the Union forces might attack with their superior weapons while his guns were wet and out of commission.

When the rains stopped and the sun began to shine, water became scarce. Large numbers of dead horses and mules had been dumped into the Mississippi River, and the water next to the banks swarmed with maggots and was unfit for use. The only water available to the Texans, from shallow wells at the rear of their camp, was hardly sufficient for cooking and drinking, and Ashbel posted sentinels by the wells to see that no water was wasted for the "purpose of cleanliness." Three ounces of musty cornmeal and pea flour were issued daily to each man. Every eatable vegetable, every half-grown peach, every green berry around the fort was gathered and eaten. Helplessly Dr. Smith watched his men become weak and emaciated and with his trained eye observed that, although only two or three died from outright starvation, many had symptoms of incipient scurvy.[58]

One day toward the end of the siege Ashbel was informed that there were no more cartridges for the Enfield rifles with which his men were armed. He counted the ammunition and found that only fifty-four rounds to a man were left. Clearly they could not hold out much longer. After General John Pemberton formally surrendered to General Grant on July 4, 1863, the men of the Second Texas Infantry marched through the line of Union sentinels, "tired, dirty, covered with vermin, ragged, barefoot and hungry," as Colonel Smith reported to his commander. "But," he added, "when I think of their cheerfulness and courage under the circumstances, it appears to me that no commendation of these soldiers can be too great."

The men of the Second Texas were paroled pending their exchange and sent to a camp outside Brandon, Mississippi. The men had a natural and intense desire to return to their homes in Texas, and Ashbel had all he could do "by command and appeal to their honor" to keep them with him until he could secure their orders to return home. On July 17 he managed to see General Pemberton, who gave the regiment a forty-day furlough, instructing Ashbel to collect and reassemble his men in Texas after that time.[59]

[58] Ibid.
[59] General orders, July 17, 1863, ibid.

The Connecticut Rebel 159

Many years after the war a private in the Second Texas recalled Ashbel's leadership. He reminded Ashbel that he had stayed with him on his outpost duty and recalled the first time he had noticed Ashbel in battle. It was at Shiloh, when the colonel was in front of his company "shouting them on." The soldier also remembered the colonel at Vicksburg, fixing fuses to shells, "whilst I threw them over and on the yanks." But the most vivid memory of the former Confederate soldier was of a "long, bloody day" at Vicksburg

when you stood out on the Hill and encouraged the Masourians and Arkansas troops on to our assistance. I can see you now. *There you stand*, in full view of the assaulting colums. I can hear your voice *Come on My Brave Masourians*. Come and *Help my Boys*. I can see the Shot and Shell tare the ground at *your feet*. I can see the bullets pierce your clothes. I can hear the Shouts of our Supporters as they came up the Hill. The charge in the Road and the yanks going fleeing down the Slope.[60]

Although Ashbel conceded that the Second Texas had been defeated—not by Union soldiers but by "want of subsistence and want of ammunition"—he did not admit that they were spiritually beaten. In fact, he claimed: "The 2nd Texas Infantry achieved one victory—they utterly destroyed any prestige which the enemy might have heretofore felt when the soldiers they should encounter should be Texians."[61]

[60]: H. H. Merritt to Ashbel Smith, April 17, 1879.
[61] Ashbel Smith, report on siege of Vicksburg, n.d., Ashbel Smith Papers.

CHAPTER NINE

Now Is the Seed Time
(1863–1872)

WITH stiff, swollen legs and cheeks hollow from privation, the survivors of the Second Texas Infantry made their way back to the homes that many of them had not seen in more than two years. Their commanding officer, however, did not spend his leave days in relaxation. Texans were hungry for factual news of the war, and he was pressed to write articles for local papers and to make speeches. Complying with these requests, he praised the behavior of the Confederate troops and spoke encouragingly of an ultimate victory for the South—if the people remained united.

Underneath his facade of confidence lay serious anxieties, which he reported to his superiors. He had taken the opportunity of talking with his Union captors after the fall of Vicksburg and was astonished to learn of the detailed plans the enemy had made to force Texas to supply beef to the Union armies. He warned the Texas leaders to pay careful attention to the defenses of the Texas-Louisiana border, because the Union officers had extensive knowledge of the topography, weather, and feasible routes of the area.[1]

After the furlough period Ashbel was separated from his regiment for a time, having been named chief inspector general of the state troops. He applied himself with his usual thoroughness to the job, which involved writing and receiving innumerable reports and also extensive traveling to inspect the troops. He found that many of their guns were not serviceable. A few men had Springfield rifles, which he praised as excellent, but in his opinion the guns manufactured in Texas

[1] Ashbel Smith to Capt. Edmund P. Turner, November 6, 1863, Confederate Southern Army Trans-Mississippi Department, correspondence and circulars, 1863–65, Ashbel Smith Papers.

Now is the Seed Time

were "utterly worthless, projecting the ball neither with force nor accuracy."[2]

Willing himself to work as long as his mind and body could function, he had no patience for laxness or laziness. When an officer reported that his men refused to cut and burn bushes or load steamers, Ashbel replied that such work under certain circumstances was indeed "proper employment for soldiers" and advised the officer to inflict "such discipline as the cases may require."[3]

On his return to Texas, Ashbel had discovered that an important presence had passed out of his life. Sam Houston had died in July, 1863, while his friend and physician was making his way back from the battlegrounds in Mississippi. Margaret Houston had taken her children to Independence to be near her mother and her beloved Baptist Church. She wrote to Ashbel offering him a large tent for the men in his regiment who most needed shelter from "weakness, sickness or any inability to bear exposure" and giving him directions for obtaining it from Cedar Point.[4] Happily, Sam Houston, Jr., was recovering from the serious wound he had received at Shiloh, from where he had been taken to a Union hospital, as Ashbel had surmised.

In late November, when Federal troops captured Brownsville and moved up the coast as far as the Matagorda peninsula, the Second Texas was first ordered to Velasco. The camp was on the open beach, and when blue northers roared through, it was so miserably cold that the men feared they might freeze to death. After a few weeks the regiment was moved to Camp Slaughter, on Oyster Creek, where heavy timber provided welcome protection from the wind. There Ashbel had under his command, in addition to the Second Texas Regiment, the First, Second, Third, and Fourth regiments of infantry state troops.[5] The camp was kept in readiness for an enemy attack. Ashbel issued orders that guns were to be placed so that the men could find them in the dark and that if it became necessary to abandon horses, mules, or cattle the officer in charge was to have them killed.

At times during the coldest part of the winter supplies ran low. Periodically Ashbel had to order investigations of alleged pilfering of

---

[2] Ashbel Smith to Lt. Col. I. D. McAdoo, November 1, 1863.
[3] Ashbel Smith to Col. K. B. DeWalt, November 9, 1863.
[4] Margaret Houston to Ashbel Smith, October 26, 1863.
[5] General Order December 31, 1863, 243, *The War of the Rebellion*, 26:562. Special Order 344, December 16, 1863, Military Order Book, Ashbel Smith Papers.

the local farmers' smokehouses and potato banks by the soldiers. But he was indignant when he felt that red tape was keeping supplies from his men. On January 2 he demanded that the quartermaster furnish his men with meat *immediately*, adding, "No excuse will be taken for not supplying them."[6]

On January 8 there was naval action at the mouth of Caney Creek, and on the twelfth Ashbel Smith was ordered to take the Second Texas Infantry and as many of the state troops as had arms to guard the mouth of the San Bernard River, with instructions that "under no circumstances will the enemy be permitted to gain possession of the mouth of the Bernard."[7] A week later several Union gunboats were sighted near Fort Caney. It was assumed that the Federal forces were planning an invasion at that point, and Colonel Smith was put in command of the fort. His friend H. P. Bee, now a brigadier general, called it "the Post of Honor" and said, "It appropriately belongs to 2nd Texas."[8] The men under Ashbel's command formed a brigade, designated the Second Brigade, Second Division, and composed of the Second Regiment Texas Infantry, Waul's Legion, Hobby's Regiment, and Wilkes's Battery.

The leading Confederate generals in the area, Kirby Smith and John B. Magruder, considered abandoning the Matagorda peninsula and pulling the troops back into the interior. All but two of the officers they consulted agreed with this plan; the two were Joseph Bates and Ashbel Smith. Years later Bates testified that the "determination and positiveness" with which Colonel Smith declared that he could hold his position persuaded the generals to hold the ground and resulted in "saving Texas from invasion."[9]

Working with his engineer, Colonel Smith selected strategic positions and submitted plans for strengthening the fort by building redoubts and rifle pits. His plans were approved, and the works, including a bridge, were constructed under his close supervision. The work was often done at night because of the daytime bombardment of the coast by Federal vessels. In recognition of his efforts the garrison, on

---

[6] Special Order 13, January 2, 1864, Military Order Book, Ashbel Smith Papers.

[7] W. T. Mechling, Asst. Adj. Gen., to Ashbel Smith, January 20, 1864, *The War of the Rebellion*, 34:899.

[8] General H. P. Bee to Ashbel Smith, January 28, 1864. H. P. Bee was the son of Ashbel's close friend, Barnard E. Bee.

[9] W. P. Ballinger to Joseph Bates, October 9, 1879.

the left bank of the Caney, was named Fort Ashbel Smith, in line with the policy of naming garrisons for prominent soldiers and citizens.[10]

While the Second Texas was enduring hardships on the coast, Ashbel received word that the Confederate command east of the Mississippi had misplaced the Second Texas and its commander and that they had been reported absent without leave. He fired off an angry four-page letter, with copies of his orders, to the appropriate officials, detailing every movement of the Second Texas since its induction and ending: "I respectfully ask that the status of the 2nd Texas Vol. Infantry in your Department be rectified, and that the reproach of absence without leave whether imputed through ignorance or misplaced punctilio be utterly expunged."[11]

In March, 1864, Ashbel was detached to Houston to serve on a board of examination for disabled, disqualified, and incompetent officers. He was elected president of the board, which in June was ordered to Galveston, where it was to hold its sessions.[12] The vulnerability of the island city was demonstrated when Union ships made an expedition into Galveston Bay during the first week in July. In his absence Ashbel's regiment had been moved to Galveston and was being enlarged from 460 to 760 men. On August 12, Ashbel was released from his duties on the board of examination and resumed command of his troops on Galveston Island.

In September an epidemic of yellow fever broke out on the island, and the city was placed under strict quarantine. The Tremont House was turned into a hospital for the soldiers, who showed a new kind of courage in nursing their stricken comrades through a disease they believed to be deadly contagious. Ashbel Smith's own iron health broke down, and he was ill for several weeks, probably with malaria. When Brigadier General James M. Hawes, commander of the Galveston defenses, contracted yellow fever, Colonel Smith, the ranking officer, was well enough to take over the command. The problems he inherited were both large and small, and he attacked them with vigor.

It was discovered that Union boats were reconnoitering the beach

[10] Captain E. P. Turner to Gen. H. P. Bee, February 17, 1864, Military Order Book, Ashbel Smith Papers, Special Order 45, February 25, 1864, ibid.

[11] Ashbel Smith to Gen. G. Cooper, February 27, 1864.

[12] General Magruder, Special Order 69, March 9, 1864, Military Order Book, Ashbel Smith Papers; Special Order 86, March 28, 1864, ibid.; Special Order 170, June 18, 1864, ibid.

at night, and rumors reached Galveston that Admiral David G. Farragut was at New Orleans outfitting his ships for an attack on Galveston. Colonel Smith reacted to this news by strengthening the pickets to form a continuous line along the beach and issuing orders that a detachment was to sleep in each battery at night.

Ashbel also learned that deserters were keeping the watchful Federal forces "cognizant of everything transpiring on the Island." To put a stop to this, he asked for authority to convene courts martial for immediate trials of deserters caught in the act.[13] He also sent out a notice that prisoners who had escaped after being ordered executed for desertion were to be captured and brought back to Galveston with a renewal of the order for their execution, saying, "Such an example is much needed in this command, and will doubtless exercise a salutary influence on preventing desertion hereafter."

There were shortages of wood, water, and food on the island. One gallon of cistern water was issued to each man a day, and detachments were sent into the countryside to search for foodstuffs. Other shortages made it necessary to send a message to the commander of the United States forces off Galveston informing him that the Confederates could not supply sufficient clothing and blankets for Union prisoners and asking whether the Federals wanted to supply them.[14]

Several times during the winter and spring of 1864–65, Ashbel was on detached duty, serving on courts martial in various Texas cities. When, however, Brigadier General Hawes asked to be relieved of his assignment, Ashbel Smith became the permanent commander of the Galveston defenses. Ashbel received permission to have his nephew Ashbel Smith Kittredge assigned to duty as his acting assistant adjutant general.

The shortage of usable arms had become a serious problem for the Galveston troops, and Ashbel, after polling the large cotton growers along the southern coast, devised a complex plan for using cotton in exchange for guns or money to purchase guns. Because cash was scarce, his plan involved sending an agent to England to obtain the guns.[15] He urged that "every man who is able ought to subscribe $500 or 8 bales of cotton—small sums will not answer in this emergency."[16]

[13] Ashbel Smith to Capt. W. A. Smith, October 22, 1864; October 26, 1864, ibid.
[14] Ashbel Smith to Capt. I. B. Marchand, November 25, 1864, ibid.
[15] Ashbel Smith to Capt. A. H. May, February 7, 1865, ibid.
[16] Ashbel Smith to Col. H. Washington, March 7, 1865.

When this scheme failed to produce weapons, Ashbel wrote to Governor Pendleton Murrah, advising him that some patriotic citizens wanted to advance $50,000 for the purchase of a number of Whitworth, Armstrong, or Blakeley guns to be used by the troops guarding Galveston. He asked if the governor would be willing to issue state bonds to cover the amount.[17] Murrah expressed "gratification" at the offer and assured Ashbel that as soon as the guns were purchased he would issue bonds at 7 percent interest to cover the amount.[18] Ashbel was skeptical of Murrah's promises, however, observing to a friend, "You and I know that Governor Murrah is a hopeless trickster."[19]

The Confederate commanders in the coastal area did not share Colonel Smith's belief that Galveston was "invincible." General Kirby Smith wrote to General J. G. Walker:

I shall endeavor to strengthen your means of defense at Galveston by increasing its garrison, but so apparent is the natural weakness of the position that I am daily more strongly convinced of the impracticability of making a successful defense against an attack in force. . . . A show of strengthening it should be made, whilst secretly preparing for the evacuation.[20]

After the fall of Charleston and Wilmington, many Texans thought that it was only a matter of days before the Union navy attacked Galveston Island in force. Many of them were resigned to "giving up the coast" to the enemy, but Ashbel Smith had other ideas. He wrote to David Burnet that an attack seemed imminent but added, "Gloomy as our affairs seem to be at this moment, I am by no means despondent."[21]

Sanguine by nature, Ashbel remained optimistic about the outcome of the war longer than many other Texans because he held one firm belief that buoyed his hopes. Because of his firsthand knowledge of British and French diplomacy he looked to those nations for help, for he was convinced that they would not permit the war to end in a way that would allow the Confederate states to be rejoined to the United States. He expressed this confidence in a long letter about Texas's foreign relations which was published in the *Houston Daily Telegraph* on February 20, 1865, and reprinted in other Texas papers.[22]

[17] Ashbel Smith to Governor P. Murrah, March 1, 1865.
[18] Governor P. Murrah to Ashbel Smith, March 1, 1865.
[19] Ashbel Smith to Col. Wm. J. Hutchins, January 17, 1865.
[20] General E. K. Smith to Maj. Gen. J. G. Walker, January 30, 1865, *The War of the Rebellion*, 48:1353. General Smith was a distant relative of Ashbel.
[21] Ashbel Smith to David Burnet, March 9, 1865.
[22] Ashbel Smith to *Houston Daily Telegraph*, February 20, 1865.

After the appearance of his letter some of his friends urged him to run for governor, and editorials supporting him for that office appeared in the *Houston Telegraph* and the *Galveston News*. Ashbel told his friends that he would run only if he became convinced that he could serve Texas better in that position than in his present one. As letters pressing him to run continued to arrive by every mail, he began sounding like a candidate. In a letter to Colonel C. G. Forshey he described the man Texas needed as governor: "We need a man of practical experience. . . . It is . . . desirable that our next Governor should . . . be one who has served in the Army, that he may understand the wants of our soldiers and have an active sympathy with them. . . . We want a solid brain, large experience, high purposes, firmness, clean hands." He told Forshey that he had "nearly arrived at the conclusion that if the people shall choose to elect me for Governor, I shall be most grateful for their confidence and will serve them to the best of my ability."[23] There were several candidates but Ashbel Smith had strong support, especially in west and central Texas, and his chances seemed good. The election, of course, would never be held.

Heavy spring rains that flooded prairies and raised rivers to their banks made an overland invasion into Texas unlikely and gave Texans some relief from tension. The threat from the sea did not diminish, however, and Ashbel continued to cajole and importune for the arms he desperately needed. He assured his superiors that he could hold the city against any attack by sea *if* he had sufficient guns.

When news of Lee's surrender reached him, Ashbel issued a message of encouragement to his men:

22 April 1865

. . . The Colonel Commanding takes this opportunity to say that there is nothing in the news received this day of our misfortunes in Virginia, which should dampen our ardor. On the contrary, the news serious as it is should stimulate us to redoubled efforts to defend our homes. Our hopes are still high. . . . The resources and means of defence in the Trans Mississippi Department are immense and when viewed in connection with the advantages which we possess in our position and in the remoteness from the source of Yankee supplies of subsistence, munitions and men, are calculated to give us great encouragement.

Let every man be of good cheer, there is life in the Old Land yet.[24]

[23] Ashbel Smith to Col. C. G. Forshey, March 21, 1865.
[24] Ashbel Smith, General Order 28, April 22, 1865, Military Order Book, Ashbel Smith Papers.

On May 3 the *Wren* arrived in port, bringing eight pieces of artillery, eighty-seven cases of Enfield rifles, and ammunition. The supplies were welcome but woefully inadequate. Ashbel found it necessary to issue orders to "fire on the enemy whenever they come within range of your guns, be sure and not fire an ineffectual ball, but let each one tell; for we have no ammunition to waste and when you do fire blow them out of the water."

As the news from the East became more grim, Colonel Smith became more determined to hold Galveston. He kept the men at work on the fortifications for long hours, working himself into the early-morning hours. He secured a horse so that he would be prepared to lead his men in battle when the enemy appeared on the beaches of Galveston.

The troops did not share his optimism, and short rations did not improve their morale. Some of the men were reportedly begging meat and bread from Galveston citizens. Ashbel reminded his officers and men of standing orders prohibiting them from messing and lodging with citizens and instructed his officers that these orders were to be "strictly enforced."[25] As insubordination spread, Ashbel received an anonymous threatening letter from several of the soldiers.[26]

On May 14 a mass desertion was attempted. Having been forewarned, Colonel Smith placed a trustworthy guard unit at the Galveston City end of the railroad bridge and another at the draw on the bridge. The unit on the bridge was prepared to stop the train by turning the draw if the deserters boarded the cars. Ashbel went to the bridge just after dusk and intercepted 200 to 300 men attempting to leave. After calming their fears about being able to withstand an enemy attack, he informed them that his guards were determined to prevent them from leaving. The men dropped away and the next morning were back on duty. Colonel Smith had the leaders arrested and put to work on the fortifications under strong guard. Then he reported, "The ninety-eight deserters and jay hawkers are hard at work," adding, "I feel competent and have at all times felt competent to maintain the subordination of these troops."[27]

His authority was daily becoming more tenuous, however, as

---

[25] Ashbel Smith to Lt. Col. Fulcrod, April 22, 1865.
[26] Anonymous letter to Col. Smith, May 16, 1865.
[27] Ashbel Smith to Capt. E. P. Turner, May 15, 1865, Military Order Book, Ashbel Smith Papers.

truths, half-truths, and lies about the fortunes of the Confederacy continued to reach the troops on Galveston Island. One of the most persistent rumors was that the Federal forces intended to destroy the railroad bridge, cutting off the island from the mainland, and then burn the city to the ground. Ashbel kept a strong guard on the bridge with orders to blow Union surveying parties out of the water and also set men to work constructing pontoon bridges for emergency use.

By the last week in May, Ashbel's officers were telling him that they could no longer hold their men on the island. Telegrams flew between the Confederate district headquarters in Houston and Colonel Smith's office. On May 21 he received orders to evacuate the island, and General Magruder telegraphed him to try to "induce a sufficient number of soldiers to remain at Galveston to garrison the place. If necessary try to get citizens to volunteer."[28]

Ashbel drew up plans for an orderly evacuation designed to keep confusion to a minimum, but he was fighting a losing battle. The demoralized troops, who had not been paid in months, looted quartermaster and commissary stores and took ammunition and arms and other Confederate property, including transportation vehicles. On the night of the twenty-first a blockade-running steamer, the *Lark*, arrived at Galveston harbor. Instead of coming to anchor and reporting, as regulations required, the ship came directly to the wharf before dawn. Soldiers boarded the ship and with hardly "a remonstrance" from the captain began plundering her stores. The guard was unable to halt the looting until most of the Confederate goods had been carried away. Realizing that this "taste of plunder" might soon lead some of the soldiers to ignore the bounds between public and private property and begin robbing private homes, Ashbel began immediately to move the troops in small groups to towns away from Galveston, where their commanders could ask the Houston district office for dispersal orders.[29]

On May 23, Governor Murrah telegraphed Ashbel asking him to serve as one of two commissioners representing the state of Texas at negotiations for peace terms with Union officials in New Orleans. Ashbel agreed to serve, and he and the other commissioner, William P. Ballinger, were furnished with funds of $500 each. On May 25 they boarded the United States steamer *Antona* and four days later arrived in New Orleans. There they found that the convention of surrender

---

[28] Gen. Magruder to Ashbel Smith, telegram, May 22, 1865, ibid.
[29] Ashbel Smith to Maj. Gen. Gordan Granger, June 23, 1865.

had already been signed by both sides, and after "mature consideration" they decided to admit that surrender was an accomplished fact and work for the best terms they could achieve. They explained frankly to the Union leaders that most Texas soldiers had "disbanded themselves" and had probably returned to their homes. They disclosed that most of the Confederate army's ordnance, commissary supplies, and transportation equipment had been seized by the troops. The two representatives assured the Union officials that the people of Texas were ready, "in sincere good faith," to return to a "loyal, obedient" relationship with the United States of America.

The Union officials informed the Texans that an immense cavalry force under General Philip Henry Sheridan had been preparing to "sweep over Texas" and "desolate it." While they listened politely to the requests of the commissioners, they were not inclined to yield on the major issues. Among the terms that the Texans urged were that the soldiers in Texas be allowed to keep their arms and ammunition, that the impending election be allowed to take place, that Negroes be allowed to remain on the plantations until the cotton crop was picked, and, above all, that military rule not be set up in Texas. After an interview with General Sheridan, neither commissioner felt hopeful that the requests would be granted. There was no more to be done in New Orleans. Ballinger stayed on for a few days to investigate the feasibility of going to Washington to speak in Texas's behalf, while Ashbel returned to Texas to report to Governor Murrah.[30] Before Ashbel arrived in Texas, however, the governor, along with some other Texas leaders, had fled to Mexico for sanctuary.

In Galveston, Colonel Smith formally turned over his command to Union Major General Gordon Granger, whom he found to be personally courteous and friendly but officially harsh and unyielding. The cause that Ashbel pleaded for most earnestly was that the men be allowed to keep their guns. He pointed out that most of them had brought their own guns with them when they enlisted. He emphasized that in the sparsely settled rural areas, where each farmhouse was its own castle, firearms were indispensable for the defense of property and person and of the honor of women from "jayhawkers and lawless

---

[30] Ashbel Smith to Gen. Magruder, June 1, 1865; W. P. Ballinger Diary, May, 1865; Ashbel Smith, memorandum on negotiations with Union officials, May 29, 1865; W. P. Ballinger to Gov. Pendleton Murrah, June 1, 1865; Ashbel Smith and W. P. Ballinger to Maj. Gen. E. R. S. Canby, May 30, 1865, *The War of the Rebellion*, 48:675–76.

negroes," for procuring meat for subsistence, for protection against destructive or dangerous wild animals, and, in the frontier counties, for defense against Indians. To take away the weapons of the good and peaceful citizens would be to leave them at the mercy of felons, he argued. Such arguments made little impression on the Union officials.[31]

Since the fortunes of most Texans, particularly those of slaveowners, had been swept away by the war, Ashbel found irony in the $20,000 property-ownership limit imposed by the federal government. Writing to a friend, he said that he did not know anyone in *his* county with an estate worth $20,000, and that he feared that heavy taxation would be a practical confiscation of most of the property that was left. His inclination, he declared, was to retire to Evergreen and abstain from public life. The idea was fleeting, of course, and he was soon geared up to take on the new opponents. "In view of the plans of the radical destructionists it becomes the duty of every good member of society to qualify himself to vote and to exercise this right as a solemn duty," he said. "Sullen indifference is not only in bad taste—it is wrong."[32]

In speeches and letters Ashbel urged Texans to look to the soil for their salvation and to diversify their crops to increase their income:

The land is left us, this goodly land, and we still have the stout hearts of our countrymen. . . . Our business, our duty is to retrieve our condition, to reestablish the prosperity, the comfort, the protection of local laws which once were ours. Our manly pride which forbids us to remain cast down; our love for the women of our land, the patrotic glow which every generous heart feels in the honor of his state and in the generations who shall come after us that we may not leave them an unworthy heritage, all, all impel us to retrieve our condition.[33]

On October 12, 1865, he took the oath of amnesty, and his name was placed on the register of voters of Harris County. Wanting a place where he could make his opinions heard, he took the advice of his friends, ran for a seat in the Texas house of representatives, and was elected to the Eleventh Legislature. The members of the house were mostly conservative, but there was a sharp division between the conservative Unionists and the former Secessionists led by Ashbel and

---

[31] Ashbel Smith to Maj. Gen. Gordon Granger, June 23, 1865; Ashbel Smith Journal, June 30, 1865.
[32] Ashbel Smith to Gen. James Barnes, June, 1865.
[33] Ashbel Smith speech, n.d. (ca. June, 1866), Ashbel Smith Papers.

Now is the Seed Time

others. The contest for speaker for the house was a close one between Unionist Nat Burford of Dallas County and former Secessionist Ashbel Smith of Harris County, with Burford winning by a vote of 39 to 30.

The Eleventh Legislature faced a number of touchy problems in getting Texas back into the Union on the best terms that could be won or wrested from the federal government. One of these problems was the election of two United States senators. Ashbel wrote to David Burnet urging him to accept the nomination, assuring him, "There is no man in the State . . . so universally acceptable, so endeared in the affections of the people as yourself."[34] Burnet reluctantly accepted the nomination, though he protested that he could not sign the required "ironclad" oath, and so in all likelihood would not be allowed to take his seat.[35] Ashbel's preference for the other senator was Judge John Hancock, but on the final ballot he voted for Judge O. M. Roberts, for he felt that one senator should be from the eastern part of the state. In the end neither Burnet nor Roberts was seated, since neither would take the test oath, which barred from election to national office practically everyone who had controlled state policies in the rebel states before the war.

As chairman of the federal-relations committee, Ashbel drafted a report expressing gratitude to President Andrew Johnson for his proclamation on August 20 that the insurrection in Texas was at an end. The report praised the president for this evidence of his confidence in the people of Texas.[36] When, however, the Fourteenth Amendment to the Constitution of the United States was submitted to the legislature, the chairman of the federal-relations committee took off his gloves. In a scathing statement Ashbel Smith listed his objections, and those of most southerners, to the amendment: (1) it was a "nullity," as the states most concerned were not represented in the Congress which created it; (2) its clear intent was to take away certain powers and rights of the states over their citizens and to give these powers to the federal government; and (3) by permitting wholesale Negro suffrage and practical disfranchisement of whites, its intention was to degrade the governments and social institutions of southern states. Ashbel's committee declared that the amendment was prompted by "passion and malig-

---

[34] Ashbel Smith to David G. Burnet, September 30, 1866.
[35] David G. Burnet to Ashbel Smith, October 10, 1866.
[36] *Journal of the House of Representatives of the State of Texas, Eleventh Legislature*, 1866, pp. 268–69; hereafter cited as *Texas House Journal*.

nancy." It acknowledged the danger in rejecting the amendment, a danger already made clear by threats from the radicals. Nevertheless, the committee recommended its rejection for the sake of "honor." Their recommendation was sustained by a vote of 70 to 5.[37] Despite the rejection by the Texas legislature and by other state legislatures, the Fourteenth Amendment became the law of the land, and Ashbel morosely concluded that "the Constitution of the United States as it was, is gone forever."[38]

Other committees on which Ashbel served included the judiciary committee, which dealt with the division of Texas into congressional districts and with liquor laws; a committee investigating the establishment of a state geological bureau; a select committee on reorganizing the state militia; and a committee to petition President Johnson to release Jefferson Davis.[39]

Legislation introduced by Representative Smith included a bill to allow his friend former Governor Lubbock to adopt a son and measures pertaining to railroads, the use of convicts for labor on public works, the incorporation of the Houston Chamber of Commerce, and the appointment of a state superintendent of public instruction as provided for by the new constitution of 1866.[40]

Problems arising from the activities of the Freedman's Bureau took up much of the time of the federal-relations committee, which tried unsuccessfully to have the powers of the militia over Freedman's Bureau affairs transferred to local civil officials.[41] In October, Chairman Smith delivered a report from the committee deploring the allegations of Brevet Major General J. B. Kiddoo, the assistant commissioner of the bureau, that white citizens of Texas had been committing crimes and outrages against Negroes. Denouncing Kiddoo for unfairness in citing isolated cases, the committee report listed a number of murders and other atrocities committed by Negroes and white federal soldiers, including the "wanton, outrageous, and unprovoked burning of the town of Brenham."[42]

Five of the acts passed by the Eleventh Legislature pertained to

[37] Ibid., pp. 577–84.
[38] Ashbel Smith to Gen. G. J. Jennings, August 29, 1867.
[39] *Texas House Journal, Eleventh Legislature*, pp. 201, 248, 252, 373–74, 897–99.
[40] Theodore Uglow Lubbock to Ashbel Smith, August 19, 1866; *Texas House Journal, Eleventh Legislature*, p. 379.
[41] Ibid., pp. 288–89.
[42] Ibid., pp. 528–33.

Now is the Seed Time

special concerns of Representative Smith. Two were acts to incorporate companies of which Ashbel Smith was a director: the Planters Mutual Insurance Company and the American Industrial Agency. The purpose of the latter was to invest in "bonds and shares of railroad companies and in other public and private securities."[43]

Another organization incorporated by the Eleventh Legislature was the Houston Dramatic Association, with Ashbel Smith as a shareholder.[44] Still another in which he was involved was the Houston Scientific Institute, which was granted the right to pursue various means of "increasing and diffusing scientific knowledge."[45] Probably the act that pleased Ashbel most was one establishing an orphans' home at Bayland, across the bay from his plantation. Serving with Ashbel as trustees for the home were his cousin Henry Gillette and W. P. Ballinger.[46] It was a project to which Ashbel would devote much time in the future.

One of the acts of the Eleventh Legislature was to order the removal of the body of General Albert Sidney Johnston, the hero of Shiloh, from its temporary burial place in New Orleans to the State Cemetery in Austin.[47] Colonel Ashbel Smith was named to lead the joint select committee which undertook to carry out the transfer of the "sacred remains" in January, 1867. Ashbel, it will be recalled, had served under Johnston when the latter was secretary of war for the Republic and again when Ashbel had led his company under Johnston's command at Shiloh. The two had been friends when Johnston lived in Galveston in the early days of the Republic, and Ashbel accepted the assignment as an honor, though he knew that there would be difficulties in performing it.

No announcement was made of the quiet exhumation ceremony in the New Orleans cemetery, but a large crowd attended. There was no martial music, and no military uniforms were worn, not even by the former Confederate generals in attendance, who included P. G. T. Beauregard, Braxton Bragg, John Bell Hood, Richard Taylor, James Longstreet, Simon Bolivar Buckner, and Randall Lee Gibson. When the boat carrying the body and the committee reached Galveston, Ash-

---

[43] H. P. N. Gammel, *Laws of the State of Texas*, pp. 393, 400.
[44] Ibid., pp. 390–99.
[45] Ibid., pp. 350–55.
[46] Ibid., pp. 37–39.
[47] *Texas House Journal, Eleventh Legislature*, pp. 453–54.

bel found that the United States officials there had canceled the planned funeral procession. He ordered that the body lie in state on the central wharf. Thousands came to view it and followed it to the special train that carried it to Houston the next day. Indignant about the arbitrary actions of the Federal officials in Galveston, the citizens of Houston did everything possible to show honor to the fallen hero. Houses and stores were draped in mourning crepe from roofs to foundations, and businesses were closed. A large band escorted the coffin to the Houston Academy, where it lay covered with flowers and with burning tapers in silver candlesticks at the head and foot. A picture entitled *The Weeping Confederacy* hung on the wall. Two days later bells tolled all over the city as a mile-long cortege followed the coffin, borne on a black-draped hearse pulled by six white horses with sable plumes. Prudently no federal military officials showed their faces on the streets of Houston on that day.

On February 2, Ashbel Smith presented the remains of General Johnston to Governor James W. Throckmorton in the hall of the house of representatives. A few days later the hero of the Battle of Shiloh was buried as he had wished, with a "handful of Texas earth" on his breast.[48]

After completing his legislative assignment, Ashbel retired to Evergreen to oversee his crops and livestock and take comfort in his beloved books. Although he believed himself barred from holding any office, "civil or military, State or National," by the passage of the Fourteenth Amendment, he did not despair. He told a friend: "I anticipate that the time will come and while many a day shall still remain for you and me when we can safely think freely and speak boldly."[49]

For a few months the secluded life as a scholar and farmer contented Ashbel. That he considered Evergreen an idyllic retreat is seen in his poetic description of it:

. . . the velvet green lawn skirting the water—the winding shore jutting out here and there into a promontory studded with evergreen groves—the broad walk of white shells formed by the heaving of the waters along the margin of the Bay. Evergreen Island in front with other islands and peninsulas and the opposite shores diversifying the prospect.—The myriads of wild fowl dabbling

[48] William Preston Johnston, *Gen. Albert Sidney Johnston*, pp. 694–715. Gammel, *Laws of Texas*, 5:79–80.
[49] Ashbel Smith to Gen. G. J. Jennings, August 29, 1867.

in the water during the winter months and far off to the left the broad expanse of Galveston Bay stretching to the city of the same name.[50]

As 1868 opened, Ashbel emerged from his seclusion to get into the thick of politics again. He joined F. R. Lubbock, John H. Reagan, and others in calling a meeting of Democratic leaders at the Harris County Courthouse on January 20.[51] Ashbel was named chairman of the only important committee, the committee on resolutions, though he at first declined the nomination, preferring to have a place on the floor. As he told Throckmorton, he was much vexed because he did not have his own way in anything. He did manage to stifle some "flummary" resolutions, but several passed against his will.[52]

With the main purpose of the Houston meeting—to assure white leadership of the state government—he was in complete accord, but he believed that the members made a serious mistake in recommending that Texans vote against holding a state constitutional convention, since he believed that it was bound to take place. By their action in "unnecessarily" raising the issue, Ashbel felt that the Democrats had lost the chance to create a "large compact party" that could have prevented the ratification of any constitution it considered unfavorable.[53]

He particularly blamed Judge John Reagan's "earnest and personal" appeals for the actions of the convention and speculated that the judge had felt it "necessary to be a little ultra in order to rehabilitate himself with the state from which his letters had isolated him."[54] Ashbel considered Reagan's ability "great" but much mistrusted his "judgment."

The Democrats failed in their aim to keep conservative whites in control of the constitutional convention, which was to meet in June. One of the reasons was the new Loyal Union League, whose purpose was to encourage and influence the Negro vote. Ashbel condemned the league as a political machine run by "officeholding and office seeking Radicals scalawags and carpet baggers . . . an engine of intimida-

---

[50] Ashbel Smith, "Description of Texas," speech, n.d.
[51] *Dallas Herald, Flake's Daily Bulletin*, January 5, 1868.
[52] Ashbel Smith to J. W. Throckmorton, February 4, 1868.
[53] Ashbel Smith to Col. C. C. Gillespie, February 10, 1868.
[54] Ibid. Ashbel Smith is referring to letters Judge Reagan wrote urging Texans to accept reality and allow the freed Negroes their rights of citizenship and voting privileges to avoid even harsher treatment by the radicals.

tion mixed up with some bribery," which through threats of "terrible penalties" forced Negroes to swear to vote for candidates recommended by the league.[55] He did not, however, approve of the methods or actions of the Ku Klux Klan, which was established to counteract the influence of the Loyal Union.

Trying to explain his role in Texas politics to his nephew Henry G. Kittredge, Ashbel claimed that he was not an "unreconstructed rebel" and told him: "Though an outlaw in the land of my fathers, I have no other country. In regard to the government, my single wish is that liberty may be restored and that the administration of the government may, if possible be again pure, honest, just—a government of law and not of malignity and plunder—that I may again before I die, revere it."[56]

When the executive committee of the Democratic party of Texas appointed Ashbel a delegate at large to the National Democratic Convention to meet in New York on July 4, he welcomed the opportunity to make a trip to the North. At the same time he received the appointment, Ashbel also received an invitation to address the Texas State Teachers Convention. In sending his regrets, he said that the desire to withdraw from politics and devote himself to the cause of education was becoming stronger with him. He compared the condition of citizens of Texans with that of a farmer in winter: "Now is the time to prepare for that which is to come. Now though the weather is still chilly, and ungenial, now is the time to prepare the land, now is the seed time."[57]

He urged the teachers to oppose the threatened division of Texas into several states, saying that it "would be disastrous to the cause of education among us." He predicted that if the state was fragmented there would be only "little colleges" instead of a "noble" university where the poorest son or daughter could obtain an education that would allow him or her to "commence the career of life" on an equal footing with the "curled darling of the wealthiest."[58]

Ashbel watched the proceedings at the National Democratic Convention in New York with morose interest. When the Democrats drafted Horatio Seymour, former governor of New York, as their presi-

---

[55] Ashbel Smith, "Negro Voting in Texas," n.d., Ashbel Smith Papers.
[56] Ashbel Smith to Henry G. Kittredge, April 13, 1868.
[57] Ashbel Smith to Pres. Hancock, June 22, 1868.
[58] Ibid.

dential candidate, Ashbel thought that the strongest objections to Seymour in the North would be "the friendly and generous sentiments" that he had expressed toward the South during the war.[59] Ashbel found that many people in the North were "hopelessly blind," failing to see that the Reconstruction Acts were intended by the radicals to effect the "permanent disfranchisement and crushing out of nearly all that is good and intelligent and reliable among us."[60]

While he was in New York, Ashbel spent half a day in the Appleton bookstore, coveting the new books, which he could not afford. "It seemed that a thousand or two dollars would furnish me with delightful society for the balance of life," he sighed.[61] He also took time to examine every laborsaving agricultural implement that he thought suitable for use in Texas, and he also studied the "industrious and economical habits" of northern farmers. He thought that southern farmers, now without slave labor, must make changes in their methods if they were to survive. He also spent hours with Henry Barnard, discussing the state of education in the South. And he was reunited with his family for the first time in nearly ten years.

Three days after he returned to Evergreen, Ashbel suffered a fall from a high ladder while he was gathering grapes. The accident left him semi-invalided and unable to travel to Houston or Galveston for about six weeks. With him on the plantation were fifteen to twenty of his former slaves, living in cabins and working the farm on shares. While he was still crippled, the sharecroppers made fifty to sixty tons of excellent hay. About this time Ashbel began experimenting with grapes and wine making.

He was convinced that grapes would be a profitable crop for Texans. For sweet-eating grapes he preferred the fruit of the vines that had been brought to Texas from France. His wines, however, were made from native grapes, which grew in great quantities on the coast.

In an article Ashbel described the five common grapes of Texas: mustang, muscadine, summer, post-oak, and El Paso. He deplored the name "mustang" as "a barbarous unmeaning word that ought to be eliminated or appropriated alone to wild horses." He described the hardy, prolific grape with the detestable name in romantic imagery:

[59] Ashbel Smith to Col. C. C. Gillespie, July 10, 1868. Ashbel was related to Horatio Seymour.
[60] Ashbel Smith to Dr. William McCraven, July 28, 1868.
[61] Ibid.

"When ripe it covers smaller trees or clusters of small trees with a black and green mantle. Its grapes hang from the tops of trees 40 feet high, like a broad black carpet, to the ground, or in huge black festoons 20 or 30 feet long dangling to the wind." He noted that both birds and hogs feasted on the ripe fruit. Not considered sweet enough for a good table grape, the mustang made a wine suitable to serve with meals or as a tonic for "enfeebled health." He gave four pages of precise directions for making and keeping the wine. He considered his mustang wine better than any claret that could be purchased in a restaurant or wine shop. He was careful to add, "No whiskey drinker whose palate has been debauched with whiskey can appreciate a wine or judge of its quality."[62] When he mailed his essays on wine making to editors of the local papers, he sent along samples to prove his claims. He also wrote a paper on vinegar making, declaring that no vinegar should be imported; it should be made at home. He himself made vinegar from persimmons, peaches, and grape juice (the last the best, in his opinion).[63]

In June, 1869, when the Texas Medical Association awoke from its comatose state, Ashbel took time out from his wine making to assist in the re-creation of that organization. The meeting was held in Houston's leading hotel, the Hutchins House, and it lasted three days. Most of the time was taken up with problems of organization in the hope that this time the association would "take"—a hope that was fulfilled. After business was completed on the third day, the president called for reports on subjects of interest, and Ashbel was one of the volunteers, giving, it was reported, "a most learned and interesting talk on the treatment of malarial fever by the use of leaves and bark of the willow tree as a substitute for quinine."[64] Since he hated taking quinine, one wonders whether he had experimented with this treatment on himself.

When the Southern Historical Society was organized in New Orleans in 1869, outstanding men from all over the United States were named vice-presidents to head their state branches. The list included General Robert E. Lee for Virginia, Admiral R. Semmes for Alabama, Wade Hampton for South Carolina, and Colonel Ashbel Smith for Texas. Ashbel immediately began corresponding with Texas leaders,

[62] Ashbel Smith to E. H. Cushing, editor, *Houston Telegraph*, April 9, 1869. Ashbel Smith to Col. W. Richardson, ed., *Galveston News*, June 7, 1869.
[63] Ibid.
[64] Pat Ireland Nixon, *A History of the Texas Medical Association, 1853-1953*, pp. 36-40.

such as Governor Frank R. Lubbock and General Thomas N. Waul, whose help he asked in planning a state organization that would be simple, inexpensive, and efficient. For convenience and to save traveling expenses for many of the prospective members, he decided to hold the organizational meeting in Houston concurrently with the First Annual State Fair of the Agricultural, Mechanical, and Blood Stock Assocation in May, 1870.[65] At the fair Ashbel Smith received an elaborate certificate for having entered "The Best Still Wine Made of Texas Grape."

Two weeks after the meeting ended, Ashbel attended the second annual meeting of the Texas State Medical Association, also held in Houston. He was appointed to several committees, including the Committee on Credentials and the Committee to Memorialize the Legislature. In the absence of an essayist, Dr. Smith was invited to address the group on the second day. He chose to discuss pneumonia and his experiences in treating it. The talk was well received, and the group passed a motion asking him to write it up for publication.[66]

In December, 1870, Ashbel lost another cherished friend with the death of David G. Burnet. The two men, so different in their personalities and in their feelings toward Sam Houston, had come to appreciate each other over the years. Ashbel, who had once characterized Burnet as a "man John Knox would have hugged with grim delight," kept the older statesman posted on politics and urged him from time to time to attend certain public meetings. In one such invitation Ashbel described Burnet as "venerable by your years, venerable by your wisdom, venerable by eminent public services, venerable in the spotless purity of your private life."[67] Burnet replied that Ashbel's personal kindness had the savor of "old wine" and told him that he and his wife, Hannah, found Ashbel's visits as refreshing "as mid-summer rains." In his last letter to Ashbel he sent along a toast to the government of the United States—"as it was."[68]

Texans were greatly occupied with railroad building and financing during the 1870s. After considering possible routes, Ashbel wrote an

---

[65] Ashbel Smith to James Jones, M.D., July 28, 1869; Ashbel Smith to General Waul, August 5, 1869; Ashbel Smith to Hon. F. R. Lubbock, August 4, 1869; Ashbel Smith to Dr. J. W. Caldwell, January 3, 1872.

[66] *Proceedings of the Texas Medical Association,* 1870.

[67] Ashbel Smith to David G. Burnet, April, 1868.

[68] David G. Burnet to Ashbel Smith, April 20, 1868.

eleven-page letter to the publisher of the *Galveston News* about how important it was that the city have a "cheap, speedy, certain and profitable" railroad connection with the rest of Texas and eventually all the rest of the United States. He pointed out the most feasible routes with respect to topography, habitation, crop and cattle raising, the depth of water on sandbars and in shallows, the availability of timber for ties and bridges, areas protected from saltwater worms (which destroyed pilings), the number of trestles and drawbridges necessary on various routes, distances, and quite a few minor details.[69]

In 1871, Ashbel decided to return to planting cotton. He purchased a new gin and experimented with different kinds of cotton and different growing seasons. He noted that the seeds which he planted late seemed to be less seriously bothered by cotton worms, as did those planted next to his sugarcane, a favorite resort of partridges, hummingbirds, and mosquito hawks. He found that Sea Island cotton could yield 200 to 300 pounds of lint per acre and that baled cotton was worth a little over a dollar in gold a pound in Liverpool. He compared the Sea Island cotton of the Texas coast with cotton from near Vicksburg and with that of the Carolina and Georgia coastal islands and found it equal in quality and quantity.[70]

Ashbel took some of his cotton to the Grand State Fair, sponsored by the Agricultural, Mechanical, and Blood Stock Association at Houston, and offered to superintend or take charge of working the ginner at the fair if there was no one else qualified to run it. He also scolded the directors for having "scarcely recognized the importance of Sea Island cotton as a crop of Texas already considerable and in the progress of rapid development."[71]

In the fall of 1871, Ashbel went with friends to west Texas on a deer-hunting trip. They camped on the bank of the San Saba River, enjoying successful hunting by day and long talks around the campfire at night. A hint of danger added spice to the excursion, for they were in Indian country. Although they saw smoke signals and signs of Indian trails, they did not encounter any trouble.[72]

As the administration of Governor E. J. Davis and the Radical Republican program became more unbearable, Ashbel felt compelled to

[69] Ashbel Smith to Col. W. Richardson, February 24, 1871.
[70] Ibid., March 27, 1871.
[71] Ashbel Smith to Hon. John T. Brady, April 21, 1871.
[72] Ashbel Smith, clipping, n.d., Ashbel Smith Papers.

speak out against this "terrible maladministration" and "its corrupt and ruffian police." The declaration of martial law in some counties, he claimed, was "only another name for the abrogation of all law."[73]

In June, 1872, Ashbel attended the state Democratic convention in Corsicana and was again elected a delegate to the national convention, to be held in Baltimore later that year. Noting Ashbel's presence at the state convention, the editor of the *Fairfield Daily Statesman* called him "one of the old landmarks of Texas." But some of the younger members of the party resented Ashbel's cavalier dismissal of their abilities because they were "young and untried."[74]

Arriving in Baltimore, the Texas delegates found that "everything was predetermined," leaving them the choice of bolting the convention and the party or going along with the choices that had been made. To bolt, the Texans felt, would be to align themselves with the party of scalawags and carpetbaggers and to lose for their state the sympathy of all other southern states. At first Ashbel had strong misgivings about the nomination of his old adversary Horace Greeley for president, but he came to agree with John Reagan, the leader of the Texas delegation, that the editor was the strongest man the Democrats could have chosen. Ashbel was named one of the committee assigned to inform Greeley of his nomination, and he spent some time at Greeley's country home outside New York City, where he came to have even more favorable feelings toward the Democratic candidate.[75] Returning to Texas, Ashbel wrote letters, made personal appeals, and gave speeches at the inevitable barbecues promoting Greeley and condemning "Granticism," but he knew that the odds were against his man. When the balloting was over, although Greeley won the majority of Texas's votes, Grant had won on the national level by a landslide. "Hell is hard to conquer," swore Ashbel Smith.

As he traveled around postwar Texas, Ashbel found it sadly changed. In his diary he wrote an elegy, reminiscent of the Old English poem *The Wanderer*—a lament for what had been lost. Everywhere he found "dull monotony, the unrelieved cheerlessness, the dearth, the death of all the high social culture which once bloomed in these now farming regions." He asked:

---

[73] Ashbel Smith to "My Dear General," December 31, 1871.
[74] *Fairfield Daily Statesman*, June 28, 1872.
[75] Ashbel Smith to Richard Westcott, July, 1872.

Where has gone the social culture, the mental culture, the high intellectual culture of former days? Where is the gentleman who welcomed with both hands the comer to his mansion, who made him feel that he the host and not the visitor was the obliged party—who talked history, statesmenship, the economic policy of our own and other countries, interspersed with personal anecdotes of our own great men of that day? Where is this grand, genial gentleman scattered all through the agricultural districts of the South before the war . . . ? He exists no longer, he is not.

And he pictured the present:

But in his place you meet the farmer, he takes your horse, unsaddles him, feeds him, bids you in the meantime to walk into the house. He spreads, that is his wife does, a fair plain supper, talks of the weather, is afraid of a glut of rain and the cotton worm or of drought and a short corn crop, tells you about his own crop. He shows you a bed, goes to bed himself and this soon after the chickens. In the morning his bill is a dollar and a quarter, he goes to his work and lets you pursue yours, with or without a dry goodbye.[76]

[76] Ashbel Smith Journal, July 11, 1880.

CHAPTER TEN

A Very Broad Stage (1873–1880)

ASHBEL'S papers contain little information about his private activities on his trip north in the summer of 1872, but he must have seen his mother for the last time, for Phoebe died on November 16, 1872, just before her eighty-third birthday. Ashbel was her oldest son, and she had been only sixteen years old when he was born. Her letters to him were signed "Your loving mother and friend," and he always showed deep concern and affection for her. Strangely, just at the time he lost the person most closely associated with his early life, Ashbel took steps that would give him a family in his old age. Almost inadvertently he acquired a foster daughter.

Several years earlier, along with some of the other outstanding citizens of the area, Ashbel had helped organize the Bayland Orphans' Home for Children of Confederate Soldiers, which the Eleventh Legislature had incorporated. Ashbel's cousin Henry F. Gillette became the superintendent, and Ashbel donated his services as physician to the orphanage, which was across the bay from his plantation. He won the affection of many of the children, who wrote him letters, called him "Uncle," and begged him to visit them.

Little Anna Allen, whose father, a farmer, had been killed in the war, was one of the orphans whose condition and courage stirred Ashbel's compassion. After her husband's death Mrs. Allen had taken her three children to stay with a sister but had soon become ill and died. Knowing that her aunt could not afford to keep three extra children, Anna applied for admission to the orphanage. When Ashbel became acquainted with the eleven-year-old Anna, she was suffering from a severe eye disease that had made her nearly blind; yet in spite of her affliction she worked at making candles.

Ashbel began a series of treatments on her eyes, but the trip from his plantation to the orphans' home took several hours by boat and horseback. When he decided that Anna's eyes should be treated twice a day, he arranged for her to stay at Evergreen temporarily. Anna was tiny but sturdy and independent. The attraction between the lonely bachelor and the orphaned child was strong. She lacked formal education but had a quick mind, and in the evenings Ashbel read her the stories of Hans Christian Andersen and a great deal of poetry, which she quickly memorized, to his delight.

Anna, wanting to please the man who had rescued her from blindness and life in an institution, began taking over as many of the domestic chores at Evergreen as she could manage as her eyesight gradually returned to normal. By mutual consent Anna became Ashbel's housekeeper, and in January, 1873, he wrote to John Bowers, "She and I consider her permanently at home at Evergreen."[1]

As their feelings for each other became stronger, he offered to adopt her to give her a sense of security and to prevent others from assuming that she was his hired servant, a mistake she hated. But the strong-minded Anna did not want to take the name Smith, for a number of the detested carpetbaggers she had known as a little child had been named Smith. Therefore, they did not formalize their relationship, but in their correspondence he frequently called her "My dear child," and she called him "Uncle Ashbel," "My beloved Colonel," and "My beloved friend." He came to think of her as his child, and she came to have the power to cause him the extremes of joy and anguish that his own child would have done.

In the spring of 1873, Ashbel was again involved in a railroad dispute. In the press he strongly advocated payment of the bonds which had been granted to three lines by the Texas legislature but were now being repudiated. Ashbel considered it a debt of honor, and the president of the Houston and Great Northern Railway Company congratulated him for being the "first man in the state who boldly advocated in the press the payment of the bonds *over his own signature.*"[2] Eventually the issue became moot when land grants were substituted for bond payments.

Another article that Ashbel wrote in support of railroads con-

---

[1] Ashbel Smith to John Bowers, January 4, 1873.
[2] James W. Barnes to Ashbel Smith, May 29, 1873.

cerned the charge made against them—particularly by the granges—that they were monopolies. The railroads' "excellence and *raison d'être*" Ashbel claimed, were that they *were* monopolies in furnishing transportation of every kind "cheaper, speedier, safer and more regularly and more reliably than any other land carriage could do." He went on to point out that railroads were not as bad as other commercial and financial "rings," such as gold and cotton monopolies. He cited the wharf company of Galveston as a "hideous" ring that charged excessively and iniquitously both the producer and the consumer.[3]

With his Democratic friends Ashbel rejoiced at the victory of Richard Coke over E. J. Davis in the race for governor, and he went to Austin in January, 1874, to join in the inauguration festivities. Presumably he witnessed there the struggle that occurred when Davis and his "police force" tried unsuccessfully to prevent Coke from taking office. Along with 1,500 other happy Texans, Ashbel Smith attended the grand inaugural ball.

Caroline's younger son, Henry G. Kittredge, arrived in the early summer to visit Ashbel and Anna before leaving for a trip to Europe, after which he was to enroll at Yale. The holiday was filled with crabbing, swimming, horseback riding, and feasting on peaches, watermelons, and blackbird and wild-duck pies. In the evenings Henry received sage advice from his uncle on how to get the most from his time in Europe and at Yale. It was a visit that Henry Kittredge still recalled with pleasure as an old man. Ashbel was pleased with his nephew and impressed by his "clear thinking." When Henry enrolled at Yale, Ashbel sent him $100 to buy a microscope. After Henry completed a year at Yale and went into the cotton-factoring business in Boston, the two continued to correspond regularly, discussing business and other matters of interest to them both, and Henry frequently handled the sale of his uncle's cotton and wool.

Education again claimed Ashbel's time and attention as he neared his seventieth year. There was now a state superintendent of public instruction, and each county had its own superintendent as well. In the 1874 elections Ashbel was elected to the Board of School Directors for Harris County, and the board in turn named him county superintendent. The job involved much paperwork and tedious detail, but he set about it with enthusiasm, writing long letters of requests and sugges-

[3] Ashbel Smith, essay, July 31, 1873, Ashbel Smith Papers.

tions to the state superintendent and publishing letters of information in the local papers for parents and prospective students.[4]

By inclination and by background Superintendent Smith was well suited to his position. He had been a teacher, had served as trustee for schools, and had kept in close touch with Henry Barnard and other friends in educational circles. He had read widely in educational journals and had made himself familiar with textbooks so that he could advise parents authoritatively. Ashbel observed that not a few teachers seemed to have adopted the teaching profession as a means of maintaining themselves with the least possible physical labor until "something better turned up." Since such applicants were invariably the most "importunate in forcing themselves on the trustees," he proposed to take upon himself the job of screening all applicants to ensure that the students would have the best-qualified teachers who could be found.

In one of his long letters to State Superintendent O. N. Hollingsworth, Ashbel expressed his opinion on various questions connected with free public schools. He opposed a recommendation to change the school attendance ages from six through eighteen years to eight through sixteen years for several reasons, two being that young men "precipitated too early into money-making become sordid" and "the young woman released from her studies too early is very likely to become hard and precocious." He argued that a great advantage of beginning school at six was that young children could easily learn other languages idiomatically and with a correct accent while older children seldom mastered them. He favored changing the school term from four months to ten, arguing that the longer school year would attract more able teachers and improve the quality of teaching.[5]

On April 7, 1874, at the opening session of the annual meeting of the Texas State Medical Association in Dallas, Ashbel made an "elegant and eloquent" response to the welcoming address. He took an active part in this milestone meeting, which had "fully a hundred members in attendance." As a member of the Committee on Special Legislation, he presented some amendments to an act passed by the Texas legislature the year before in an attempt to regulate the practice of medicine in the state. The committee recommended that every doc-

---

[4] Ashbel Smith to Editor, *Houston Age*, February 7, 1874.
[5] Ashbel Smith to Hon. O. N. Hollingsworth, November, 1874.

A Very Broad Stage 187

tor should be required to be a member of the medical association of his county. It also urged that the legislature pass a law requiring that a permanent record of all births, marriages, and deaths be kept in the district-court records of each county. On a lighter note the committee suggested that any person not a citizen of Texas who came to the state and advertised to perform surgical operations or cure diseases should have to pay into the county treasury the same tax paid by "persons exhibiting a circus performance or menagerie." A serious problem underlay this humorous proposal, and Ashbel made a speech attacking the "montebanks and impostors" in the profession and castigating newspapers that allowed advertising by quack doctors.[6]

The society passed a resolution offered by Dr. Smith that the TMA use its influence to obtain a legislative appropriation for the Texas Medical College and Hospital, which had been chartered the previous year.[7] When the old Galveston Medical College was dissolved in 1873, the Texas Medical College and Hospital had risen phoenix-like from its remains, and Ashbel Smith had been named one of the trustees. He soon became the president of the board. As one of their first acts the trustees appointed a board of examiners to give competitive oral and written examinations to prospective professors of the new school.

Dr. Ashbel Smith served as the examiner in charge of selecting the doctor to fill the chair of surgery. After examining the applicants, he announced that Dr. Greensville S. Dowell was the best-qualified candidate. The choice was a courageous one because, although Dr. Dowell was a brilliant scientist who several years later would make the connection between yellow fever and mosquitoes, he was an object of controversy in Galveston medical circles. In fact, the dissolution of the earlier medical college was credited to his autocratic rule. Ashbel, however, determined to recruit the best teachers available for the new school, recognized Dowell's ability and persisted in his choice.[8]

Seven professors were selected, and clinical teaching began at the Galveston City Hospital, at Ninth Street and Strand Avenue. The state legislature appropriated $5,000 a year to the school, with a provision that supplemental funds could be made available for care of indigent

[6] Nixon, *A History of the Texas Medical Association*, pp. 51–57; *Proceedings of the Texas Medical Association*, 1874.

[7] Gammel, *Laws of Texas*, pp. 870–75.

[8] *The University of Texas Medical Branch at Galveston: A Seventy-five Year History of the Faculty and Staff*, pp. 9–10.

patients as needed. Thus the Texas Medical College and Hospital began under the firm guidance of Ashbel Smith. It was the nucleus to which he would point as he battled a few years later to persuade Texans that the state medical school should be established in Galveston.

About mid-June, Ashbel acquired firsthand medical information on the treatment of snakebite. On a Saturday evening at dusk as he walked up the hill from the bay shore, he felt a heavy scuffling around one of his legs and a pain like the bite of sharp teeth. At first he thought that his assailant was a wildcat or some such animal, but when he reached the house, he saw by the light three small wounds just above his ankle. There were two punctures at each wound, and he realized that they had been made by the fangs of a snake. Although the attack had occurred only five minutes earlier, the leg was already swollen. Nevertheless, he decided to delay treating himself and observe the effects of the poison.

In fifteen minutes the pain was excruciating. He took a half teaspoonful of saturated tincture of iodine in a wineglass of water and repeated the dose four times over the next several hours. He also had the wounds touched several times with iodine and his leg, now swollen from ankle to knee, painted with iodine. Over the next four hours the pain gradually abated. About 1:30 A.M. he fell asleep and awoke at dawn to find his swollen leg stiff and sore to the touch. He slowly got better, but for days he had to keep the injured leg elevated, for it became livid if it hung down for a few minutes. Impressed by the efficacy of the iodine treatment, Ashbel described the experience in a letter to his friend E. H. Cushing, who had the letter published in the *Houston Telegraph*.[9]

Ashbel considered it the most severe snakebite he had ever seen and conjectured that his attacker had been a large rattlesnake. Having acquired confidence in iodine through using it in his practice, he told Cushing that he had decided to give it a "fair showing in my own case, unaided and unobstructed by any other medication." He was sure that without the treatment he had followed the bite would have been fatal in a matter of hours. Some northern papers copied the article from the *Telegraph*, and Ashbel received congratulations from friends and fellow physicians who were impressed by his cool, scientific attitude under the circumstance.

[9] Ashbel Smith to E. H. Cushing, June 24, 1874.

A Very Broad Stage   189

As soon as he could hobble around, Ashbel returned to superintending the activities of Evergreen and of his newest industry, a brickyard on Cedar Bayou, which he had acquired as partial payment of a debt. The yard included all the necessary brickmaking equipment, a cabin, and other improvements and could turn out 1,500 bricks a day.[10] Since, however, he was not particularly interested in the business, he advertised the yard for lease.[11] In the meantime, while he waited for a taker, he continued to produce and sell bricks, estimating that most of the bricks used in construction in Galveston came from Cedar Bayou. He was also selling timber, hay, cotton, wool, and some vegetables, such as onions.

From time to time he went to Houston to buy or sell goods, catch up on world affairs, and talk politics and philosophy in the bookstore of his good friend E. H. Cushing. Cushing had been a teacher and long-term editor of the *Telegraph*, which during the Civil War he had printed on brown wrapping paper and wallpaper. Ashbel had supplied him with many articles for the paper, and Cushing had backed and encouraged Ashbel in his political activities. Cushing's wife, Matilda, was fond of Ashbel, who sometimes acted as the Cushings' physician. Matilda was kind to Anna, sending her ruffles to sew on her dresses and giving her motherly advice. The Cushings' son, Edward, and Anna enjoyed each other's company, and Ashbel often invited the boy, who was a few years younger than Anna, to Evergreen so that she could have a companion near her own age. Edward looked forward to these "roistering" times on the bay and seemed to think of Ashbel as an uncle too.

In the spring of 1875, Ashbel addressed the Texas Veterans Association, a group he had helped organize two years earlier. Its membership was restricted to those who could produce proof of service to Texas before annexation in 1845. "You and I belong to a past generation," Ashbel told the aging soldiers, and shared with them the credo that guided his last years: ". . . life has duties to perform to its last moment; this world is not a resting place. Man to be true to his destiny should die in harness."[12]

As was his custom, Ashbel kept up with pending state legislation.

---

[10] Deed between D. W. Hinkle and Ashbel Smith, June 11, 1874.
[11] John M. Cookes to Ashbel Smith, June 18, 1874.
[12] Ashbel Smith, speech to Texas Veterans Association, 1875.

When a bill making it unlawful for "horses, cattle, sheep, goats, and hogs" to run at large was under consideration, he opposed it vigorously. He believed that such a law would work "incalculable mischief and injury" to the small stock owners, who could not afford herders and who would be unable to fence in the grazing land they needed. The newly invented barbed wire had not yet found acceptance in Texas, and wooden fences could easily be burned, especially on the open prairie. Ashbel predicted that fence burning would increase if the stock law was passed.[13]

As a farmer and a stockman Ashbel knew both sides of the question. Once, after cattle belonging to a neighbor had repeatedly broken into his fenced cotton field, he angrily shot and killed two of the cows that "perversely" refused to be driven out of the field. Instantly regretting his impulsiveness, Ashbel sent his overseer to the neighbor with a note of apology and the assurance that he would pay all damages promptly.[14]

In the fall of 1875, Texans were agitated about the new state constitution being drawn up by the convention elected the previous year. Ashbel wrote several long letters to members of the convention setting out his views on what should and should not be included in the constitution on a number of subjects including education, railroads, and immigration.[15]

In mid-November, Ashbel went to Austin to attend the fair. He particularly wanted to look at the agricultural implements on display. He was convinced that Texas farmers could greatly increase their profits if they would become willing to use more laborsaving devices, but he understood their reluctance to buy equipment without having seen it in operation. Except for a number of good plows he found the display "very meagre," and he felt that the same could be said of fairs in Dallas and Houston. Writing to his cousin B. F. Avery, who manufactured farm equipment, Ashbel suggested that displaying farm-implements at Texas fairs, especially those in the larger cities, would be advantageous to the manufacturers as well as to the farmers.[16]

The Galveston Historical Society, composed of such substantial

---

[13] Ashbel Smith to Samuel W. Allen, February 11, 1875.

[14] Ashbel Smith to Col. John Manley, August 17, 1875.

[15] Ashbel Smith to Hon. C. S. West, September 1, 1875. Ashbel Smith to Horace Cone, November 15, 1875.

[16] Ashbel Smith to B. F. Avery, November 30, 1875.

citizens as John Sealy and Henry Rosenberg, invited Ashbel to deliver an address to the group at its annual meeting on December 15, 1875. The invitation asked him to relate personal recollections of his "long continued connection with the public affairs of the Republic and State of Texas." The speech, which he entitled "Reminiscences of the Republic of Texas," was probably the most important address he ever made, and in it he came closest to answering the many pleas that he write a history of Texas from his unique vantage point.

In addition to giving an exhaustive history of the annexation of Texas, he sketched the history of Texas from the time of its conquest by Spain. Sam Houston, Santa Anna, Lamar, Anson Jones, Lord Aberdeen, Louis Philippe, David Burnet, James Pinckney Henderson, and scores of minor characters marched across the stage as Ashbel unfolded the drama of the evolution of his adopted state.[17]

The members of the society were so impressed by the wealth of historical information and insight in the address that they ordered 100 copies printed. Ashbel managed to obtain at least 20 to send to relatives and friends. In his letter of thanks Benjamin Silliman, nephew of the great chemist who had influenced Ashbel at Yale a half century earlier, urged his friend to write his autobiography, saying: "Your life has not been like those of all your peers who began life with you—each cribbed, confined in a single, narrow groove. You have borne a conspicuous, important, useful and honored part on a very broad stage."[18] In a review of the published speech the *Galveston News* said, "No one better than Ashbel Smith could give us reminiscences of the history of the Texas Republic . . . all of which he saw and part of which he was."[19]

During the winter of 1876 the Texas legislature argued over bills aimed at obtaining for the state federal money which had been promised at the time of annexation. Guy M. Bryan, a fellow rancher and political friend, urged Ashbel to join with him in writing open letters to the *News*, spelling out why the United States owed Texas not only these monies but also a great deal more that had been promised by United States officials. Ashbel eagerly contributed two long letters quoting dates and times and naming specific officials who had made such promises. After offering proof that Galveston was to be *the* great

[17] Ashbel Smith, "Reminiscences of the Texas Republic," speech to the Historical Society of Galveston, December 15, 1875.
[18] Benjamin D. Silliman to Ashbel Smith, April 17, 1876.
[19] *Galveston News*, August 6, 1876.

entry port of that region of the United States, he called upon the United States Congress to build "dikes, substantial works on the Gulf side of the city." The danger from hurricanes was periodic but real, he warned; without a sea wall "the devastation may be great, terrific."[20] Fifteen years after his death the sea wall still had not been built, and the devastation wrought by the great storm of 1900 was indeed "terrific."

In April, Ashbel attended the annual Texas Medical Association meeting, held in the opera hall in Marshall, a town with tree-lined streets and well-tended lawns. The Civil War and the subsequent depression had left the citizens of the town impoverished, but they gave the doctors warm welcomes into their homes. An unusual feature of this convention was the performance of two operations before the assembled members. The use of hypodermic syringes was discussed, and it was predicted that before long every physician would carry them as a part of his equipment.[21]

Politics also occupied Ashbel's time that spring. He was a delegate to the National Democratic Convention, which nominated New York Governor Samuel J. Tilden as its candidate for president. Back again in Texas, Ashbel served as president of the county Democratic convention and took the opportunity to endorse again the Texas and Pacific Railway Company and its president, Thomas A. Scott, and to denounce the actions of Collis P. Huntington, vice-president of the Central Pacific Railroad. With satisfaction Ashbel described his performance to an officer of the Texas Pacific: "I 'fed fat' my scorn, indignation and denunciation etc.—amidst most emphatic and nearly universal opprobation of the convention."[22] The editor of the *Houston Age* was not as pleased with the performance and accused Ashbel of ignoring some pertinent facts in order to make his points.[23]

The highlight of America's centennial celebration of 1876 was the Great International Exhibition in Philadelphia, and Ashbel Smith was appointed by the United States Centennial Commission to act as an

---

[20] Ashbel Smith, *Inducements for the Annexation of Texas to the United States and the Pledges Made by That Government to Texas, Fully Shown by Letters from Cols. Guy M. Bryan and Ashbel Smith*; "Ashbel Smith to M. R. Jefferds, General Manager of the Galveston & Camargo Railway, for Use in Jefferd's Memorial to the Texas Legislature on Bill H.R. 2067."

[21] Nixon, *A History of the Texas Medical Association*, pp. 65–70.

[22] Ashbel Smith to John Blown, August 16, 1876.

[23] *Houston Age*, August 14, 1876.

A Very Broad Stage 193

"international" judge on the Jury of Awards.[24] The *Austin Daily State Gazette* jokingly suggested that Texas should send Ashbel Smith to the centennial exhibit as one of its historic relics.[25]

As a war veteran and a friend of railroad men in high places, Ashbel traveled to Philadelphia on passes. He discovered that, although it took him only three and a half days to reach Philadelphia from Houston, he missed the intimacy and stimulation he had enjoyed on slower trips, during which he never failed to make some interesting acquaintances. He complained that in the sleeping and parlor cars of the trains he met only long-distance travelers and so "learned nothing of the country through which I was passing." Efficient it might be, but he decided that it was a "boring" way to travel.[26]

While he was away, Anna went to Houston to stay with the Cushings and attend school. The bachelor father and his foster daughter exchanged letters that breathed their affection for each other. His letters, characteristically, were packed with instructions and advice. He fretted that it was Anna's first time out on her own "sole responsibility" and begged her to be "ladylike" at all times.

When the exhibition opened, Ashbel was assigned to the jury that was judging horned cattle. In his leisure time he thoroughly inspected all the "treasures" of the fair. He was chagrined that Texas had sent nothing to exhibit its wealth of resources, produce, or manufactures. Like most other visitors to the fair, he was impressed by the Kansas House, with its magnificent displays of natural resources and products. He visited the Kansas House many times, eavesdropping in the crowds that thronged the building and fuming that Texas could have sent specimens "equal to and better" than every item displayed by Kansas. His chief regret was that Kansas would attract hundreds of thousands of immigrants by this form of advertising and that Texas could have done the same.

[24] W. H. Parsons to Ashbel Smith, July 29, 1876.
[25] *Austin Daily State Gazette*, August 13, 1876.
[26] Dr. D. F. Stuart, who accompanied Ashbel, told this anecdote: One day as they and some friends rode on a crowded streetcar in Philadelphia, deeply absorbed in conversation, a woman approached the platform on which they were standing. Seeing that the men were blocking the doorway, the cab driver seized Ashbel roughly by the arm, exclaiming, "Make way for a lady!" Then, Dr. Stuart reported, "Dr. Smith jerked a small knife from his pocket and pointing it ominously at the throat of the astonished driver said to him, in the suppressed, earnest tones of wounded honor, 'Dare you, sir, to teach me how to be polite to a lady!'" (James D. Lynch, "Life and Character of Dr. Ashbel Smith," *Daniel's Medical Journal*, April, 1886, pp. 441–55).

Among the agricultural implements Ashbel was impressed by the English double Macarthy roller gin, which could gin both short-staple and Sea Island cotton nearly twice as fast as the American-made Macarthy gin. Another laborsaving implement on which he commented was the riding, or sulky, plow. He was pleased to find that the Avery plow, manufactured by his relatives, was far superior to other models he examined.[27]

During his stay in Philadelphia, Ashbel boarded in a private home to save money, but he bought Anna a pair of "cuff buttons" at the Turkish exhibit. And he had his portrait made because she wanted one. The picture shows him at seventy-one, his hair thinned and his beard gray, but his posture still ramrod straight, and his eyes bright and penetrating. He dressed in the conventional black suit, white shirt, waistcoat, and black bow tie of the period. When he was at home on his plantation, he added a broad-brimmed black hat, his Confederate overcoat, and short English boots into which he packed his trouser legs.

When Ashbel returned to Texas, he learned that the legislature had passed an act to establish an "Agricultural and Mechanical College of Texas, for the benefit of the Colored Youths" and that Governor Richard Coke had appointed Ashbel Smith one of three commissioners charged with setting up the school.[28] One of the first duties of the commission was to choose a site for the college. Notices were published, soliciting donations in money and land—at least 500 acres suitable for agricultural purposes.

Ashbel wrote an article—titled "Education of the Negro" for the *Texas Christian Advocate*. In it he pointed out that the freedom of Negroes was a fact which neither stupid indifference nor false logic could change. He argued that the time had passed when the illiteracy of the Negro was a safeguard against plotting and insurrection. Now that the Negro was likely by the force of "oppressive circumstances" to take his place at the ballot box, the great question, Ashbel told his readers, was how his power and influence could be made to harmonize with the "common good" of both races. The answer, of course, was education. Ashbel chided Texans for not taking the matter seriously enough. He blamed "stupid prejudice" for lack of action, while "yankee school teachers are instilling their dangerous propaganda into the

---

[27] Ashbel Smith, "Centennial Exhibition at Philadelphia," Ashbel Smith Papers.
[28] Gov. Richard Coke to Ashbel Smith, September 26, 1876.

Negro population." He declared: "In proportion to the intelligence of a people is their value increased as good citizens, masters of their own actions, and a power for good or evil among us. . . . *The Negro must be educated; and educated by the people among whom he lives.*"[29]

The next year the commissioners selected a site for the college five miles east of Hempstead and one mile north of Prairie View. The school was at first called Alta Vista Agricultural College. When it failed for lack of students, it was changed to a training school for teachers of Negro children and renamed Prairie View State Normal School.[30]

From the close of the Civil War to the end of his life Ashbel was a frequent contributor of articles on agricultural subjects to newspapers and journals such as the *New England Farmer*, the *Boston Ploughman*, and the London weekly *Cotton*. He wrote a paper on Louisiana rock salt for *Home and Farm*, a journal published by a northern branch of his Avery relatives, praising the salt mined in the Petite Anse mines as the purest and best obtainable, citing his personal experience in using it to preserve the hogs and beef slaughtered at Evergreen. Since there were other Avery relatives on Avery Island, off the coast of Louisiana, he had reason to have inside information on the mining operations there.[31]

In an article on growing sugarcane in Texas, he estimated that it could be cultivated to yield an average of 1,000 pounds of sugar and 100 gallons of molasses per acre over successive seasons. He suggested that sugar was a better-paying crop than cotton for Texas farmers, whom he constantly exhorted to "diversify, diversify." Out of his own experiments came specific instructions for planting the cane, protecting it from cold, and making molasses, including a breakdown of costs of the equipment needed. The "secretiveness and mystery" with which professional sugar boilers had invested their craft was nonsense, he declared, adding, "It is less difficult than to learn to make domestic soap." In the same article Ashbel summed up his philosophy of farming:

In addition to his main crops—cotton or sugar cane—every good and prosperous farmer will add a considerable breadth in corn, sweet potatoes, and

---

[29] Ashbel Smith, "Education of the Negro," Ashbel Smith Papers.
[30] Webb and Carroll, eds., *Handbook of Texas*, 2:406; *Texas House Journal, Sixteenth Legislature*, 1879, pp. 268–69.
[31] Ashbel Smith to Editor, *Home and Farm*, January 22, 1877.

minor crops sufficient to bread his family, forage his teams and raise his meat. The Texas farmer who buys his meat after the first year is a bad manager. He is a bad manager if he goes outside of his farm to buy any article for his table, except flour, sugar, coffee, and salt and a few articles of inconsiderable cost, as condiments, until his net income authorizes the use of luxuries.[32]

By 1877, Ashbel had done an about-face in his opinion on fencing. In one of a series of letters on Texas to the *Boston Ploughman* he spoke of good fencing as indispensable before "any considerable improvement can be made in Texas cattle."[33] For the *Ploughman's* readers in addition to cattle raising he discussed clover, forage grasses, coal, schools, and immigration in Texas.

At various times in his farming career Ashbel swore off raising cotton, but he always came back to it, and several of his articles discussed it at length. Edward Atkinson, the editor of the *Ploughman*, sent Ashbel seeds of a "new" Egyptian, or Bamian, cotton which Ashbel grew with considerable success. He exhibited it at the state fair at Dallas and received a number of requests for seeds from Texas farmers, who hoped that it might be more resistant to the cotton worm than the fine, silky Sea Island variety. The commissioner of the United States Department of Agriculture wrote to ask Ashbel for a full description, a specimen, and seeds of "your newly discovered Egyptian cotton mentioned in the Texas papers."[34]

Galveston was the meeting site of the Texas Medical Association in 1877. A hot controversy arose over the appointment of some "irregular practitioners" to sit on a board of examiners in Austin. Seeking to quell the bitter dispute, Ashbel suggested to the doctors that if they could not get all they were entitled to they should take what they could get and get the rest in installments. He said: "Liberty has been defined . . . as the right to go to hell in any way the traveler in that direction might elect, and so all the people of Texas, in the exercise of their sovereign rights, may patronize and will patronize medicine or homeopathy . . . and this convention is powerless to remedy the evil." One of the most enlightened papers presented at this meeting, on the subject of preventive medicine, presented the theory that infectious diseases

---

[32] Ashbel Smith to Edward Atkinson, *Ploughman*, April 16, 1877.
[33] Ibid., May 9, 1877.
[34] E. H. Stevens, Librarian, Department of Agriculture, to Ashbel Smith, December 5, 1877.

were caused by "living germs" and that water contaminated by evacuations of patients suffering from cholera or enteric fever might be dangerous.

The president of the association spoke on the poor quality of the education of many young physicians.[35] Ironically, Ashbel and his colleagues at the Texas Medical College and Hospital in Galveston were struggling with the opposite problem. After their strenuous efforts to secure excellent professors for the school, the teachers often lectured to roomfuls of empty chairs.[36]

In the fall of 1877, Ashbel received a touching letter from young Ed Cushing, who wrote on his mother's behalf and his own, asking Ashbel to persuade the ailing elder Cushing to take a desperately needed vacation from work.[37] Ashbel responded to the appeal, obtained railroad passes, and took a traveling vacation with Cushing to various towns in Texas, including Dallas, where they attended the fair.

By 1878, Ashbel had grandnieces and nephews, for both Ashbel Kittredge and Henry Kittredge were married and had offspring, as did some of Curtis's children. Ashbel repeatedly invited his nieces and nephews and their children to visit him, and several of them did so. Caroline's daughter Jessie had married a man named Edmund Hull, and at Ashbel's invitation, Hull stayed at Evergreen while he looked around for land for a farm.[38] Hull eventually settled on a farm near Evergreen. Ashbel soon began to be disturbed by Hull's habits, which included sleeping late and spending too much time in Galveston, which Ashbel considered an "entertaining, expensive and profitless place for a farmer." The extent of Hull's weaknesses had not yet been revealed, however, and Ashbel had other important things on his mind.

The Paris International Exposition promised to be the most exciting event of the year, and naturally Ashbel Smith wanted to be part of it. He saw it not only as an opportunity to go to Europe again but also as a chance to promote immigration to Texas. Consequently, he was pleased when Governor Richard B. Hubbard nominated him as one of the two honorary commissioners from Texas, and President Rutherford

---

[35] Nixon, *A History of the Texas Medical Association*, pp. 71–76.
[36] William Penny et al. to Ashbel Smith, March 3, 1877.
[37] Ed Cushing to Ashbel Smith, September 2, 1877.
[38] E. D. Hull to Ashbel Smith, January 2, 1878.

B. Hayes made the appointment official.[39] No clerical help or expense money went with the honor, and, like most other Texans in the late 1870s, Ashbel had little spare cash. But he agreed with Cushing, who told him, "You will have to go to Paris even if you have to live on fish and oysters for a year after you return."[40]

As Ashbel prepared for the trip, he was swamped by requests from individuals and companies to take samples of Texas goods to display at the exposition.[41] Among other items he took samples of cotton, lumber, shingles, and handmade quilts. He arranged for Edmund Hull to take charge of Evergreen and for his cousin Henry Gillette to help oversee the sheep shearing, the care of the livestock, and the planting of sugarcane, corn, sorghum, and cotton.

Ashbel's chief concern was for Anna's welfare during his absence. It was arranged that she would stay with her married sister in Marlin for some weeks and then return to Houston to stay with the Cushings. Shortly before he was due to leave, Ashbel suffered a bout of fever, which caused him to have some misgivings about undertaking the arduous trip and deeply distressed Anna.[42] He found, however, that travel was much more comfortable and swifter than it had been on previous trips. It took him only three and a half days to reach New York from Houston, and another ten days on the *City of Redmond* brought him to Liverpool. The sea voyage restored his strength and rested him, and by the time he reached London he had gained about ten pounds.

As usual, Parisians honored Ashbel Smith for his learning and for his intellect and named him one of the judges of agricultural products. The judges were invited to a constant round of entertainments, and the balls, receptions, and banquets undermined Ashbel's newfound health and his purse. "However," he told George, "as I neither smoke, nor drink champagne, or load myself with finery, I am not in debt nor broke."[43] In open letters published in Texas papers, Commissioner Smith described in detail the events of the exposition. In spite of the opposition of the Prince of Wales, he insisted on field trials for ag-

---

[39] "Notification of Appointment as Honorary Commissioner to Represent Texas at International Industrial Exposition in Paris," February 7, 1878.
[40] E. H. Cushing to Ashbel Smith, March 16, 1878.
[41] Polk Smith to Ashbel Smith, March 30, 1878.
[42] Anna Allen to Ashbel Smith, April 17, 1878.
[43] Ashbel Smith to George Smith, August 1, 1878.

A Very Broad Stage   199

ricultural implements. He had his way, and the trials were held. In reporting the results of these trials of reapers, binders, and mowers, Ashbel exulted, "The American machines were triumphantly victorious."

Some of the international congresses he attended were "diplomatic, literary, scientific, speculative, practical, commercial, financial, transportation," and others that he summed up as "talkative." In analyzing for his Texas readers the complicated political alliances in Europe, Ashbel commented, "Happy America separated by 3,000 miles of ocean!" He was particularly impressed by the power and strength of the German Empire under the leadership of Otto von Bismarck.[44]

On August 1, Ashbel sailed for New York on the *City of Berlin*. He had planned to visit Caroline in Keene, Henry Kittredge in Boston, and his brothers, George and Henry, in Memphis. News of a yellow-fever epidemic in Houston, however, made him eager to return to Texas as quickly as possible. On his arrival he found the outbreak severe and Houston under a quarantine "tight as a drum." Anna was well, however, and he was able to take her back to the relative safety of Evergreen.

Soon after his return, Ashbel himself became ill with an attack of fever, which kept him bedridden for weeks and left him weak and feeble for a long time. Cushing worried about his friend's health: "These dragging and continually recurring fevers are very dangerous at your time of life"[45] Ironically, Cushing who was almost a quarter of a century younger than Ashbel, had himself only a few weeks to live.

While Ashbel was abroad, his cousin Henry Gillette and other friends, including Cushing, had been working (with Ashbel's consent) for his nomination for a third term in the Texas legislature. Ashbel's opponents were "Greenbackers." He described the race as "intense, hot, all absorbing," and he won.[46]

In the same election Cromwell Jones, Anson Jones's son, was elected a judge. Writing to congratulate his young friend, Ashbel mentioned a writing project that he was planning as a rebuttal to articles that had appeared in the *Galveston News* during the fall of 1878. Ashbel believed that these articles reflected the "animus of the *Civilian* and the

[44] Ashbel Smith to E. H. Cushing, July 24, 1878.
[45] E. H. Cushing to Ashbel Smith, October 26, 1878.
[46] Ashbel Smith to Edward Atkinson, May 24, 1879.

News of thirty-five years ago toward Anson Jones."[47] He was distressed to realize that Texas history was likely to be compiled from sources that he considered inaccurate and prejudiced. The *Houston Telegraph*, when it was edited by Dr. Francis Moore, was in his opinion the organ of "blind, conceited, malicious fanaticism"; the *News*, "openly bitterly hostile, . . . always suspicious"; the *Civilian*, animated by the same spirit, "more insidious but not less malignant." Ashbel dismissed Foote's history as "rhapsodical, dashed off under the influence of General Lamar and his personal adherents," and Yoakum's history as "hasty, prejudiced, ignorant, . . . incorrect, incomplete, . . . a burlesque of history."[48]

A writer of Texas history whom Ashbel respected was Homer S. Thrall, a Methodist minister who had come to Texas as a missionary in the days of the Republic. In 1879, Thrall wrote Ashbel letters on his newfangled "type-writer," asking for information about historical events and also requesting Ashbel's endorsement of his latest history of Texas. Although he found fault with most histories of Texas, Ashbel was not tempted to follow the advice of his friend Senator S. B. Maxey to write one himself. "How many histories are written," Ashbel told Maxey. "How few live." He did, however, begin work on a history of the "diplomatic correspondence, intercourse, and relations of the Republic of Texas with other countries" and asked Maxey to help him obtain permission to examine some of the documents in the State Department files in Washington. Maxey secured a qualified permission for Ashbel to use the papers, but unfortunately he never completed the project.[49]

On the first day of 1879, Ashbel received a telegram informing him that his brother Henry had died suddenly of a heart attack at his home in Memphis. After the Civil War, Henry had been appointed a judge on the Supreme Court of Tennessee and had achieved considerable success in his law practice. His second marriage had been turbulent, however, and in his will Henry had made generous provision for Caroline Kittredge and her children but had left to his wife, Har-

---

[47] Ashbel Smith to Hon. C. Anson Jones, November 11, 1878.

[48] Ibid. Ashbel is referring to *Texas and the Texans* by Henry Stuart Foote (for which Ashbel wrote an appendix) and *History of Texas from Its First Settlement in 1685 to Its Annexation to the United States in 1846* by Henderson King Yoakum.

[49] Ashbel Smith to Hon. S. B. Maxey, November 10, 1879; Secretary, United States Department of State, to S. B. Maxey, June 8, 1882.

riet, only as much as the law required. Furious, Harriet tried to break the will, producing fictional letters slandering her late husband. Ashbel wrote to her, telling her kindly but firmly that she could not break the will and would only waste a great deal of money on lawyers' fees if she tried. But the scorned widow was not deterred and continued her efforts to discredit Henry. Finally, to stop her character assassinations, Ashbel and George decided to have a pamphlet printed containing their letters to each other about Harriet, Henry's memoranda about her, and a sample of the least vicious of her letters—with the threat to print the others if she did not drop her accusations against their dead brother. In the opening letter Ashbel wrote: "A man's good name after his death, the memory of a man eminent for the purity of his life, and distinguished by public services, is not only dear to his friends and kindred, but it is also to be guarded as a sacred truth, especially by his kindred." Ashbel wrote George: "It is painful to speak ill of a woman, but . . . she can no longer claim the forbearance due to the sex she has disgraced. Let the truth in its hideous infamy be shown." George replied, "'Let the galled jade wince.'" In the end Henry's estate was distributed as he had intended.[50]

Ashbel was in Austin attending to his legislative duties when he received word of the death of E. H. Cushing. He sent Anna a message, "Our dear good friend Mr. Cushing died Wednesday night," and made a hurried round trip to Houston to attend the funeral and comfort Cushing's widow, Matilda. Cushing's health had been deteriorating for a long time, and Matilda, who also suffered from many physical complaints, had frequently sought Ashbel's medical advice. Two weeks before Cushing's death she had written to Ashbel: "You are my St. Ashbel. . . . it is as if I sat in a dismal dungeon and this [Ashbel's concern] the sole ray of light that has penetrated the gloom. . . . I have been holding on to you all this year."[51] After Cushing's death she continued to hold on to Ashbel, writing him in the dead of night when her insomnia and depression kept her awake. Matilda was only forty years old, thirty-three years younger than Ashbel, but clearly she worshiped him and would have welcomed the idea of forming a closer relationship with him. She addressed her letters "My dear, dear friend," and in one

[50] *Letters between Ashbel Smith and George A. Smith pertaining to Henry G. Smith and Harriet Nooe Smith, 1868–1880.*
[51] Matilda Cushing to Ashbel Smith, January 1, 1879.

she cried out, "I need you . . . I want you." At seventy-three Ashbel Smith obviously still had his old charms.

During the regular session of the Sixteenth Legislature, Representative Smith received a number of suggestions from his constituents. They included establishment of an "inebriate asylum" for drunkards, a law to protect the well-being of hogs, and legislation to suppress gambling, which the correspondent described as a "mania" in Galveston.

Ashbel was the chairman of the Committee on Public Health, which had been assigned for study a bill to support a national quarantine law. He made a strong report opposing transferring this power to the federal government, believing that it belonged to the state. He also had professional objections to the bill, but in the end he supported it because he was convinced that his constituents were almost "universally" for it.[52]

Representative Smith of Harris introduced and pushed through the house resolutions to authorize lending state-owned mineralogical and geological specimens to the International and Great Northern Railroad Company to display "the rich and varied products of Texas" to easterners.[53] A few years later he had cause to regret this generosity when he had problems getting the specimens back for use in the University of Texas mineralogy department.

He also offered a resolution to exempt native Texas wines from the United States internal revenue tax, declaring that wine made from the native grapes, especially from the mustang, without "any admixture whatever" except sugar was, besides water, the "best and healthiest beverage for this climate, is sanitary as a preventive in all epidemic diseases, and is also a great means of promoting temperance." All foreign wines, he said, contain "alcoholic liquors, which are injurious to health and good morals."[54]

Under economy-minded Governor O. M. Roberts finances were a hot issue for the legislators. Ashbel understood why the philosophy of the greenbackers appealed to Texans who like him were hard up for ready cash, but he considered it a kind of "financial heresy." He thoroughly agreed with Roberts's "pay as we go" policy. One of the lighter

[52] *Texas House Journal, Sixteenth Legislature*, regular session, p. 634; extra session, p. 198.
[53] *Texas House Journal, Sixteenth Legislature*, regular session, pp. 565, 583, 598.
[54] Ibid., pp. 617–18.

moments during the session occurred when a young member decided to tease the venerable Dr. Smith by tickling the back of his neck with a spider made of rubber tied to a string and hanging from a pencil. Twice Ashbel absentmindedly brushed the "spider" away. Then, discovering that he was the butt of a practical joke, he jumped from his seat and agilely chased the laughing jester down the aisle, kicking at him as he went. When the chairman called for order, Ashbel bowed courteously and said, "Mr. Speaker, I pay as I go."[55]

When Ashbel addressed the house on schools, he began his speech by announcing that he would not tolerate being called an enemy of public schools because he refused to join in backing the present "wretched, inefficient, and expensive" state public school system. On the contrary, he proclaimed, he was the strong, unwavering friend of public education. He believed that every Texas child was entitled to an education and that four months in a country school with poor teachers was not furnishing it. Texas children, he lamented, "read slowly," had "sprawling handwriting" and "hideous spelling," and were "conspicuously ignorant of all higher attainments." The only successful schools in the state used local funds or local taxes, he pointed out, citing Houston schools as examples of the best schools in Texas. They operated ten months a year and were financed by the city and by a liberal donation from a private fund. He also cited the excellent schools of San Antonio and Denison, which were financed by municipal funds.[56]

As usual, Ashbel was involved in the presidential campaign. He was elected president of the state Democratic convention and worked for the election of the Democratic presidential candidate, General W. S. Hancock. After the Republican candidate, General James A. Garfield, won the election, Ashbel found a bright side to the defeat. Now, he hoped, Texans would realize the futility of their efforts to control national offices and devote "their purposes, their energies, their labors and their hopes to home affairs and to home interests."[57]

In the spring of 1879 a portrait of Thomas J. Rusk was presented to the state of Texas by a Kentucky artist. As a member of a committee appointed to solicit paintings of Texas heroes, Ashbel was among the

---

[55] Norman G. Kittrell, *Governors Who Have Been and Other Public Men of Texas*, p. 19.

[56] Ashbel Smith, "Speech on Financing of Public Schools," n.d., Ashbel Smith Papers.

[57] Ashbel Smith to "My dear old Friend," January 1, 1880.

speakers at the dedication of the portrait. His speech, which the newspapers dubbed "The Key to the Continent," covered the early history of Texas, with emphasis on the Battle of San Jacinto as a key factor not only in the fate of Texas but also in the destinies of Arizona, New Mexico, and California.[58]

During some of the tedious legislative reports Ashbel wrote to Anna at his desk on the floor. When she failed to write as often as he wished, he pleaded: "Why, my dear child, this silence, this neglect . . . ? My anxiety is very great. . . . I am crowded with business, yet I make time to write to you."[59] Ashbel continued to be concerned for the fate of orphans. One piece of legislation that he took particular interest in introducing and pushing through the House was an emergency-aid bill for the Bayland Orphans' Home.

Ashbel was disturbed when he learned that Anna was thinking seriously of marrying a young man whom he did not consider good enough for her. Matilda Cushing's view of the match (which did not materialize), probably did not console Ashbel—if she meant it to be consoling. Matilda wrote:

Anna is a *creation* of yours—but she springs from the same kind of stock she is marrying into—and while with you she is much in the condition of a person under the application of a galvanic battery—remove your influence and she will be superior in a measure to those people, but not enough so to render her miserable.[60]

Consciously or unconsciously, Matilda Cushing was jealous of Anna, who obviously had the stronger pull on Ashbel's affections. Matilda showed the same ambivalent feelings toward Mary Johnson, an orphan who had been reared by the Cushings as their own daughter. Mary grew up to be strikingly handsome, talented, and sweet-natured. When she decided on teaching as a career, and "Uncle" Ashbel helped and encouraged her, Matilda for a time could not bear Mary's presence.[61]

During the vacations between the regular and special sessions of the Sixteenth Legislature, Ashbel went to Evergreen, where George was paying a visit. One day Matilda Cushing sent for Ashbel, telling

---

[58] Ashbel Smith, "Presentation of Gen. Rusk's Portrait," speech, Ashbel Smith Papers.
[59] Ashbel Smith to Anna Allen, March 14, 1879.
[60] Matilda Cushing to Ashbel Smith, April 14, 1879.
[61] Matilda Cushing to Ashbel Smith, April 2, 1879.

him, "You are the only rest and peace I have." In June, Ashbel returned reluctantly to Austin. "My thoughts go back to Evergreen at least a hundred times a day," he wrote to Anna.[62] He left for the capital pleased with himself for having brought the gentle Mary Johnson to the plantation to stay with Anna. Now, he thought, Anna would have a companion. Mary could supervise Anna's lessons, and the two girls could enjoy many pastimes together.

Like many another parent the idealistic bachelor father discovered that his "child's" view of the situation was quite different from his own. A few days after he reached Austin, he was dismayed and shaken to receive a letter from Anna in which she accused him of caring more for Mary than for her. Since Mary was taking her place in his affections, she would leave Evergreen. She knew that she was "too hateful" to live there any longer.[63] Bypassing an important committee meeting, Ashbel sat down to answer the letter. He told Anna: ". . . you have grown into my heart; no person, no thing can tear you out from it . . . your happiness is a part and parcel of my own happiness. . . . Alas, alas, alas, my dear Child, that you whom I do love, whom I do cherish, who is so intertwined with every fibre of my soul should utter and feel such words and feelings." He compared his love for Anna and for Mary with the love a parent can feel for two children. "Do I not love you both, cherish you both? You may wrong me, you may hate me. I shall ever love you as I now do, dearly."[64] This letter, which Ashbel told Anna to keep and read over when she felt unhappy, apparently soothed her, and she and Mary settled into a peaceful coexistence—at least on the surface.

During the month-long special legislative session, which was mostly concerned with matters of finance, Ashbel served as chairman of the Committee on Insurance, Statistics, and History and of the Committee on Public Health, Vital Statistics, and History of Texas. His committees dealt with legislation concerning levying and collecting taxes on public lands, public sanitation measures, defining insurance agents, and regulating medicine, surgery, and pharmacy.[65]

Back at Evergreen, one of Ashbel's first concerns was to see Mary

[62] Ashbel Smith to Anna Allen, June 8, 1879.
[63] Ashbel Smith to Anna Allen, June 17, 1879.
[64] Ibid.
[65] *Texas House Journal, Sixteenth Legislature*, extra session.

through her examinations before the Houston Board of Examiners. He was pleased with his protégé and used his influence to try to find her a teaching position.[66] In the meantime she continued to live at Evergreen.

On his trips to Houston, Ashbel stayed at the Hutchins House. After taking care of his business, he often visited Matilda Cushing, who found great solace in long talks with him—even though he sometimes went to sleep during them. When the New Year arrived, Matilda wrote Ashbel a letter of good wishes, which included a wish for "renewing" his youth and another that he would move from Evergreen to a place nearer her.[67]

In March, Caroline finally made a long-promised and often-postponed visit to Evergreen. She was "charmed" by the plantation and delighted with Anna. She wrapped Ashbel's foster child in a motherly affection to which Anna responded wholeheartedly. Caroline's visit lasted about six weeks, and after she went home, she wrote Anna loving letters and sent her small gifts.[68]

As president of the Board of Trustees of the Texas Medical College and Hospital at Galveston, Ashbel was present to hand out the diplomas and congratulate the graduates of the 1879–80 session for choosing the "noble" profession of medicine. The growth of the school had been disappointing. The eight faculty members outnumbered the six graduating students, though the trustees had tried various inducements to attract students, such as reducing fees and making dissecting material "abundant and free." The school also advertised that "good board" could be had in Galveston for four to six dollars a week.[69]

In April, Ashbel attended the annual meeting of the Texas Medical Association in Brenham, where he made a cantankerous contribution to the proceedings. After a heated controversey over the new "occupation tax," a resolution was offered to thank the Honorable George Finlay for having opposed the tax in the previous legislature. Ashbel rose to say that he had heard Finlay's speech, "which consumed two hours' time of the House," and that Finlay had only alluded to the tax as burdensome on lawyers and had not mentioned doctors. Furthermore, Ashbel said, he felt that doctors were willing to support the state

[66] Ashbel Smith to E. D. Clopper, December 22, 1879.
[67] Matilda Cushing to Ashbel Smith, December 24, 1879.
[68] Caroline Kittredge to Anna Allen, June 26, 1880; August 29, 1880.
[69] Circular, Texas Medical College and Hospital, Galveston, 1879–80.

A Very Broad Stage 207

government, and he failed to see that Finlay had done anything for which the physicians should thank him. The resolution was rejected.[70]

When Ashbel's friend Senator Maxey asked him to analyze Texas's currency and finances, Ashbel responded with a long letter tracing the history of Texas's economic ups and downs since the days of the Republic. Impressed, Maxey used the letter in his arguments against greenbackism and asked for permission to have the letter published.[71]

Since his arrival in Texas in 1837, Ashbel had worked for the cause of immigration to his adopted state, both publicly and privately. He received frequent queries from friends, acquaintances, and strangers in America and in Europe about what Texas was really like. He answered their questions painstakingly, with detailed descriptions of the climate, geography, people, economic condition, educational facilities, religious institutions, and commercial possibilities. As Texas's minister to England and France, he had recruited and screened immigrants to the Republic. Since annexation he had seized opportunities to promote and encourage immigration.

In September, 1880, he published letters in the *Galveston News* and in northern papers in which he analyzed the population growth of Texas. He was especially concerned that the immigration rate was much lower than he and others had predicted several years earlier. He named four important causes of the arrested immigration:

1. a number of infamous land frauds
2. exaggerated publicity given to crimes in newspapers
3. criminal laws that favored the criminal rather than the victim
4. quarantine laws that like the "yellow flag of a pest house" waved off immigrants; whereas, the whole security against yellow fever lay in one thing—*sanitation*.[72]

As president of the Board of Trustees of the Texas Medical College and Hospital at Galveston, Ashbel again conferred degrees on the new doctors in March, 1881. Perhaps to amuse himself, he gave his address in Latin. The *Galveston News* reported that, although they were impressed, most of his audience remained unenlightened. When asked

---

[70] *Proceedings of the Texas Medical Association*, April, 1880, pp. 25–26.

[71] Herbert T. Hoover, "Ashbel Smith on Currency and Finance in the Republic of Texas," *Southwestern Historical Quarterly* 71 (January, 1968): 419–24.

[72] Ashbel Smith to Alfred Richardson, July 27, 1880; Ashbel Smith to Edmund Atkinson, August 16, 1880; September 9, 1880; *Galveston News*, September 30, 1880.

their opinions of it, the faculty members called the speech "splendid" and "outstanding," but none of them ever revealed its content.[73]

The year 1881 contained a number of significant events for Ashbel Smith, but undoubtedly the one with greatest personal meaning for him was Anna's marriage on February 20 to George Wright. The couple were married in Christ Church in Houston with Ashbel Smith and Mary Johnson as witnesses.[74] A resident of the bay area, Wright was a hard-working man with whom Ashbel had done business in connection with his brickyard. The bachelor father gave his blessings to the match and made the newlyweds a gift of about seventy-five acres of Evergreen so that they could establish their own farm near him. George and Anna built their house close to Evergreen so that Anna could visit often, and she continued to look after the plantation during Ashbel's absences. She shared his garden, making catsup from his tomatoes and pickles from his cucumbers, as well as doing other household tasks for him.[75]

In time the Wrights had a baby girl, whom they named Caroline. Their second daughter, Mary, died at the age of three, but four sons survived to adulthood. At the time Ashbel gave Anna the land for her farm, he told her that one day the land would make her rich. Little did he know what truth he spoke. When oil was found at Goose Creek in 1916, the Wrights' home and the old Evergreen homestead were in the middle of the field. At the time of her death in 1944 a Texas newspaper referred to Anna Allen Wright as the "wealthiest woman in Harris County."[76] Ashbel Smith, who frequently exhorted Texans to develop their natural resources, never dreamed that he was growing cotton and sugarcane on top of a spectacular pool of oil.

[73] *Galveston News*, March 17, 1881.
[74] Wright family bible, in possession of Anna Pearl Wright Thomas, Baytown, Texas.
[75] Anna Allen Wright to Ashbel Smith, June 29, 1881.
[76] *Dallas Morning News*, December 29, 1944.

CHAPTER ELEVEN

Father of the University
(1881–1885)

IN 1839 the Congress of the Republic of Texas set aside fifty leagues of land to provide for "two colleges or universities." In 1854, under Governor E. M. Pease's administration, the legislature set aside $100,000 in United States bonds for endowing a university. Four years later, in 1858, under the leadership of Governor Hardin R. Runnels, the legislature had made further financial provisions for a state college, and a university fund was established. During the hard times of the Civil War and Reconstruction the state had borrowed from the school fund for other urgent needs, and it was not until the constitution of 1876 paved the way that action was finally taken to found a "first class" state university.[1]

In addition to providing for the Prairie View School, which Ashbel had helped establish, the constitution of 1876 made the Agricultural and Mechanical College of Texas, situated at Bryan, a branch of a nonexistent University of Texas. On October 4, 1876, the A&M College of Texas opened its doors and got off to a shaky start. Another five years passed before the Texas legislature, on March 30, 1881, passed an act establishing the University of Texas. The act provided for the voters to decide on the location of the university and for the governor to appoint eight regents to organize and manage its affairs.[2]

As a consequence of the legislative action Ashbel's interests in medicine and education were combined as he fought to have the medical branch of the new state university established in Galveston. In January, 1881, he had testified before the house education committee,

---

[1] Webb and Carroll, eds., *Handbook of Texas*, 2:821.
[2] General Laws of Texas, chap. 75, p. 79, cited in O. M. Roberts, "Establishment of the University of Texas," *Historical Association Quarterly* 1 (April, 1898): 243–46.

presenting arguments for choosing Galveston as the site for the medical school, and in the spring he wrote an article for the *Texas Journal of Education*, setting out his views on the college. He considered Austin the only suitable location for the main branch of the state university; it was "preeminently healthy," was easily accessible by railroad from every part of the state, and, being the seat of government, would give the students the advantage of observing the running of the state firsthand. He was opposed to the building of "huge structures" for dormitories or common dining halls. Experience had proved, he contended, that private boarding houses provided cheaper and better living conditions and were "favorable to better conduct."[3]

On April 5, Governor Oran M. Roberts appointed Ashbel to the university's first board of regents, whose job it was to organize the school "from the foundation to the capstone." The regents received no pay and had no secretarial assistance. The first board included Throckmorton, Ashbel's fellow physician, who expressed to Ashbel the feeling of most of the other members: "In what we will have to do as regents we will have to rely wholly upon your judgment and knowledge."[4]

The duties of the board members were, as Ashbel realized, both basic and comprehensive. They were to define the general plan of the university buildings, set up a curriculum, select a faculty, and take all other steps necessary for perfecting the organization of the school. Ashbel was pleased that they had a clear field with "no rubbish of former attempts" to clear away and "no grease vested interests" to contend with. He was determined to keep the university free of the "cancer" of party politics.[5]

After the board elected him president, Ashbel learned that he had the additional burden of approving disbursements from the university fund to pay the bills of the university, Texas A&M, and Prairie View Normal School.[6] This meant that he had to become familiar with the financial operations of all three colleges and check their accounts regularly, which meant a great deal of traveling, correspondence, and other paperwork.

Governor Roberts set September 6, 1881, as the date for the vot-

[3] Ashbel Smith, essay on education, *Texas Journal of Education*, March, 1881.
[4] J. W. Throckmorton to Ashbel Smith, June 5, 1881.
[5] Ashbel Smith to Rev. Theodore D. Woolsey, May 29, 1881.
[6] O. M. Roberts to Ashbel Smith, December 5, 1881.

ers to choose the location of the proposed university and to decide whether or not the medical branch should be separate and, if so, where it should be located. Although a few other cities had their supporters, Austin had little serious competition as the site for the main campus, but the debate over where to locate the medical branch was heated.

When the Texas Medical Association met in Waco in April for its annual session, fourteen doctors took part in the debates, which filled thirteen pages of the minutes. Ashbel spoke at length on the advantages of Galveston, pointing out its size—it was the largest city in Texas—its general healthiness, its wealth and industry, the opportunities it would provide for medical students to observe the diseases of patients who arrived on ships, the "nobility" of its citizens, and most important, the medical college which was already in operation, with a "first class" faculty and excellent clinical and dissecting facilities.[7]

In spite of Ashbel's eloquence, some members of the association were vehemently opposed to "dismembering" the university. Others opposed Galveston as a site because of the danger of hurricanes and yellow-fever epidemics. One doctor unkindly pointed out that it had already been proved that the location would not make for a successful school, since the medical college, which had been operating at Galveston for almost fifteen years, averaged no more than a dozen students a session.[8]

Before the TMA closed its meeting, it voted Ashbel Smith president-elect for the following year—an honor many thought was long overdue. In his acceptance speech Ashbel told his fellow physicians:

In our profession of medicine, every professional act to any and every human being is, or ought to be to do good to that being. In so doing, the physician obeys that command of our Saviour, to be like our Father which is in Heaven, who makes his sun to rise on the evil and on the good, and sends his rain on the just and on the unjust. Gentlemen, our profession is indeed a noble one.[9]

It was one of the paradoxes of Ashbel Smith's character that he could with sincerity on this and many other occasions refer to his profession

---

[7] "Proceedings of the Texas State Medical Association, Thirteenth Annual Session," *Texas Medical & Surgical Record*, June, 1881, pp. 219–44; *The University of Texas Medical Branch at Galveston*, p. 13.

[8] "Proceedings of the Texas State Medical Association, Thirteenth Annual Session," *Texas Medical & Surgical Record*, June, 1881, pp. 234–36.

[9] Ibid., p. 245.

in idealistic terms and at other times, realizing how many illnesses and injuries were beyond the skill of the physician, acknowledge that the doctor could be a "nuisance" who might do more harm than good.

The TMA also elected Ashbel a delegate to the annual session of the American Medical Association, to be held in Richmond, Virginia, during the first week in May. The timing of the meeting fitted in with Ashbel's plans for a trip east and north that summer. He had several reasons for the trip. His primary purpose was to visit eastern and northern universities to gather information and lay the groundwork for recruiting the faculty and setting up the curriculum for the new university.

He turned first to his alma mater, Yale, for guidance. He made plans to attend the commencement on June 29 and wrote to Yale's President Theodore Woolsey, asking him to be prepared to recommend competent professors for the new school. Ashbel stipulated that they should be "gentlemen of scholastic attainments," that they should have "tact" in imparting knowledge and administrative talent, and that they should be "improvable." He assured Woolsey that there would be no prejudice against men of "Northern birth."[10]

On his journey Ashbel visited Vanderbilt University at Nashville, and he may have made brief stopovers at other schools. But the university that Ashbel studied most closely in formulating his ideas was the University of Virginia, founded by Thomas Jefferson, whom Ashbel admired as a statesman and as an educator. Many of Jefferson's theories about education had long been assimilated into Ashbel Smith's thinking.

Probably the living man with whom Ashbel was most eager to confer was Henry Barnard. Barnard congratulated his old friend for having the opportunity for "a great work to start right a great institution." He invited Ashbel to stay with him in Hartford—wherever he might be living when Ashbel arrived. The dedicated leader of American education was in danger of having his mortgage foreclosed because of "sacrifices" he had made to keep the *Journal of Education* going. Cheerful as ever, Barnard was hoping, Micawberlike, for "something to turn up."[11]

In addition to university business, Ashbel had family matters to take care of in the North. He planned a visit to his half-brother, Curtis,

---
[10] Ashbel Smith to Rev. Theodore D. Woolsey, May 29, 1881.
[11] Henry Barnard to Ashbel Smith, May 16, 1881.

Father of the University 213

who was now living in Kirkwood, Illinois, on the Chicago, Burlington and Quincy Railroad route. "Come!" Curtis urged. Of Curtis's six living children, the one with whom Ashbel kept in closest touch was the oldest boy—his namesake nephew, Ashbel Grattan Smith. Many years later, just before World War I, when Ashbel Grattan had become the patriarch of the Smith clan, he wrote a letter concerning his uncle that was among the memorabilia enclosed in the cornerstone of the first library building of the University of Texas.[12]

In Keene, New Hampshire, Ashbel found Caroline's household gloomy. Caroline's husband, Dr. Kittredge, was in critically poor health, and the behavior of Jessie's husband, Edmund Hull, had become impossible. Ashbel confirmed the reports about Edmund's drinking and associations with other women. After agonizing family conferences, it was decided that Jessie should get a divorce, and Ashbel promised to help her win it. In their distress both Caroline and Jessie leaned on Ashbel's strength. Subsequently, with the help of attorneys and detectives, Ashbel had papers served on Edmund and arranged for depositions about his nephew-in-law's behavior to be sent to a judge in Keene, who granted Jessie a divorce.[13]

As soon as he returned to Texas, Ashbel began making plans to attend the great International Cotton Exposition to be held in Atlanta in the fall. He made a speech in Houston praising Texas agricultural and industrial resources and pleading with Texans to have enough pride to send a respectable number of samples of their products for display at the exhibition. He himself carried pillowcases full of Sea Island cotton from Evergreen. He went to the exposition as an official representative of the Galveston Cotton Exchange, and after his arrival he was appointed a vice-president by the fair executives.[14]

Ashbel was pleased by the showing Texas made, and he reported to the editor of the *Houston Post* that the exhibition was "a wonderful display of things useful to the South, surpassing all expectations, riches better, more various for the use of the South than was ever before collected any where on earth, or is likely to be again soon collected." He was extremely annoyed by the inadequate news coverage of the exposi-

[12] Ashbel G. Smith to Clara Newman Murray, June 12, 1904.
[13] Caroline Kittredge to Ashbel Smith, July 10, 1881. Jessie Hull to Ashbel Smith, July 14, 1881. D. H. Woodward to Ashbel Smith, September 2, 1881. Albert Mills to Ashbel Smith, September 19, 1881.
[14] Ashbel Smith to Edward Atkinson, October 20, 1881.

tion and accused reporters of being interested only in gaining advertisements and subscriptions. With such an attitude the reporters, he felt, were not informing the people of Texas about the many implements exhibited that might be of great use to them. To make up for this shortcoming, Ashbel wrote long, detailed letters to the *Post*, describing the equipment displayed at the fair that was suitable for use by Texas planters. He proudly reported the judges' comments on his own Sea Island cotton, which was declared "beautiful . . . . Magnificent . . . the best cotton of this kind at the Exposition."[15]

In October the regents of the University of Texas were notified that the voters of Texas had chosen Austin as the site of the main campus of the college and Galveston as the site of the medical branch. Ashbel Smith was pleased. The trustees of the Texas Medical College and Hospital of Galveston decided to close the school to clear the way for the new medical branch, which they expected to open soon.[16] No one, least of all Ashbel Smith, imagined that it would be ten more years before his hard-won dream of a university medical school would become a reality—or that he would not live to see its birth.

When the university regents met officially for the first time on November 15, 1881, funding for the school was so uncertain that some questioned the wisdom of continuing with plans for it. But the enthusiasm and momentum for founding a great university had been generated, at least among those who cared about education, and the regents decided to go ahead and trust that the money would be forthcoming. The seven regents attending the first session were Ashbel Smith, Thomas D. Wooten, R. B. Hubbard, Smith Ragsdale, T. J. Devine, T. M. Harwood, and A. N. Edwards. J. W. Throckmorton was ill and unable to attend (he later resigned because of poor health). With other regents Ashbel served on the executive committee, the committee on university departments, and the committee to choose a design for the university seal.[17]

The board adopted a general plan for the necessary construction and advertised for plans and specifications for the west wing, which

[15] Ashbel Smith to Editor, *Houston Post*, November 2, 1881.

[16] *The University of Texas Medical Branch at Galveston*, pp. 13–14.

[17] The design suggested and accepted was "a Texas star inscribed within a circle, leaving a narrow space between the two circumferences on which shall be engrossed the Latin words 'Universitas Texana.' The remaining space to be filled with some appropriate design—as a vine or branch with leaves. The space between the points of the star to be filled with the Latin motto 'Non sine pulvere palma.'"

was to be three stories high. The regents' academic plans called for nine divisions, or schools, with one professor each, and a department of law, with two professors.[18] Plans were also made for the medical branch, but in the ten years that passed before it opened, those plans were extensively modified.[19] The board respectfully asked that the state repay, with interest, the money that had been borrowed from the university fund. After three days of meetings the regents reported their proceedings to the governor. The last paragraph of the report read:

> In conclusion, the board would state, after careful review of the entire subject, that substantial grounds exist for the belief that the design of a University, entertained and cherished by the fathers of the Republic and the State of Texas, will be carried out to a successful termination, and that the State of Texas, at no distant day, will possess a University resting on foundations broad and deep, growing with the growth, and keeping step with the population, the wealth and intelligence of the State of Texas.[20]

One of the most important duties of the regents was the selection of a faculty. Ashbel insisted that the selection not be hurried. He wanted the "ablest and most famous professors" who could be induced to come to Austin. Governor Roberts agreed and supported Ashbel's stand, but some newspapers and many prominent Texans were annoyed by the slowness of the board in choosing a faculty. Reporters were also disgruntled that they were not allowed to attend the regents' meetings, and attacks in the press became so virulent that when two members of the board resigned the governor had difficulty finding suitable replacements. Ashbel growled, "Competent gentlemen do not willingly accept an office which subjects them to damaging misrepresentation by irresponsible newspaper correspondents." He met the criticisms of the regents head on and vigorously defended them against "incorrect and unjust disparagements of newspaper newsgatherers."[21]

Most of the burden of corresponding with and interviewing prospects for the faculty fell on Ashbel and the able new secretary of the board, Alexander Penn Wooldridge. Recommendations came to the re-

---

[18] Minutes of the Board of Regents of the University of Texas, 1881–83, microfilm, Barker Texas History Center, University of Texas, Austin; hereafter cited as Regents' Minutes.

[19] Ibid.

[20] Roberts, "Establishment of the University of Texas," pp. 252–61.

[21] Ashbel Smith to *Galveston News*, May 21, 1882; A. P. Wooldridge to Ashbel Smith, August 10, 1882.

gents from inside and outside the state. Teachers at a number of institutions—as well as their wives—wrote to Ashbel. So did old friends, such as Throckmorton, who suggested a son-in-law of Sam Houston (the husband of Nettie Houston Bringhurst) to chair modern languages.[22]

During the winter and spring of 1881–82, Ashbel spent so many late nights at his correspondence on university matters that he severely strained his eyes. He diagnosed his ailment as "nervous exhaustion of the eyes" caused by "excessive exposure to the glare of the kerosene lamp." He was forced to rest his eyes for several weeks until they returned to normal. The episode frightened him a little, for he had always had exceptionally good eyesight and had never needed glasses, even in old age.[23]

In the spring of 1882 not all of Ashbel's thoughts were on his public duties. Although he was well past three score and ten, his thoughts still turned to love—or at least to affection and companionship. The family that Ashbel had created for himself had dissolved. Anna had a growing family to care for, and Mary was settling into a teaching career. Ashbel wrote to Radcliffe Hudson, asking his opinion of matrimony at Ashbel's time of life. The woman was almost certainly Helen M. Owen, a cousin of Ashbel's who was living in the bay area. She was handsome and intelligent, knew French, and shared Ashbel's love of reading. In his will Ashbel named her, along with his brother George, as executor of his estate and left her one-sixth of his property. Radcliffe remembered that when he met her briefly on a visit to Evergreen she seemed to "brighten up all the surroundings." His advice was that, since Ashbel was still as "vigorous and active as a forty year old, . . . if you think it will add to your comfort, marry—and as you said to me—*chance it!*"[24] As usual, however, Ashbel's talk of marriage came to nothing. If he did feel lonely, he did not take time to brood over it. Besides his voluminous correspondence on university affairs, he wrote long memorandums and letters to state and national congressmen on such matters as mail delivery and railroad routes.

Moreover, he had important medical business at hand. As president of the Texas Medical Association, he was responsible for summoning members to the annual meeting in Fort Worth in April. The atten-

[22] J. W. Throckmorton to Ashbel Smith, November 1, 1881.
[23] Ashbel Smith to Edward Atkinson, March 26, 1882.
[24] Radcliffe Hudson to Ashbel Smith, May 20, 1882.

dance was the largest ever recorded, even though some doctors from San Antonio boycotted the meeting because of a grievance over some of the association's policies. Ashbel's presidential address summarized the changes in the medical profession in the state in the past half century. He had much to say about education and about the schools of the state. One of the sessions that drew the most interest and discussion was on Darwinism. In contrast to previous meetings, this one was noted for the large number of admissions to membership, harmony, and not least the amount of dues collected.[25]

In June the State Teachers Association held its annual meeting at Galveston, and Ashbel attended along with Governor Roberts. Both men addressed the teachers, asking for their support and encouragement of the new university.[26] Ashbel also journeyed to other Texas cities alone and with other board members to address groups on the same theme.

About the first of August, Ashbel received a letter from the university architect, F. E. Ruffini, informing him that work had begun on the west wing of the university building: "The excavation is well under way, stone is being hauled."[27] Another pleasing piece of news was that John William Mallet, of the University of Virginia, had accepted the regents' invitation to become professor of chemistry and physics. Mallet, whom Ashbel had wooed all summer, was president of the American Chemical Society, a fellow of the Royal Society, and an associate fellow of the American Academy of Arts and Sciences and had seventy-one research papers to his credit.[28] Later, when Mallet was selected as faculty chairman in charge of the day-to-day operation of the university, Ashbel thought he was a fortunate choice for the school, which was to be run, like the University of Virginia, without a president.

At their August meeting the regents, having received the bad news that the legislature had not voted them additional funds, took steps to economize. The number of academic departments was reduced from nine to six. Despite the tight budget, however, Ashbel prodded the regents to set the faculty salaries as high as possible to

[25] *Texas Medical & Surgical Record*, 1882, pp. 203–205.
[26] Roberts, "Establishment of the University of Texas," p. 263.
[27] F. E. Ruffini to Ashbel Smith, August 2, 1882.
[28] Frank E. Vandiver, "John William Mallet and the University of Texas," *Southwestern Historical Quarterly* 53 (April, 1950): 423–42.

attract the best professors obtainable. In the face of harsh criticism for their extravagance the regents set the following salary schedule:[29]

School of English and History	$3,500
School of Chemistry and Physics	3,500
Mathematics, Pure and Applied	3,500
Mental Philosophy, Logic, and Ethics	4,000
Latin and Greek	3,500
Modern Languages, French, Spanish, and German	2,500

The date on the cornerstone of the first building of the University of Texas reads "November 16, A.D. 1882." Because of inclement weather on that day, the ceremony was postponed to the following day, when the stone was laid on College Hill with an impressive ceremony that gray skies and chilly breezes did not diminish. By 11:30 the grand procession had formed near the courthouse. A marching band led the parade, followed by the regents, the officers of the university, the heads of state departments, and the mayor and aldermen of Austin—all in carriages. Prominent county officials and colorfully costumed groups such as the Odd Fellows, the Knights of Pythias, and the Knights Templars followed on foot. The Austin Greys in their dress uniforms acted as escorts to the ladies of the female seminary. A large group of public school students joined to make the parade a half mile long, and many private carriages followed to extend it another half mile.[30]

At the building site Governor Roberts introduced Regent Smith to the crowd of over two thousand. "We have come together to do a great work," Ashbel told the assembled Texans. In his address he emphasized that the university would offer a first-class curriculum taught by first-class professors. He compared the founding of the University of Texas with the founding of the University of Virginia by Thomas Jefferson and quoted some of Jefferson's ideas about education. He noted that it would be as easy for the poor boy to get an education at the university as for the rich boy. He pointed out that Texas women would be able for the first time to obtain a decent education in their own state. "And who will say that her intellect is inferior to that of a man?" he challenged his listeners. Prophetically he told the audience: "Texas holds embedded in its earth rocks and minerals which now lie idle be-

[29] Ruth Ann Overbeck, "Alexander Penn Wooldridge," *Southwestern Historical Quarterly* 67 (January, 1964): 341.
[30] *Austin Weekly Democratic Statesman*, November 23, 1882.

cause unknown, resources of incalculable industrial utility, of wealth and power. Smite the earth, smite the rocks with the rod of knowledge and fountains of unstinted wealth will gush forth."[31] His promise was dramatically fulfilled in 1923, when oil was discovered on university property.

After the speeches the regents, with the help of the Masons, the Knights of Pythias, and the Odd Fellows, laid the cornerstone. Among the articles in the lead box embedded in the stone were copies of six Texas newspapers, laws pertaining to the establishment of the university, a photograph of the new capitol, a Bible, plans and drawings of the university building—and a picture of the Queen of England contributed by a man confined in the county jail.[32]

Immediately after he returned to Evergreen, Ashbel was struck with a "sudden catarrh and fever" that incapacitated him for about a week. Again in the spring of 1883 he had a protracted illness, which he told acquaintances was "pulmonary congestion." To his family and to a few old, close friends like Radcliffe Hudson, however, he admitted that he thought he was suffering from angina pectoris.[33]

Nevertheless, his labors for the university did not lessen. Every mail brought him ten to twelve letters concerning faculty selection, building problems, financial difficulties, and other matters on which he had to make decisions, find solutions, or offer advice. Unable to afford a secretary, he took care of all the correspondence himself. The significance of what he hoped to accomplish kept him going. Writing to M. W. Humphreys, of Vanderbilt, to offer him the chair of Latin and Greek, Ashbel said:

If I supposed there even any likelihood that the University of Texas ever be an institution of shriveled proportions, one in which instructions shall be given chiefly in some Latin & Greek, mathematics & belles lettres & limited to modest acquisitions in these departments of education, such an institution in short as are most of our American colleges, . . . I would not devote my good leisure to any such University of Texas.[34]

The university's financial picture looked brighter to Ashbel. He wrote to Leslie Waggener, who had been named professor of English

---

[31] Ashbel Smith, "Address on the Laying of the Corner Stone of the University of Texas," November 17, 1882, Ashbel Smith Papers.
[32] *Austin Weekly Democratic Statesman*, November 23, 1882.
[33] Maria Hudson to Ashbel Smith, March 6, 1883.
[34] Ashbel Smith to Prof. M. W. Humphreys, December, 1882.

and history, telling him that the Texas legislature had appropriated a million acres of land to the support of the university, which, added to the million acres set aside for the school by the state constitution, made two million. "There also belong to the University interest bearing Bonds amounting to about $600,000." In cash funds, Ashbel estimated, the university had in hand $59,000, plus $50,000 due on September 1, and an "annually accruing interest from and after 1st September of about $35,000." The university, Ashbel assured Waggener, was on a "solid financial basis."[35] In a few months he was to find that his optimism had been premature.

At their April 30, 1883, meeting the regents had to referee a dispute between the architect, Ruffini, and the building contractor, A. H. Cook, over the use of wood netting instead of iron for ceilings. Cook said that iron would sag, but Ruffini disagreed. The board voted with Ruffini. The rest of the meeting was largely concerned with means of deriving revenue from the lands owned by the university, the details of organizing the departments of the school, and the procurement of equipment.[36]

There were many letters and several more regents' meetings before the faculty selections were announced, and there was some infighting among the members over the candidates. Ashbel strongly supported General Kirby Smith for the chair of mathematics, but the general was defeated by what Ashbel called "intrigue" in Austin, and Leroy Broun was chosen. Ashbel consoled himself that "we can mount our University independent of any single man, and successfully."[37]

When the names of the new faculty members were finally released, and it was learned that most of the professors came from Virginia, Tennessee, and Kentucky, there was bitter criticism. Some of it came from disgruntled losers such as Alex Hogg, a professor at Texas A&M, who had wanted the chair of mathematics. Hogg accused the board of setting up a policy reading "No Texas man need hope to enter here" and sarcastically suggested that the university be moved to Tennessee or Kentucky to be more convenient for the faculty members.[38]

As a matter of fact, early in the summer a preliminary meeting of the faculty *was* held in Nashville for the convenience of the new fac-

[35] Ashbel Smith to Leslie Waggener, April 18, 1883.
[36] Regents' Minutes, April 30, 1883.
[37] Ashbel Smith to A. P. Wooldridge, November 24, 1882.
[38] Alex Hogg to Ashbel Smith, August 23, 1882; May 11, 1883.

ulty. The business of the meeting was to make plans for the first term and set up the curricula.

Although there were construction problems and delays, Ashbel confidently assured the teachers that at least part of the main building wing would be ready for use when the first term opened in September. As the summer progressed, however, prospects that the building would be ready in time diminished. In August the bricklayers struck, first for six dollars a day and later for seven. Then, on August 20, came the sudden death of the man who was to do the galvanized ironwork for the cornices, which had to be in place before the roof could be installed.[39] The university had to "borrow" the temporary capitol to hold classes, and plank walls were hastily installed to partition off classrooms. The partitions proved inadequate, too thin to keep out noise and full of knotholes that the students used for passing notes between rooms.[40]

In spite of all obstacles the University of Texas opened on September 15, 1883, with 166 students enrolled in the academic department and 52 students enrolled in the law school. The law department had as its faculty the only native Texas instructors, O. M. Roberts, the former governor, and Robert S. Gould, former chief justice of the Texas Supreme Court. The large crowd that gathered for the opening convocation heard addresses by Governor John Ireland and Regents President Smith and by Professor Mallet on behalf of the faculty. At the close of his speech Ashbel introduced the faculty to the audience. With pride he called them "the officers in charge of the educational interests of the people."[41] As part of the ceremony the sculptor Elisabet Ney, whom Ashbel introduced as the granddaughter of "Marshal Ney of the Army of Napoleon," presented a bust of Governor Roberts to the university.[42]

A crisis threatened in early October, when Mallet, disenchanted with conditions at the university and distressed over the declining health of his son John, who had tuberculosis, asked to be relieved of his duties so that he could return to the University of Virginia. A meeting of the regents was called, but before it convened, Mallet withdrew his

[39] A. P. Wooldridge, August 20, 1883; September 26, 1883.
[40] Milton W. Humphreys, "The Genesis of the University of Texas," *Alcalde* 1 (1912): 6.
[41] Regents' Minutes, September 15, 1883; Humphreys, "The Genesis of the University of Texas," p. 9.
[42] Regents' Minutes, September 15, 1883.

resignation, at least for the term.[43] As a gesture of sympathy and because he believed in its effectiveness as a tonic, Ashbel sent Mallet's son some bottles of his homemade wine. Not all the regents valued Mallet as highly as Ashbel did. Regent James Clark, of Bonham, wrote Ashbel that the university would survive the "calamity" of Mallet's withdrawal, adding, "A mallet is not the hammer of Thor, after all."[44] In October there was a call from Wooldridge for Ashbel to come to Austin to light a fire under the dilatory builders, authorize payments for equipment, and oversee the installation of the laboratory.

A visit from George in November cheered Ashbel, but his responsibilities in connection with the university were unrelenting. As the year drew to a close he wrote to a friend:

It is a common expectation that when life is protracted beyond the period of vigorous labor, declining years will be a period of mental & physical leisure with time for frequent reminiscence—for garrulity about former scenes and for pleasant memorandums chastened and corrected by the wiser judgment of grey hairs. Such is not my good fortune. I work harder, have fewer moments for recreation and for society than at any period of my former long life.[45]

Advice and constructive criticism from well-wishers could sometimes be almost as trying as outright attacks by enemies of the university. At times Ashbel felt besieged on all sides as he fought against "ignorance, prejudice and insidious friends."[46]

In the spring of 1884, Regent Wooten sent Ashbel some good news and some bad news about the university. The bad news was that lightning had knocked down a chimney and had done other damage to the building. The good news was that the one million additional acres voted to the university by the legislature in 1883 was at last to be so designated by the land office and that the board would be able to make use of funds obtained by leasing the land.[47] On the heels of Wooten's letter came one from another regent, Wooldridge, accusing Wooten of misinterpreting the board's intentions about leasing the lands and accusing him of wanting "to dominate everybody and everything connected with the university." Wooldridge added ominously, "this . . .

---

[43] A. P. Wooldridge to Ashbel Smith, October 10, 1883; October 13, 1883.
[44] James B. Clark to Ashbel Smith, October 17, 1883.
[45] Ashbel Smith to Fannie Darden, October 1, 1883.
[46] James H. McNeilly to Ashbel Smith, December 19, 1882.
[47] Thomas D. Wooten to Ashbel Smith, February 14, 1884.

Father of the University

will surely breed discontent and trouble."[48] This letter was soon followed by one from a faculty member, Debray, informing Ashbel that Wooldridge seemed to be acting high-handedly in the land affair and had offended the land board. Debray appealed to Ashbel to referee the differences between Wooten and Wooldridge.[49]

At their May meeting the board dealt with a number of items, including fire insurance, furniture, lightning rods, employment of a "lady assistant" to act as guardian and adviser to the women students, holiday schedules, and sewer connections.[50] In addition to the altercation between the two regents Ashbel had to deal with the resignations of two faculty members. Mallet, whose son had died in February, had definitely decided to return to the University of Virginia. Broun, who had been elected faculty chairman to replace Mallet, had also sent in his resignation. Broun was a close friend of Mallet's and perhaps was influenced by Mallet's discouragement over the university's prospects. Broun too had family problems; his wife had recently died, and his daughter was in poor health.[51] There was no scarcity of applicants for the positions, but it was laborious work to screen them carefully and choose the right men.

Furthermore, finances were not in as good shape as Ashbel had thought they were. The university was richer in land than in money. At the Texas Medical Association meeting in Belton in April, the doctors wanted to know why they had heard nothing about the establishment of the medical department of the university. Ashbel readily supplied the answer: the legislature had not appropriated funds for it.[52] He was, however, optimistic about the future of the medical school, prophesying, "This Medical Department when properly organized as it needs must be, will . . . be the leading, paramount school of Medical Instruction of the great Southwestern region of the American Union."[53]

There were some enjoyable experiences for Ashbel during the university's first year. One of the school's three literary societies was

---

[48] A. P. Wooldridge to Ashbel Smith, March 18, 1884.
[49] H. B. Debray to Ashbel Smith, March 19, 1884.
[50] Regents' Minutes, May 16–17, 1884.
[51] T. D. Wooten to Ashbel Smith, June 26, 1884; O. M. Roberts to Ashbel Smith, July 25, 1884; Humphreys, "The Genesis of the University of Texas," p. 13.
[52] Nixon, *A History of the Texas Medical Association*, pp. 110–11.
[53] Ashbel Smith to Secretary, Galveston County Medical Club, January 10, 1885.

named the Ashbel Smith Society by its women members in recognition of his strong stand on equal education for women.

On June 14, 1884, the law department held its first commencement. With flourishes Ashbel introduced the orator for the occasion: the president of Tulane University, William Preston Johnston, the son of General Albert Sidney Johnston. Professor Roberts presented the candidates for graduation to Regents President Smith, who declared the young men entitled to all the honors and rights of bachelors of law "here in Texas or elsewhere among men."[54]

Ashbel prepared his *Report as President of the Board of Regents of the University of Texas for 1884* and sent printed copies to leading businessmen and educators, as well as friends and relatives. Henry Barnard congratulated Ashbel on the progress of the university and suggested that he write a book about his experiences with educational institutions and leaders and rescue "from oblivion" pioneer leaders in American education.[55] Barnard's suggestion fell on deaf ears, as did all suggestions that Ashbel write a comprehensive history of the state. Ashbel Smith was too busy making history to record it.

At the time he received Barnard's letter, Ashbel's energies and talents as a diplomat were taken up settling quarrels between regents, between the regents and factions in the legislature, and between the faculty and the governor. Early in 1885, Regents Harwood and Wooten wrote to Ashbel sounding the alarm that there was a "scheme on foot" to take the university out of the hands of the regents and turn it over to a board of education and warning him that a bill to that effect was pending in the legislature. Governor Ireland, who approved of the bill, charged that the regents had been extravagant in handling the university's resources. Wooten believed that the governor was bent on the destruction of the present organization of the university, "probably more through ignorance of what a university ought to be than from any malicious intent." Wooten and Harwood urged Ashbel to come to Austin to lobby against the bill. Ashbel took the next train to Austin and stayed there until the bill was defeated.[56]

When the academic department of the University of Texas held its

[54] *Addresses at the Commencement Exercises of the University of Texas. Delivered June 14, 1884.*
[55] Henry Barnard to Ashbel Smith, March 16, 1885.
[56] T. D. Wooten to Ashbel Smith, January 19, 1885; February 8, 1885. T. M. Harwood to Ashbel Smith, January 15, 1885.

Father of the University

first graduation exercise and awarded the bachelor's degree to Samuel Clark Red, the lone student in the class of 1885, Ashbel Smith rejoiced. For him and his fellow regents it was truly a commencement and a promise that their years of hard work and frustration would bear fruit.[57] Former governor Roberts, perhaps the only person who knew how much of himself Ashbel Smith had given to the university, told him that he could never be repaid for his "interest, annoyance and actual labor in connection with the University of Texas."[58]

Acknowledgment of his dedicated service was to come, however. In 1886, in a special meeting of the regents immediately after Ashbel's death, the regents passed resolutions affirming that the school was the "living monument to the high and noble aims of Ashbel Smith," adding:

It may be said of him that he was insofar as the practical inauguration of the University is concerned the "Father of the University of Texas."[59]

[57] Samuel Clark Red, who became a distinguished physician, was the nephew of Ashbel Smith's old friend Dr. D. F. Stuart, of Houston, and the son of Rebecca Stuart Red, with whom Ashbel was associated in organizing Stuart Female Seminary.
[58] O. M. Roberts to Ashbel Smith, May 29, 1883.
[59] Regents' Minutes, January 29, 1886.

CHAPTER TWELVE

This World Is Not a Resting Place (1885–1886)

FOR years some of Ashbel's old friends and schoolmates at Yale, including Benjamin Silliman and E. W. Leavenworth, had cherished the idea of securing for him an honorary degree from their alma mater. Hoping to surprise Ashbel, they had privately collected letters from such influential Texans as Judge John Reagan, Judge John Hancock, and former governor Throckmorton in his behalf. They had pulled every string that might lead to the honor, including friendships and kinships with other Eli men, but the degree had not been forthcoming. Finally his two aging friends wrote to Ashbel to enlist his aid in suggesting people who might influence the awards committee and also to have him send them a sketch of his life.[1]

The idea of receiving an honorary degree from Yale pleased Ashbel immensely. One of the men with whom he corresponded about it was Oscar H. Cooper, a brilliant young Yale graduate and at the time a tutor at Yale. Ashbel had first met Cooper while serving as a legislator in Austin. Despite the almost fifty years' difference in their ages, a friendship had grown up between the two men, who shared a love of classical languages. Cooper had hoped for the Latin and Greek chair at the University of Texas. When it was awarded to Humphreys, Cooper was deeply disappointed, but he retained his warm feelings for Ashbel.

Cooper's efforts, however, were no more effective than those of Ashbel's older friends at Yale, and the degree was not awarded. Silliman and Leavenworth were exasperated and expressed their feelings in a joint letter to Ashbel: "If to be angry would do any good, . . . we

---

[1] E. W. Leavenworth to Ashbel Smith, May 1, 1884; Benjamin D. Silliman to Ashbel Smith, June 19, 1883.

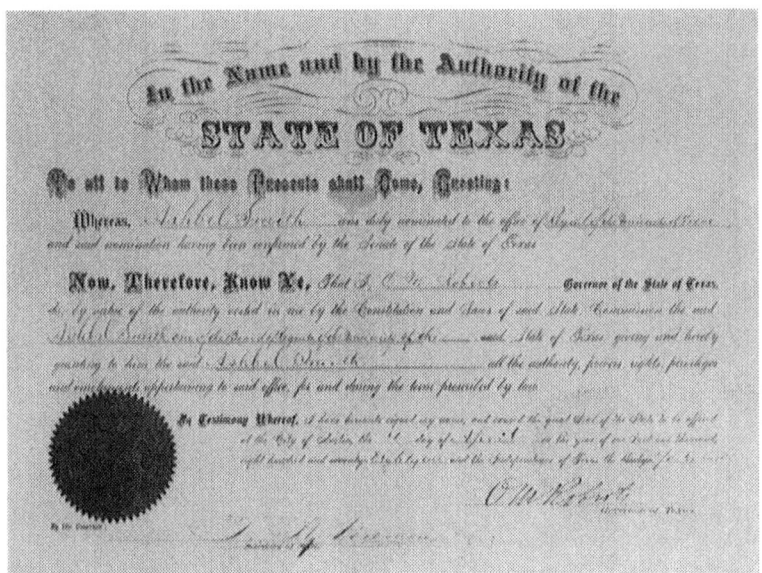

Ashbel's appointment to the Board of Regents of the University of Texas, April 4, 1881. *Courtesy Barker Texas History Center, University of Texas at Austin*

Laying the cornerstone of Old Main Building of the University of Texas, November 17, 1882. *Courtesy Barker Texas History Center, University of Texas at Austin*

West wing of Old Main on the University of Texas campus after its completion in 1883. *Courtesy Barker Texas History Center, University of Texas at Austin*

Cornerstone of the west wing of Old Main, the first building on the University of Texas campus, erected in 1882–1883. The cornerstone is now located on the portico of the present Main Building of the university in Austin.

Ashbel Smith Building ("Old Red") at the University of Texas Medical Branch, Galveston, as it appeared about 1896. *Courtesy Moody Medical Library, UTMB, Galveston*

Bust and plaque in front of the Ashbel Smith building on the campus of the University of Texas Medical Branch. *Courtesy Moody Medical Library, UTMB, Galveston*

Medallion awarded annually to the Ashbel Smith Distinguished Alumnus of the University of Texas Medical Branch, Galveston. *Courtesy George Valter Brindley, M.D., Temple, Texas*

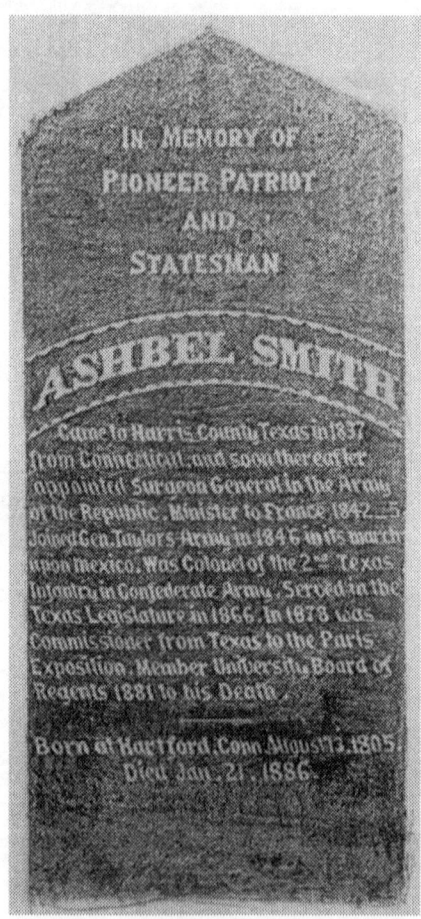

Rubbing of the gravestone of Ashbel Smith in the Texas State Cemetery, Austin.

two should be in a paroxysm of rage and almost disposed to commit matricide on Mother Yale."[2] For the remaining years of Ashbel's life his old friends faithfully but futilely tried to win the degree for him.

The biographical sketch that Ashbel sent to Yale was becomingly modest. In summation he said:

> His career had not been one of unvarying applause. He was twice burnt in effigy for his alleged opposition in 1845 to the annexation of Texas. He was subsequently burnt in effigy for his denunciation of Know-Nothingism. He had, nevertheless, had as full a share of public esteem and popularity, as in his own opinion, he merited.
>
> He has ever been a hard money Democrat and advocated a rigid maintenance of public faith, opposing repudiation in every shape. A sickly youth, a robust manhood, and a hearty age; never a teetotaler, but always strictly temperate. He has never had a family, though for 40 years keeping house. The corruptions of these latter years have not made him falter in his confidence in American representative institutions.
>
> He has ever been firm in his faith in our savior; he hopes to die in this confidence and this faith.[3]

When the Texas Medical Association held its annual meeting in Houston in April, 1885, Ashbel was unable to attend, and the members were told that the aged doctor was lying "upon his bed dangerously sick." His recovery was slow; the illness left him weak and lacking in appetite for many weeks. Dr. Wooten urged him to come to Austin to stay in his home so that he could see that Ashbel received proper medical care and nursing during his convalescence.[4] George was at Evergreen, however, and Ashbel preferred to remain at home, where he could ride about when he felt like it or just sit on his porch, watching the steamers plying back and forth between Galveston and Houston and enjoying spectacular color panoramas as the sun set beyond Hog Island. For his "solace" there was his library, which over the years filled the walls of one of the separate buildings clustered near the main house at Evergreen.

Although he had long ago given up the formal practice of medicine, Ashbel could not refuse occasional calls for his medical skill. By word of mouth from patients and their relatives he had acquired a reputation over the years of having "cured" a number of cancers by sur-

[2] Leavenworth and Silliman to Ashbel Smith, July 18, 1884.
[3] Biographical Sketches of the Class of 1824, Yale University.
[4] T. D. Wooten to Ashbel Smith, May 3, 1885.

gery, and he continued to receive requests to take patients who had, or feared they had, the dread disease. His friends and neighbors regularly sent for him to tend them or their hired help when sudden illness or an accident occurred. Often at considerable inconvenience he traveled long distances by horseback, carriage, or boat to answer such calls. He continued to care for the orphans at the Bayland Home, treating them for everything from pneumonia to a swallowed whistle. Dr. Sam Burroughs, who accompanied Ashbel to the home on one occasion, observed, "While making the necessary examination, Dr. Smith gently stroked these patients on the forehead with his hand, reassuring them of their early recovery with encouraging words."[5]

Ashbel enjoyed entertaining at Evergreen and especially delighted in visits of old friends like Maud Jeannie Fuller Young, who was a writer. She in turn enjoyed visiting him and gathering material for a "scrap-bag sort of history" she planned to write. In the evenings she and any others who happened to be visiting the plantation gathered around the blazing fire in the main house to listen to the stories of the "old sage." One story he liked to tell was of the encounters he had had with Don Manuel Godoy, "Prince of Peace," prime minister of Spain under Charles IV of Spain, and a favorite of the queen as well as the king. When Ashbel met Godoy, the aging statesman was living in exile in Paris almost as a recluse. After Ashbel won his confidence, Godoy told the young diplomat about events of his years as prime minister, and particularly about one that concerned the province of Texas (which Godoy claimed the king had given to him to be an appendage of the House of Godoy). The king had assigned to him the task of taking young women in female asylums in Spain to Texas, together with 2,000 soldiers, to become permanent settlers of the province. The soldiers were designated, and the ships were preparing to sail when Napoleon invaded Spain, and the sailing orders were canceled. In telling the story, Ashbel liked to quote Byron's reference to Godoy in *Childe Harold* and to speculate on what might have been the fate of Texas if the colonizing plan had not been interrupted by Napoleon's invasion.[6]

[5] Scrapbook belonging to Mrs. B. F. Troxell, n.d., Sterling Municipal Library, Baytown, Texas.

[6] Ashbel Smith to Maria Hudson, August 5, 1842; *Dallas Morning News*, October 29, 1933; "Texas Bestowed on Prince of Peace," in John G. James, *The Southern Student's Hand-Book of Selections for Reading and Oratory*; Ashbel Smith Journal, n.d.

This World Is Not a Resting Place 229

Ashbel had thought of making a trip north in the summer of 1885, but he abandoned the idea and stayed home to mend his fences, literally, with a "lot of barb wire." A fall that he suffered from horseback in July was greatly exaggerated in the *Houston Post*, which lamented that he was not expected to recover. Ashbel was still capable of managing his affairs. When he learned that a rancher was laying claim to some of his cattle on Hog Island, Ashbel wrote the man threatening to prosecute to the "extent of the law" the rancher or any other person "who shall kill, mark, brand or attempt to remove any of the horned cattle on or from the island."[7]

In September, Ashbel was back in Austin for the opening of the new semester of the university and to conduct meetings of the regents. Stung by a description of the university as a "high school," he admonished the professors to improve the quality of their lectures to raise them to university standards.[8] An outbreak of dengue, or breakbone, fever in Austin caused some prospective students to delay their arrival. That was probably just as well, for most of the professors came down with the disease.[9] When the epidemic abated, a total of 171 students finally enrolled for the term. One application came to the university from a Negro in Wilmington, North Carolina. He was told that the branch for "colored boys" had not yet been established and was referred to Tillotson Institute.[10]

Ashbel's scientific curiosity was as great as ever, and when he returned to Evergreen, he sent John Bowers a long list of questions about the nature and treatment of dengue fever. Ashbel told Bowers: "I am now 80—an octogenarian. I lead a life of active work, mentally. With all agriculture I have made my peace. I ride and get about well, but soon tire physically. My mind is active, its chief failure as it seems to me is of the memory."[11] Bowers wrote back answering Ashbel's questions about dengue and congratulating him on his good health. Although he still worked hard, Bowers himself felt feeble. "I am now nearly sixty-eight years old," he told Ashbel, "and am an older man

---

[7] Ashbel Smith to P. W. Hudson, March 12, 1885.
[8] T. D. Wooten to Ashbel Smith, December 18, 1885.
[9] James B. Clark to Ashbel Smith, November 17, 1885. The architect of the university building, F. E. Ruffini, died of dengue fever during this outbreak.
[10] Ibid., August 28, 1885.
[11] Ashbel Smith to John Bowers, October 4, 1885.

than you are at eighty." His letter ended: "Goodbye my dear old friend—does it not appear strange that nearly half a century has passed over us since you first took me—a poor—forlorn—homeless Texas soldier—cared for me—gave me a home and made me what I am. May God bless you for it forever."[12]

During the last few years of his life Ashbel frequently discussed religion with his friends and relatives, asking them about their spiritual beliefs and trying to express his own. Although he never accepted Darwin's ideas on the evolution of man, he studied Darwin's writings carefully and paid "profound homage to the minute accuracy of the observations and to the admirable ingenuity of the reasoning of Darwin, Huxley and others." In a letter to Benjamin Silliman, Ashbel wrote that, although he did not question the accuracy of Darwin's observations in natural history or his patient investigation or his good faith, "when he asks me to read nature by his discoveries and hypotheses he might as well ask me to explore the universe throughout boundless space by the light of a summer lightning bug."[13]

Ashbel often expressed his feeling that, when we have "compassed" all worldly knowledge, we arrive at a "boundless, incalculable horizon": ". . . the infinite lies before us—infinite space—infinite power—infinite knowledge—infinite wisdom. Infinite space is a certain entity; and it is abhorrent to reason that power, knowledge, wisdom should not be coextensive with infinite space. Nor must we lose sight of infinite time . . . . We can only walk even if tremblingly and doubtingly by Faith."[14]

Although he was a member of the Episcopal church, he did not base his ideas or beliefs on other men's doctrines but took them from the Bible, and especially from the New Testament, of which he was a lifelong scholar. When a British committee produced a revised version of the New Testament in 1881, he, along with other classical scholars in the United States, studied it and wrote criticisms of it. Some of Ashbel's criticisms—especially those of Acts—were published in the *Galveston News*.[15]

Probably the last patient that Ashbel treated was a neighbor's rela-

---

[12] John Bowers to Ashbel Smith, October 19, 1885.
[13] Ashbel Smith to Benjamin D. Silliman, May 5, 1877.
[14] Ashbel Smith, postscript to letter, n.d. (ca. Spring, 1885).
[15] Ashbel Smith to Theodore D. Woolsey, May 29, 1881.

This World Is Not a Resting Place 231

tive who was bitten by a snake during the second week in October, 1885.[16] The last visitor he entertained at Evergreen was Oscar Cooper. In 1885, when there was no opening at the University of Texas for Cooper, Ashbel had persuaded him to take the position of principal of Houston High School and had found lodgings for him in the home of his friend Judge George Goldthwaite. During the Christmas holidays Ashbel invited Cooper to visit Evergreen for several days. On their last night together the conversation ranged widely. In the midst of a discussion of Plato, Ashbel went into his library and, bringing out a copy of *The Republic*, read it in Greek, translating into English as he went with a facility that astonished his young friend, who himself was a classical scholar. Cooper was also impressed that his aged host could read the fine print in the *Galveston News* without glasses.[17]

As the new year began, Ashbel's thoughts turned back to the time of slavery, and he wrote his final thoughts about it, calling the abolition of slavery a "national sacrifice, indispensable to the unification of the whole American people." He had finally made peace with the abolitionists but realized that, before unification could be completed, "the generation of secession and Civil War and of deep seated abolition hatred must be buried in the grave North and South and a new generation grown up."[18]

His thoughts were also on his part in the Civil War, and he began making some notes concerning the Second Regiment, Texas Infantry, but he was forced to take to his bed by a return of his old pulmonary illness. Dr. Nicholas Schilling was called and diagnosed Ashbel's illness as "bronchopleurisy" with other complications, for which he prescribed quinine, morphine, whiskey, and other drugs. By January 20 there was no improvement, and word was sent to Houston that Ashbel Smith was critically ill. As soon as they received word of his condition, Oscar Cooper and Judge Goldthwaite started for Evergreen. Before they arrived, Ashbel had died. According to his doctor, "The heart stopt acting and he passed off without a struggle."[19] Anna Allen Wright

[16] William Mills to Ashbel Smith, October 10, 1885.
[17] O. H. Cooper, "Reminiscences of Colonel Ashbel Smith," *Alcalde* 9 (1921): 1075–77. Cooper later served as a part-time professor in the University of Texas.
[18] Ashbel Smith Journal, January 8, 1886.
[19] Dr. Nicholas T. Schilling Collection, Chambers County Historical Commission, Anahuac, Texas. Copy from History of Medicine Collection, University of Texas Medical Branch Library, Galveston, Texas.

took out her treasured autograph book and opened it to the first page, on which was written:

May God bless you, my dear Child, for you are as a child to me. May I beg you on all occasions and in all matters to aim to do your duty to God as he requires it, to put your trust, your whole trust in Him, the Great Father, who never abandons His children is the prayer of your affectionate

Ashbel Smith

At the top of the page she wrote: "21/Jan/1886 died Thurs one a.m. in his Bed Chamber at Evergreen, Texas."[20]

In a magnificent casket Ashbel's body lay in state in Houston's Armory Hall. Hundreds came to place evergreen wreaths around the coffin and look for the last time at the well-known face. George arrived during the night to accompany his brother's body to Austin on a special train provided by the railroad. Aboard the train, which was draped in mourning, were many of Houston's prominent citizens and a military escort. In Austin his body lay in state in the Hall of Representatives before it was taken to the State Cemetery in a procession that included the Austin Greys and other military companies; groups of civic societies; delegations from Houston and Galveston; the governor and members of the executive and state department; the University of Texas regents, faculty, and students; and hundreds of private citizens. After an elaborate eulogy by the Episcopal bishop of Texas, the Connecticut Yankee was laid to rest with all the honors his adopted state could provide, not far from the grave of Albert Sidney Johnston.

Governor Ireland, Ashbel's sometime foe in university affairs, gave the dead statesman a glowing tribute as one of Texas's "noblest and best citizens" and confessed himself perplexed about how to praise this man whose "splendid powers and . . . energies have been so divided . . . as to leave the judgment . . . in doubt as to which side to turn the scale in weighing his honorable, upright and useful life."[21]

The same dilemma faces anyone who tries to depict Ashbel Smith—the Yankee rebel, the hot-tempered diplomat, the gregarious loner, the idealistic politician, the home-loving rover, the bachelor fa-

---

[20] Autograph book of Anna Allen Wright, in possession of Anna Pearl Wright Thomas, Baytown, Texas.

[21] Newspaper clipping folder, Sterling Municipal Library, Baytown, Texas; *Galveston News*, January 31, 1886; *Clarksville Northern Standard*, January 29, 1886; *Austin Statesman*, January, 1886.

ther, the slave-owning humanitarian, the peace-loving soldier. His complex life is so inextricably woven into the history of Texas in the nineteenth century that whenever we examine any of the burning questions of the day—finance, politics, religion, transportation, immigration, agriculture, warfare, medicine, or education—we find Ashbel Smith there, analyzing, expounding, crusading, searching for the truth to open the way to a better life for himself and his fellow Texians.

BIBLIOGRAPHY

Works by Ashbel Smith

For over fifty years Ashbel Smith was an indefatigable writer and speaker. His writings were published in medical, agricultural, educational, and general magazines and newspapers in the United States and Europe. Many of his speeches were printed as separate monographs. Below is an alphabetical listing of some of his major writings.

An Account of the Yellow Fever Which Appeared in the City of Galveston, Republic of Texas, in the Autumn of 1839; with Cases and Dissections. Galveston: Cruger & Moore, 1839. 70 pp. Reprinted, with an introduction by Dr. Chauncey D. Leake, Austin: University of Texas Press, 1951.
"Address to the Citizens of Salisbury, North Carolina, on the Fourth of July, 1825." Printed in *Salisbury Western Carolinian*, July 12, 1825.
An Address Delivered in the City of Galveston on the 22d of February, 1848, the Anniversary of the Birthday of Washington, and of the Battle of Buena Vista. Galveston: News Office, W. Richardson, 1848. 17 pp.
"Address on Education." *First Semi-Annual Report of the Public Schools of Galveston*. Galveston: Printed at the News Office, 1847.
Addresses at the Commencement Exercises of the University of Texas, Delivered June 14, 1884. Austin: Warner & Co., 1884.
Addresses Delivered in the Chapel at West Point, before the Officers and Cadets of the United States Military Academy, by the Hon. Ashbel Smith, of Texas, and Col. A. W. Doniphan, of Missouri, June 16, 1848. Published by order of the First Class of the United States Corps of Cadets. New York: W. L. Burroughs, 1848. 21 pp.
Address at first commencement of Austin College. 1853.
Address to the graduates of Rutersville College. Speeches folder, Ashbel Smith papers. Mentioned in Julia Lee Sinks, "Rutersville College," *Quarterly of the Texas State Historical Association* 2 (1899).
"Address on the Laying of the Corner Stone of the University of Texas, November 17, 1882." Ashbel Smith Papers.
"Agriculture in Texas." *DeBow's Review* 18 (1855): 200–201.
"Annexation." Letter dated August 7, 1845, to *Galveston Civilian*.
"Annexation." Letter printed in "The Galveston and Camargo Railway," Me-

morial of M. R. Jefferds, of Galveston, Texas, to 45th Cong., 2d sess., H.R., November 19, 1877.

"Annexation of Cuba." Letter dated September 21, 1849, to *New York Journal of Commerce.*

"Atlanta Exposition." Letter dated November 2, 1881, to *Houston Post.*

"A Brief Description of the Climate, Soil, and Productions of Texas." App. 2 in Henry S. Foote, *Texas and the Texans.* 2 vols. Philadelphia: Thomas Cowperthwait & Co., 1841.

The Cholera Spasmodica, as Observed in Paris in 1832: Comprising Its Symptoms, Pathology, and Treatment. Illustrated by Cases. New York: Peter Hill, 1832. 80 pp.

"Common Schools." Letter dated February 7, 1874, to *Houston Age.*

"Cotton." Letter dated March 27, 1871, to *Galveston News.*

"Cuba." Letter to London *Times,* September 5, 1851.

"The Cuban Expedition." Letter dated January 20, 1850, to *Galveston News.*

"Education of the Negro." *Texas Christian Advocate,* n.d.

"Extract from the Address of Hon. Ashbel Smith to the Veterans Association, Houston, May, 1875." In D. W. C. Baker, *A Texas Scrap-Book.* New York: A. S. Barnes and Co., 1875.

"Financing Texas' Public Schools." Speech before House of Representatives, Texas Legislature, 1879.

"Grapes and Wine Making." Letter dated April 9, 1869, to *Houston Telegraph.*

"Grapes and Wine Making." Letter dated June 7, 1869, to *Galveston News.*

"Growing Sugar Cane in Texas." Letter dated September 18, 1864, to *New York Journal of Commerce.*

Hamett, John. Review of *The Substance of the Official Medical Reports upon the Epidemic Called Cholera, Which Prevailed among the poor at Dantzig (London, 1832). American Journal of the Medical Sciences* 12 (October, 1833): 447–63.

"Immigration to Texas." Letter to *Galveston News,* September 30, 1880.

"The Inaugural Exercises (September 15, 1883). Addresses by Col. Ashbel Smith, Prof. Mallet, Governor Ireland, Ex-Governor Roberts, Hon. Seth Shepard and D. G. Wooten." *Catalogue of the University of Texas for 1883–1884.* Austin: E. W. Swindells, 1884.

Inducements for the Annexation of Texas to the United States, and the Pledges Made by That Government to Texas, Fully Shown by Letters from Cols. Guy M. Bryan and Ashbel Smith. Galveston: News Steam Book and Job Printing Office, 1876. 22 pp.

"Letter from Doctor Ashbel Smith, to the Trustees of the Memphis University, Setting Forth the Practicability and the Advantages of Establishing a University of the First Class in Memphis." Memphis: *Memphis Enquirer Press,* 1849. 7 pp.

"Letter of Gail Borden, Jr., to Dr. Ashbel Smith, Setting Forth an Important Invention in the Preparation of a New Article of Food, Termed Meat Biscuit; and the Reply of Dr. Smith Thereto; Being a Letter Addressed to the American Association for the Promotion of Science, at Their Semi-Annual Meeting, to Be Held at Charleston in March Next." Galveston: Gibson & Cherry, February, 1850. 9 pp.

Letters between Ashbel Smith and George A. Smith pertaining to Henry G. Smith and Harriet Nooe Smith, 1868–1880. Privately printed, 1880.

"Letters on Constipated Colic—Vulgarly Called 'Patent-Dry-Belly-Ache.'" *New Orleans Medical and Surgical Journal* 5 (May, 1849): 713–19.

"Letters Patent between Ashbel Smith and Gail Borden. London, July 1851." Copy in Ashbel Smith Papers.

"Likelihood of Intervention of France and England in the Civil War." *Houston Daily Telegraph*, February 20, 1865; *Marshall Republican*, March 17, 1865.

"London Great Exposition." Letters dated May 1, 1851; July 25, 1851; August 29, 1851; September 5, 1851; September 16, 1851, to *New York Journal of Commerce*.

"Louisiana Rock-Salt." Letter dated January 22, 1877, to *Home and Farm*.

"Meat Biscuit." Letter dated April, 1850, to *New York Journal of Commerce*.

"Memorandum concerning the Climate of Rowan and Adjacent Counties." N.d. Ashbel Smith Papers.

"Monopoly of Gulf Coast Trade." Letter dated January 18, 1854, to *Austin Bulletin*.

"Murders on Rio Grande Border." Letter dated June 9, 1852, to *New York Journal of Commerce*.

Notice sur la géographie du Texas, sur la variété de ses productiones, de ses animaux, de ses plantes, et de ses richesses, naturelles et commerciales. Paris: Bourgogne et Martinet, 1844. 24 pp.

"The Paris International Exposition of 1878." Letter to *Texas New Yorker*, December 31, 1877.

The Permanent Identity of the Human Race; An Oration Pronounced before the Connecticut Alpha of the Phi Beta Kappa at Yale College, New Haven, August 15, 1849. New Haven: B. L. Hamlen, 1849. 32 pp.

"Railroad Connections between Galveston and East Texas." Letter dated February 24, 1871, to *Galveston News*.

"Railroad Monopolies." Paper dated July 31, 1878. Ashbel Smith Papers.

"Remarks of Senator Ford and Hon. Ashbel Smith, on the Occasion of the Presentation of General Rusk's Portrait, in the House of Representatives of Texas, April 1, 1879." Galveston: News Steam Book and Job Printing Establishment, 1879. 8 pp.

Reminiscences of the Texas Republic: Annual Address Delivered before the Historical Society of Galveston, December 15, 1875. Galveston: Published by the Society, 1876.

"Reports from Texas, Article I; On the Climate, etc. of a Portion of Texas." *Southern Medical Reports: Consisting of General and Special Reports on the Medical Topography, Meteorology, and Prevalent Diseases.* Vol. 1, edited by E. D. Fenner, M.D. New Orleans, 1850. Pp. 453–59.

"Resources of Texas." Letters dated November 20, 1876; December 20, 1876; April 16, 1877; May 18, 1877, to *Boston Ploughman.*

"Sam Houston." Biographical sketch. N.d. Ashbel Smith Papers.

"Sam Houston." Open letter concerning Houston's condition to *New Orleans True American,* January 16, 1838.

"Second Regiment Texas Volunteer Infantry." Report in Ashbel Smith Papers.

"Sheep Husbandry in Texas—in the Coast Counties." Letter to *Galveston News,* December 30, 1874.

"Slavery." Letter dated Salisbury, May 29, 1833. Published in *National Intelligencer,* June, 1833.

"Slavery." Letter to *Galveston News,* January 30, 1852.

Smith, Ashbel, Papers. Barker Texas History Center, University of Texas, Austin. This collection includes personal correspondence (1823–86); letter press books (1839–83); intermittent diary (1830–83); notes for speeches and articles on medicine, agriculture, education, slavery, transportation, alcohol, insanity, religion, politics, Indian affairs, Mexico, and other topics; medical account books; agricultural account books; stock records; diplomatic correspondence; Civil War records; and legal papers, including contracts, certificates, affidavits, commissions, and appointments.

"Snake Bite." Letter to E. H. Cushing, June 24, 1874, printed in *Houston Telegraph,* n.d.

Speech before Texas State Agricultural Society. *Transactions of the Texas State Agricultural Society: Embracing the Proceedings Connected with its Organization, the Constitution and an Address by the President.* Austin: J. W. Hampton, State Gazette Office, 1843. 24 pp.

Speech of Mr. Ashbel Smith, on the Public Debt Bill, Delivered in the House of Representatives of the State of Texas, December 11th, 1855. Austin: "State Times" Job Office, 1856.

Speech to Yale alumni, printed in *New Haven Palladium,* August 16, 1848.

"The State University." Letter dated May 21, 1882, to *Galveston News.*

"Texas Bestowed on Prince of Peace." In John G. James, ed. *The Southern Student's Hand-Book of Selections for Reading and Oratory.* New York: A. S. Barnes, 1879.

"Texas' Crops, Elections, Liquor Laws, Railroads." Letter dated August 18, 1854, to *New York Journal of Commerce.*

"Texas' First State Fair." Letter dated April 30, 1852, to *New York Journal of Commerce.*

"Texas' First State Fair." Letter dated May 13, 1852, to *New Orleans Daily Picayune.*

"Texas University." *Texas Journal of Education* 1 (March, 1881): 148–49.

"Theater in Houston." Letter dated January 28, 1882, to *Houston Post.*

"To the Legislature of the State of Texas." Letter on education. December 26, 1851.

Yellow Fever epidemic, reports on, in *Houston Star & Telegraph,* August 23, 1854; September 12, 1854; September 15, 1854.

"Yellow Fever at Houston, Texas." *Transactions of the American Medical Association*, July, 1854, pp. 530–36.
Will. Recorded Probate Minutes. Vol. M–P, p. 435, Houston, Texas. Filed February 15, 1886. Copy in Sterling Memorial Library, Baytown, Texas.

UNPUBLISHED WORKS

Ballinger, William Pitt. Diary. Typescript. Barker Texas History Center, University of Texas, Austin.
"Bayland Orphan's Home." Typescript. In the possession of Larry Jo Enderli, Baytown, Texas.
Biographical Files. Texas Collection, Barker Texas History Center, University of Texas, Austin.
Burnet, David G. David G. Burnet Papers. Rosenberg Library, Galveston, Texas.
Confederate Southern Army, Trans-Mississippi Department. Correspondence and Circulars, 1863–65. Ashbel Smith Papers. Barker Texas History Center, University of Texas, Austin.
Curlee, Abigail. "A Study of Slave Plantations, 1822 to 1865." Ph.D. dissertation, University of Texas, Austin, 1932.
Deed Records, Harris County, 1859, 1883, 1886. Houston, Texas.
Dexter Collection. Manuscript Room, Archives, Yale University Library, New Haven, Conn.
Dorrycott, Joyce M. "Ashbel Smith and the Abolitionists." Master's thesis, Southwest Texas State Teachers College, 1976.
Faculty Records, Yale College, 1817–51. Yale University Library, New Haven, Conn.
Galveston City Tax Record Books. Ashton Villa, Galveston, Texas.
Matriculation Book. Yale College, Class of 1822. Yale University Library, New Haven, Conn.
Military Records. National Archives and Records Service. General Services Administration, Washington, D.C.
Minutes of the Board of Regents of the University of Texas, November 1881, to September, 1894. Microfilm. Texas Newspaper and Non-Textual Records Collection, Barker Texas History Center, University of Texas, Austin.
Regimental Records, Second Regiment, Texas Infantry. U.S. Government Archives, Washington, D.C.
Schilling, Dr. Nicholas T. Dr. Nicholas T. Schilling Collection. Chambers County Historical Commission, Anahuac, Texas. In History of Medicine Collection, University of Texas Medical Branch Library, Galveston, Texas.
Smith, Ashbel, Papers. Barker Texas History Center, University of Texas, Austin. Personal and business letters to Ashbel Smith, records, legal papers.
Smith, Moses. Will. Recorded Book 66, p. 301. Probate Court, Hartford, Conn.

Smither, Harriet. "The Diplomatic Service of Ashbel Smith to the Republic of Texas, 1842–1845." Master's thesis, University of Texas, Austin, 1922.
Smith Genealogical Files. Prepared by Connecticut Historical Society Library, Hartford, Conn.
Stuart, Ben C. Ben C. Stuart Papers. Rosenberg Library, Galveston, Texas.
Texas Indian Papers. Texas State Archives, Austin.
Troxwell, Mrs. B. F. Scrapbook. Sterling Municipal Library, Baytown, Texas.
Worley, John Lewis. "The Diplomatic Relations of England and the Republic of Texas." Master's thesis, University of Texas, Austin, 1905.
Wright, Anna Allen. Autograph book. Family Bible. In the possession of Anna Pearl Wright Thomas, Baytown, Texas.
Yale University Student Record Books. Microfilm, Roll 1, Historical Manuscripts 69. Sterling Memorial Library, New Haven, Conn.

PUBLISHED WORKS

Adams, Ephraim Douglas, ed. *British Diplomatic Correspondence Concerning the Republic of Texas, 1838–1846*. Austin: Texas State Historical Association, 1918.
Alcott, William A. *A Historical Description of the First Public School in Hartford*. Hartford, Conn., 1832.
"Ashbel Smith." *West Texas Historical Association Year Book* 31 (1955):27.
"Ashbel Smith Sketch." *University of Texas Medical Center News*, October, 1962.
Ashcraft, Allan C. *Texas in the Civil War: A Résumé History*. Austin: Texas Civil War Centennial Commission, January, 1962.
Babour, Lucius Barnes. *Families of Early Hartford, Connecticut*. Baltimore, Md.: Genealogical Publishing Co., 1977.
Bagg, Lyman. *Four Years at Yale*. New York: Henry Holt and Co., n.d.
Bailey, Ernest Emory, ed. *Texas Historical and Biographical Record*. Austin: Texas Historical and Biographical Record, n.d.
Barker, Nancy Nichols. *The French Legation in Texas*. Vol. 1. Austin: Texas State Historical Association, 1971.
Battle, W. J. "A Concise History of the University of Texas, 1883–1950." *Southwestern Historical Quarterly* 54 (April, 1951):391–99.
Bearss, Edwin C. *Texas at Vicksburg*. Austin: Texas Civil War Centennial Commission and Texas State Historical Survey Committee, 1961.
Beazley, Julia. "Colonel Ashbel Smith." *Texas Magazine* 2 (April, 1913): 233–36.
Biographical Encyclopedia of Texas. New York: Southern Publishing Co., 1880.
Biographies of Leading Texans. 4:696–98. Austin: Texas State Library Genealogy Collection.
Blake, Clagette. *Charles Elliot, R.N., 1801–1875*. London: Cleaver-Hume Press, 1960.

Bibliography

Branda, Eldon Stephen, ed. *The Handbook of Texas: A Supplement*. Vol. 3. Austin: Texas State Historical Association, 1976.
Brawley, James S. *The Rowan Story, 1753–1953*. Salisbury, N.C.: Rowan Printing Co., 1953.
Brown, Alma Howell. "The Consular Service of the Republic of Texas." *Southwestern Historical Quarterly* 33 (January, 1930):203.
Callahan, Sister M. Generosa. "Henry Castro and James Hamilton." *Southwestern Historical Quarterly* 69 (October, 1965):179–85.
Carter, James David. *Education and Masonry in Texas to 1846*. Waco: Committee on Masonic Education and Service for the Grand Lodge of Texas, 1963.
———. *Education and Masonry in Texas, 1846 to 1861*. Waco: Committee on Masonic Education and Service for the Grand Lodge of Texas, 1964.
———. "Houston Academy." *Texas Grand Lodge Magazine*, August, 1961.
Catalogue of the Officers and Students of Yale College, 1822–1828. New Haven, Conn.: Sterling Memorial Library, Yale University.
Catalogue of the University of Texas for 1883–84. Austin: F. W. Swindells, State Printer, 1884.
Chamberlain, Hope S. *This Was Home*. Chapel Hill: University of North Carolina Press, n.d.
Clark, C. H. "The Charter Oak City." *Scribner's Monthly* 13 (November, 1876):5–11.
Clarke, Mary Whatley. *David G. Burnet: First President of Texas*. Austin: Pemberton Press, 1969.
Clopton, A. G. *An Eulogy on the Life and Character of Dr. Ashbel Smith. Delivered at the Texas State University Commencement, before the Regents, Faculty and Students. June 15, 1886*. Jefferson, Texas: Iron News Print, 1886.
Cole, Richard. "The Regent Who Bellowed Fire." *Alcalde*, April, 1965, pp. 25–28.
Commemorative Biographical Record of Hartford County. P. 814. Hartford, Conn., 1901.
Cooper, O. H. "Reminiscences of Colonel Ashbel Smith." *Alcalde* 9: 1075–77.
Cravens, John Nathan. *James Harper Starr: Financier of the Republic of Texas*. Austin: Daughters of the Republic of Texas, 1950.
Cushing, E. B. "Edward Hopkins Cushing." *Southwestern Historical Quarterly* 25 (April, 1922).
Daughters of the American Revolution Patriot Index. Washington, D.C.: National Society of the DAR, 1966.
Decrow, William Emery. *Yale and "The City of Elms."* Boston: W. E. Decrow, 1882.
Denton, Bernice B. "Count Saligny and the Franco-Texienne Bill," *Southwestern Historical Quarterly* 45 (1941).
De Shields, James T. *Border Wars of Texas*. Tioga, Texas: Matt Bradley, 1912.
———. *They Sat in High Place: The Presidents of Texas from the First Chief*

Executive, 1835–36: Presidents of the Republic, 1836–46; and Governors of the State, 1846–1939. San Antonio: Naylor Co., 1940.
Edwards, Herbert R. "Diplomatic Relations between France and the Republic of Texas, 1838–1845." *Southwestern Historical Quarterly* 20 (January, 1917): 234–40.
Farrell, Mary D., and Silverthorne, Elizabeth. *First Ladies of Texas*. Belton, Texas: Stillhouse Hollow Publishers, 1978.
"The Fight for Cuban Freedom." *Punch, or the London Charivari* 21:115.
First Annual Circular of the Medical College of Texas. Houston: Telegraph Book and Job Printing Office, 1861.
Fletcher, Herbert, ed. *Harris County Republic of Texas, 1839–45*. Houston: Anson Jones Press, 1950.
Foote, Henry Stuart. *Texas and the Texans*. 2 vols. Philadelphia: Thomas Cowperthwait & Co., 1841.
Foote, Shelby. *The Civil War, A Narrative: Fort Sumter to Perryville*. New York: Random House, 1958.
Fornell, Earl Wesley. *The Galveston Era: The Texas Crescent on the Eve of Secession*. Austin: University of Texas Press, 1961.
Franz, Joe B. *Gail Borden: Dairyman to a Nation*. Norman: University of Oklahoma Press, 1951.
Friend, Llerna. *Sam Houston: The Great Designer*. Austin: University of Texas Press, 1954.
Gambrell, Herbert. *Anson Jones: The Last President of Texas*. Austin: University of Texas Press, 1964.
Gammel, H. P. N., comp. *The Laws of Texas, 1822–1897*. 10 vols. Austin: Gammel Book Co., 1898.
Garrison, George Pierce. *Diplomatic Correspondence of the Republic of Texas: Annual Report of the American Historical Association for the Year of 1908*. Washington, D.C.: Government Printing Office, 1911.
Geiser, Samuel Wood. *Men of Science in Texas, 1820–1880*. Dallas: Southern Methodist University Press, 1958–1959.
Greer, J. K. "Committee on the Texan Declaration of Independence." *Southwestern Historical Quarterly* 31 (October, 1927): 140–47.
Hale Collection of Connecticut Headstones. Hartford, Conn.: Zion Hill Cemetery, n.d.
Hall, William H. *West Hartford*. Hartford, Conn., 1930.
Hall of Remembrance: The Heroes and Heroines of Texas Education, the 1954 Selections. Austin: Texas Heritage Foundation, October 13, 1954.
Harris, Dilue. "Reminiscences of Mrs. Dilue Harris." *Quarterly of the Texas State Historical Association* 7 (1903–1904).
Hatch, Orin Walker. "Lyceum to Library: A Chapter in the Cultural History of Houston." *Texas Gulf Coast Historical Association* 9 (September, 1965).
Hayes, Charles W. *History of the Island and the City of Galveston*. Austin: Jenkins Garrett Press, 1974.
Henderson, Harry McCorry. *Texas in the Confederacy*. San Antonio: Naylor Co., 1955.

Bibliography 243

Henry, Robert Selph. *The Story of the Mexican War.* New York: Frederick Ungar Publishing Co., n.d.

Historical Register of Yale University, 1701–1937. New Haven, Conn.: Yale University Press, 1939.

Hoehling, A. A., et al. *Vicksburg—47 Days of Siege.* Englewood Cliffs, N.J.: Prentice-Hall, 1969.

Hogan, William Ransom. *The Republic of Texas: A Social and Economic History.* Norman: University of Oklahoma Press, 1946.

Holbrook, Abigail Curlee. "A Glimpse of Life on Antebellum Slave Plantations." *Southwestern Historical Quarterly* 76 (April, 1973): 361–83.

Hoover, Herbert T. "Ashbel Smith on Currency and Finance in the Republic of Texas." *Southwestern Historical Quarterly* 71 (January, 1968): 419–24.

Houston, Sam. *The Writings of Sam Houston, 1813–1863.* Edited by Amelia W. Williams and Eugene C. Barker. 8 vols. Austin: University of Texas Press, 1940.

Houstoun, Mrs. Matilda Charlotte. *Texas and the Gulf of Mexico, or Yachting in the New World.* Philadelphia: G. B. Zriber, 1845.

Humphreys, Milton W. "The Genesis of the University of Texas." *Alcalde* 1 (1912).

James, John G. "Texas Bestowed on Prince of Peace." In *Southern Student's Hand-Book of Selections for Reading and Oratory.* New York: A. S. Barnes, 1879.

James, Marquis. *The Raven: A Biography of Sam Houston.* Indianapolis: Bobbs-Merrill Co., 1929.

Johnson, Allen, and Malone, Dumas, eds. *Dictionary of American Biography.* 22 vols. New York: Charles Scribner's Sons, 1928–38.

Johnson, Sid S., comp. *Texans Who Wore the Gray.* Tyler, Texas: Privately printed, 1907.

Johnston, William Preston. *The Life of General Albert Sidney Johnston.* New York: D. Appleton and Co., 1878.

Jones, Anson. *Memoranda and Official Correspondence Relating to the Republic of Texas, Its History and Annexation.* New York: D. Appleton and Co., 1859.

Journal of the House of Representatives of the State of Texas, Sixth Legislature. Austin: Marshall and Oldham, State Printers, 1855.

Journal of the House of Representatives of the State of Texas, Eleventh Legislature. Austin: Office of the State Gazette, 1866.

Journal of the House of Representatives of the State of Texas, Sixteenth Legislature. First Session, January, 1879. Galveston: A. H. Belo & Co., State Printers, 1879.

Journal of the House of Representatives of the State of Texas. Sixteenth Legislature. Extra Session, June 10, 1879. Galveston: News Book and Job Establishment, 1879.

Kittrell, Norman Goree. *Governors Who Have Been and Other Public Men of Texas.* Houston: Dealy-Adey-Elgin Co., 1921.

Lamar, Mirabeau Buonaparte. *The Papers of Mirabeau Buonaparte Lamar.*

BIBLIOGRAPHY

Edited by Charles A. Gulick, et al. 6 vols. Austin: Pemberton Press, 1968.
Lathrop, G. P. "A Model State Capitol." *Harper's New Monthly Magazine* 71 (October, 1885): 715–19.
Laurent, Pierre Henri. "Belgium's Relations with Texas and the United States." *Southwestern Historical Quarterly* 68 (October, 1964): 233–36.
Leake, Chauncey D. "Ashbel Smith, M.D., 1805–1886: Pioneer Educator in Texas." *Yale Journal of Biology and Medicine* 20 (January, 1949): 225–32.
"Legislative Proceedings, Sixth Legislature." *State Gazette Appendix*, December 13, 1855. Austin: Marshall & Oldham, 1855.
Looscan, Adele B. "Harris County, 1822–1845." *Southwestern Historical Quarterly* 18 (January, 1915): 261–86; 19 (July, 1915): 37–64.
Love, William. *Colonial History of Hartford*. N.p., n.d.
Lubbock, Francis R. *Six Decades in Texas*. Austin: Ben C. Jones & Co., 1900.
Lynch, James D. "Life and Character of Dr. Ashbel Smith." *Daniel's Medical Journal* 1 (April, 1886): 441–55.
McComb, David G. *Houston: The Bayou City*. Austin: University of Texas Press, 1969.
McDonough, James Lee. *Shiloh*. Knoxville: University of Tennessee Press, 1977.
M'Neilly, James H. "Colonel Ashbel Smith of Texas." *Confederate Veteran* 27 (December, 1919): 463–65.
Maher, Edward R., Jr. "Sam Houston and Secession," *Southwestern Historical Quarterly* 55 (April, 1952): 448–58.
Mallet, John William. "Reminiscences of the First Year of the University of Texas." *Alcalde*, April, 1913, pp. 14–17.
Memorial Address and Proceedings of the Memphis Bar and Law Library Assn. on the Death of Hon. Henry Grattan Smith, Late President of the Association. Memphis: Rogers & Co., Printers, 1879.
Merk, Frederick. *Slavery and the Annexation of Texas*. New York: Alfred A. Knopf, 1972.
Middleton, Anne. "Donelson's Mission in Behalf of Annexation." *Southwestern Historical Quarterly* 24 (April, 1921): 266–69.
Muir, Andrew Forest, ed. *Texas in 1837: An Anonymous, Contemporary Narrative*. Austin: University of Texas Press, n.d.
Nixon, Pat Ireland. *A History of the Texas Medical Association, 1853–1953*. Austin: University of Texas Press, 1953.
———. *The Medical Story of Early Texas, 1528–1853*. San Antonio: Mollie Bennett Lupe Memorial Fund, 1946.
Obituary Records of Graduates of Yale University Deceased from June 1880 to June 1890. New Haven, Conn.: Tuttle, Marchause & Taylor, 1890.
Order of Exercises at Commencement, Yale College, September 8, 1824. New Haven, Conn.: Printed at the Journal Office, 1824.
Overbeck, Ruth Ann. "Alexander Penn Wooldridge." *Southwestern Historical Quarterly* 67 (January, 1964): 341.
Pease, Lucadia. *Lucadia Pease and the Governor: Letters, 1850–1857*. Edited by Katherine Hart and Elizabeth Kemp. Austin: Encino Press, 1974.

Phi Beta Kappa Directory, 1776–1941. New York, n.d. Copy in Yale University Library, New Haven, Conn.
Pierce, Gerald S. *Texas under Arms: The Camps, Posts, Forts, and Military Towns of the Republic of Texas, 1836–1846.* Austin: Encino Press, 1969.
Pioneer Sketches, Cedar Bayou to San Jacinto. Goose Creek, Texas: Robert E. Lee Library Club, Goose Creek Independent School District, 1931.
Potter, Rockwell, Harmon. *Hartford's First Church.* Hartford, Conn., 1932.
Proceedings of the Democratic State Convention. Austin, January, 1856.
Proceedings of the Texas State Medical Association, June, 1870. Galveston: "News" Office, 1870.
"Proceedings of the Texas State Medical Association." *Texas Medical and Surgical Record,* June, 1881.
Proctor, Ben H. *Not without Honor: The Life of John H. Reagan.* Austin: University of Texas Press, 1962.
The Public Statute Laws of the State of Connecticut, as Revised and Enacted by the General Assembly in May, 1821. Hartford, Conn.: Published by H. Huntington, Jr., Benjamin H. Norton, printer, 1824.
Purcell, Mabelle; Purcell, Stuart; et al. *This Is Texas.* Austin: Futura Press, 1977.
Ramsdell, Charles W. "Presidential Reconstruction in Texas." *Quarterly of the Texas State Historical Association* 12 (January, 1909): 209–24.
———. "Texas from Fall of Confederacy to Reconstruction." *Quarterly of the Texas State Historical Association* 11 (January, 1908): 208ff.
Record of the Class of 1824 in Yale College, Compiled from Authentic Documents, and Published for the Benefit of the Members. New Haven, Conn.: Yale University Press, 1875.
Red, Mrs. George Plunkett. *The Medicine Man in Texas.* Houston: Standard Printing & Lithographing Co., 1930.
Red, Samuel Clark. *Biographical Sketch of Ashbel Smith, M.D.* Houston: Standard Printing & Lithographing Co., 1929.
Report of the Chief Engineer to the Secretary of War at the Opening of the Second Secession of the Thirtieth Congress. Washington, D.C.: Wendell & Von Benthaysen, 1848–49. (Contains Report of Board of Visitors of West Point Academy for 1848.)
Richardson, Rupert N., et al. *Texas, the Lone Star State.* Englewood Cliffs, N.J.: Prentice-Hall, 1970.
Roberts, O. M. "A History of the Establishment of the University of the State of Texas." *Quarterly of the Texas State Historical Association* 1 (April, 1898): 233–65.
Roemer, Dr. Ferdinand. *Texas.* Translated from the German by Oswald Mueller. San Antonio: Standard Printing Co., 1935.
Rumple, Jethro. *A History of Rowan County, North Carolina.* Salisbury, N.C.: J. J. Bruner, 1881. Republished by Elizabeth Maxwell Steele Chapter, Daughters of the American Revolution, Salisbury, N.C., n.d.
Sandbo, Anna Irene. "Beginnings of Secession Movement in Texas." *Southwestern Historical Quarterly* 18 (July, 1914): 44–46.

Shearer, Ernest C. "The Carvajal Disturbances." *Southwestern Historical Quarterly* 55 (October, 1951): 223ff.
Sibley, Marilyn McAdams. *Travelers in Texas, 1761–1860*. Austin: University of Texas Press, 1967.
Siegel, Stanley. "Ashbel Smith and the Mexican Steamers." *East Texas Historical Journal* 4 (March, 1966): 16–22.
———. *The Poet President of Texas*. Austin: Jenkins, 1977.
Sinks, Julia Lee. "Rutersville College." *Quarterly of the Texas State Historical Association* 2 (October, 1898): 124–33.
Sketches of Yale College. New York: Saxton & Miles, 1843.
Smither, Harriet. "English Abolitionism and the Annexation of Texas." *Southwestern Historical Quarterly* 32 (January, 1929): 193–205.
———, ed. *Journals of the Sixth Congress of the Republic of Texas, 1841–1842*. Austin: Von Boeckmann-Jones Co., 1940.
Spence, Mary Lee. "British Impressions of Texas and the Texans." *Southwestern Historical Quarterly* 70 (October, 1966): 171–83.
State Gazette Appendix, Containing Official Reports of Debates and Proceedings of the Sixth Legislature of the State of Texas. Austin: Marshall and Oldham, State Printers, 1856.
Stern, M. B. "Stephen Pearl Andrews." *Southwestern Historical Quarterly* 67 (April, 1964): 510–15.
Thrall, Homer S. *A Pictorial History of Texas*. St. Louis: N. D. Thompson & Co., 1879.
Transactions of the Texas State Medical Association. Sixth Annual Session, 1874. Houston: Telegraph Steam Book and Job Print., 1874.
Transactions of the Texas State Medical Association. Seventeenth Annual Session. Austin, 1885.
Turner, Martha Anne. *Richard Bennett Hubbard: An American Life*. Austin: Shoal Creek Publishers, 1979.
U.S. Bureau of the Census. *Census for Hartford, Connecticut*. Third Census, 1810. Fourth Census, 1820. Seventh Census, 1850.
The University of Texas Medical Branch at Galveston: A Seventy-five Year History by the Faculty and Staff. Austin: University of Texas Press, 1967.
Vandiver, Frank E. "John William Mallet and the University of Texas." *Southwestern Historical Quarterly* 53 (April, 1950): 422–42.
Vedder, O. F. "The Medical Profession." In *History of the City of Memphis and Shelby County, Tennessee*. Syracuse, N.Y.: D. Mason & Co., 1888.
Walker, George Leon. *History of the First Church in Hartford*. Hartford, Conn.: Brown & Gross, 1884.
Walker, Peter F. *Vicksburg: A People at War, 1860–1865*. Chapel Hill: University of North Carolina Press, 1960.
Ward, Hortense Warner. "The First State Fair of Texas." *Southwestern Historical Quarterly* 57 (October, 1953): 163–74.
The War of the Rebellion: Official Records of the Union and Confederate Armies. 128 vols. Washington, D.C.: U.S. Government Printing Office, 1880–1901.

Waugh, Julia Nott. *Castro-Ville and Henry Castro Empresario*. San Antonio: Standard Printing Co., 1934.
Webb, Walter Prescott, and Carroll, H. Bailey, eds. *The Handbook of Texas*. 2 vols. Austin: Texas State Historical Association, 1952.
Weems, John Edward. *To Conquer a Peace*. Garden City, N.Y.: Doubleday & Co., 1974.
Wheeler, John H. *Reminiscences and Memoirs of North Carolina and Eminent North Carolinians*. Baltimore: Genealogical Publishing Co., 1966.
Winfrey, Dorman H., and Day, James M., eds. *The Indian Papers of Texas and the Southwest, 1825–1916*. Austin: Pemberton Press, 1966.
Winkler, E. W., ed. *Manuscript Letters and Documents of Early Texians 1821–1845*. Austin: Steck Co., 1937.
———. *Secret Journals of the Senate, Republic of Texas, 1836–1845*. Austin: Austin Printing Co., 1911.
Wisehart, M. K. *Sam Houston, American Giant*. Washington, D.C.: Robert B. Luce, 1962.
Wooster, Ralph A. "Wealthy Texans, 1860." *Southwestern Historical Quarterly* 71 (October, 1967): 176–77.
Wooten, Dudley G., ed. *A Comprehensive History of Texas, 1685 to 1897*. 2 vols. Dallas: Wm. G. Scarff, 1898.
Ziegler, Jesse A. *Wave of the Gulf*. San Antonio: Naylor Co., 1938.

NEWSPAPERS

Austin Daily State Gazette, October 23, 1867; August 13, 1876.
Austin Daily Statesman, June 28, 1872; April 30, 1881.
Austin Weekly Democratic Statesman, November 23, 1882.
Baltimore Sun, June 1, 1852.
Baytown Sun (Baytown, Texas), August 13, 1936.
Clarksville Northern Standard (Clarksville, Texas), January 29, 1886.
Connecticut Post, 1883–85.
Daily Texan (University of Texas, Austin), March 11, 1928.
Dallas Herald, April 11, 1874.
Dallas Morning News, October 31, 1930; April 11, 1942; October 29, 1943; December 29, 1944.
Galveston Civilian and Gazette, May 3, 1845; December 10, 1845; February 14, 1846.
Galveston News, April 22, 1845; May 18, 1847; October 4, 1852; December 2, 1862; July 7, 1865; December 28, 1867; December 30, 1874; January 25, 1876; August 6, 1876; November 22, 1877; September 15, 1878; March 3, 1880; March 4, 1880; April 8, 1880; April 9, 1880; July 30, 1880; September 30, 1880; October 1, 1880; March 17, 1881; March 22, 1881; April 7, 1881; April 15, 1881; August 14, 1881; July 13, 1883; September 8, 1883; January 22, 1886; February 8, 1886; November 1, 1962; December 2, 1962; November 1, 1964.
Galveston Tribune, June 8, 1949; June 10, 1949.

Hartford Courant, February 20, 1769; October 23, 1769; March 31, 1770; April 23, 1770; October 30, 1770; November 20, 1770; April 30, 1771; October 14, 1772; April 6, 1773; July 24, 1775; September 4, 1775; October 16, 1775; April 18, 1776; January 6, 1777; March 10, 1777; October 14, 1777; November 3, 1778; February 16, 1779; January 12, 1803.

Houston Age, August 14, 1876.

Houston Chronicle, January 25, 1914; January 9, 1921.

Houston Morning Star, 1839; 1840; May 6, 1845.

Houston Post, January 30, 1955; January 29, 1967.

Houston Press, March 2, 1928.

Houston Telegram, May 25, 1878.

Houston Telegraph, February 4, 1857; February 27, 1857; December 6, 1858; December 8, 1858; January 3, 1859; April 15, 1859; April 9, 1862; July 30, 1870; February 3, 1871; June 24, 1874.

Houston Telegraph and Texas Register, January 14, 1838.

Lincoln Journal (Lincolnton, N.C.), November 24, 1898.

Memphis Daily Avalanche, January 1, 1879; January 12, 1879.

New Orleans Commercial Bulletin, April 17, 1845.

New Orleans True American, January 16, 1838.

New York Daily Telegraph, April 18, 1868.

New York Daily Times, June 8, 1854.

New York Herald, November 5, 1848.

Salisbury Carolina Watchman (Salisbury, N.C.), January 28, 1886.

Salisbury Post (Salisbury, N.C.), April 1, 1962; April 15, 1962; April 22, 1962; April 29, 1962; May 6, 1962; March 5, 1967; April 16, 1967; May 28, 1967; September 3, 1967; September 20, 1967; October 29, 1967; November 5, 1967; November 19, 1967; December 10, 1967; December 17, 1967; August 28, 1977; September 4, 1977; September 11, 1977.

Salisbury Western Carolinian (Salisbury, N.C.), July 12, 1825; August 5, 1828; June 25, 1832; March 7, 1835; February 2, 1838; March 11, 1842.

Index

Aberdeen, Lord, 77, 86, 191; and abolition, 87, 93; and annexation, 101; and "Diplomatic Act," 93; and James Hamilton, 74–75; and Mexican steamers, 75–76, 79; on Texas, 95; and triple mediation, 81; warns Mexico, 97
abolitionism, 134, 136, 231; English attitude toward, 87, 93; and Cuba, 125–126; Smith on, 29
Account of Yellow Fever . . . (Ashbel Smith), 61–62
Adams, Abel, 3
Adams, Daniel, 3
Adams, Joseph, 3
Adams, Matthew, 3
Adams, Phoebe, 3. *See also* Smith, Phoebe Adams
Agricultural, Mechanical, and Blood Stock Association of Houston, 179, 180
Agricultural and Mechanical College for Colored Youths, 194
agricultural implements, 177, 190, 194, 198–199
Allen, Anna. *See* Wright, Anna Allen
Allen, Augustus C., 38, 45, 64
Allen, Ebenezer, 95, 138, 141–142
Allen, John K., 38
Alta Vista Agricultural College, 195
America, 124
American Academy of Arts and Sciences, 217
American Association for the Advancement of Science, 120
American Chemical Society, 217
American Industrial Agency, 173
American Journal of Science, 8

American Journal of the Medical Sciences, 25
American Medical Association, 114, 115, 130, 212
American Party. *See* Know-Nothing Party
Andrew Female College, 133
Andrews, J. P., 87
annexation, 45, 48, 71, 88, 96, 108, 141, 191; Act of, 103; "Diplomatic Act" and, 93; *Galveston News* on, 199–200; preliminaries to, 97–103; Smith on, 35; treaty of (1844), 92; Texas Congress and, 90
antislavery party, 75
Anti-Slavery Society, British and Foreign, 76
Antona, 168
Appleton and Co., D., 142, 177
Arabian John (horse), 111
Arcadia, 95
Archer, Branch, 53
Aristides, 39
Arrangoiz, J. de, 97
Ashbelites, 4
Ashbel Smith Literary Society, 224
Atkinson, Edward, 196
Austin, Stephen F., 36
Austin (Tex.), 63, 210, 214
Austin Daily State Gazette, 193
Avery, B. F., 190
Avery, Lydia, 17, 64
Avery Island, 195

Baker, Moseley, 58, 59, 64, 112, 117
Baldwin Ferry Road (Vicksburg), 154
Ballinger, William P., 168, 169, 173

INDEX

Baltic, 122
barbed wire, 190, 229
Barbey, Theodore, 78
Barnard, George, 49 and n
Barnard, Henry, 16, 29, 46, 52, 59, 105, 127, 137, 186, 224; advice of, 32; investments of, in Texas, 49; and *Journal of Education*, 138, 144, 212; marriage of, 113; and Smith, 12, 48, 177; and Smith's parents, 138; and University of Texas, 212; visits Salisury, 27–28
Barrington, 141
Bates, Joseph, 162
Bayland Guards, 147, 148, 149
Bayland Orphans' Home for Children of Confederate Soldiers, 173, 183, 184, 204, 228
Beard, John, 28
Beauregard, P. G. T., 173
Bee, Barnard E., 41, 43, 51–52, 58, 63, 76
Bee, H. P., 162 and n
Belgium, 80, 85
Bell, Peter H., 122
Berkelian Premium, 8, 9
Bexar (Tex.), 43
Bible Society, 54
Birdsall, John, 45
Bismarck, Otto von, 199
Blackstone's Commentaries, 10
board of education, 137
board of examiners. *See* medical censors
Board of School Directors for Harris County, 185
Borden, Gail: as customs collector, 44, 49–50; and meat biscuit, 120–123, 125, 126, 128–129, 133
Boston Ploughman, 195, 196
Bowditch, Nathaniel, 31
Bowers, John H., 40 and n, 46, 73, 94, 99, 151–152, 229–230
Bowie, James, 106
Bragg, Braxton, 173
Brazos Bayou (Tex.), 58
Brazos River, 57
Brenham (Tex.), 172
brick making, 189
Bringhurst, W. L., 216
Broun, Leroy, 220, 223
Brower, John H., 121, 122

Brownsville (Tex.), 161
Brushy Creek, 57
Bryan, Guy M., 191
Buchanan, James, 128
Buckingham Palace, 86
Buckner, Simon Bolivar, 173
Buffalo Bayou (Houston), 38
Buffalo Bull, 50
Bulkley, George, 49, 50
Bunker Hill, 18
Burford, Nat, 171
Burnet, David G., 45, 165, 191; death of, 179; in 1841 election, 69; in 1839 election, 63; nomination of, as U.S. senator, 171
Burroughs, Sam, 228
Byron, Lord: poetry of, 7, 228

Caldwell, D. F., 34
Calhoun, John C., 48, 76, 92, 96, 119
calomel, 9, 62, 129
Camp Slaughter (Tex.), 161
cancer, 26, 227
Caney Creek (Tex.), 162
Carbajal, José María Jesús, 127
Carlisle, Anthony, 27
Carlota, 85
carpetbaggers, 175, 181, 184
Cass, Lewis, 115, 116, 128
Castro, Henry de, 73, 78, 80
Catholicism, 89, 139
Cedar Bayou, 189
Cedar Point, 69, 145, 146, 161
Central Pacific Railroad, 192
Chalmers, John G., 69–70
Chamber of Deputies, 22
Champion Hill (Miss.), 154, 156
Charles X, 21
Cherokee Phoenix, 27
Chickasaw Bayou, 153, 154, 157
Childe Harold (Byron), 228
Childress, George C., 70–71
Chillicothe, 153
Chiswick Gardens, 87
Choate, Rufus, 118
cholera, 23, 24, 26, 117, 129
Cholera Spasmodica (Ashbel Smith), 24, 25
Christ Church (Houston), 208
Christina (friend), 138–139, 142

Index

Circle Aquiole, 83
City of Berlin, 199
City of Redmond, 198
Civil War, 147–169, 209, 231
Clark, James, 222
Coke, Richard, 185, 194
Colt, Samuel, 124
Colt revolver, 124
Columbia (Tex.), 37, 38
Columbia, 47
Confederate Army, 144, 148, 160
Confessions (Rousseau), 88
constitutional convention (1875), 190
Cook, A. H., 220
Cooper, Fanny, 23
Cooper, James Fenimore, 21, 22, 23, 25, 31, 37, 48
Cooper, Oscar H., 226, 231 and n
Cooper, Susan, 24, 30, 31
Copes, James W., 46, 49
Corinth (Miss.), 149, 152
Corpus Christi (Tex.), 152
Cossitt, Rosene, 3
cotton, 57–58, 131, 138, 164, 180, 189, 194, 196, 198, 213–214
Cotton (London), 195
Cotton Exposition (1881), 213
cotton worm (boll weevil), 131, 140, 180, 182, 196
Cox, James, 143
Crimean War, 133
Crockett, Davy, 106
Crystal Palace (London), 122, 123
Cuba, 86, 125–126
Cuevas, Luis G., 99
Cupples, George, 130
Cushing, Edward, 189, 197
Cushing, Edward H., 139, 188, 189, 197, 198, 199, 201
Cushing, Matilda, 189, 198, 201–202, 204–205, 206
Cushman, Charlotte, 101
Cuvier, Georges, 20
Cyclopedia of Practical Medicine and Surgery, 25

Daingerfield, William Henry, 87
Darwinism, 119, 217, 230
Davis, E. J., 180, 185
Davis, Jefferson, 172

Day, Jeremiah, 9, 12, 19
Debray, H. B., 223
De Kalb, 153
Democratic Party, 63, 116, 145, 175, 227; national conventions, (1848) 115, (1852) 128, (1868) 176–177, (1872) 181, (1876) 192; state conventions, (1856) 136, (1857) 139, (1860) 147, (1872) 181, (1880) 203
dengue fever, 229
Devine, T. J., 214
Dickens, Charles, 87
Diplomatic Act, 93
Donelson, Andrew Jackson, 98
Dowell, Greensville S., 187
Duchess of Kent, 83
dueling, 41
Duke of Orleans, 77
Dupuytre, Baron Guillaume, 19, 20

East India Company, 111
École de Droit (Paris), 28
École de Medicine (Paris), 20
Edwards, A. N., 214
"Education of the Negro" (Ashbel Smith), 194
Elliot, Charles, 98, 99
Élysée (Paris), 125
Enfield rifles, 158, 167
Episcopal church, 29, 89, 230, 232
Epsom Downs, 101
Europe, Smith in: 19–25; as chargé d'affaires, 73–95; at London exhibition, 122–126; as medical student, 19–25; at Paris exhibition, 198–199; as secretary of state, 99–101
Everett, Edward, 74
Evergreen (Smith plantation), 126, 140, 170, 184, 189, 199, 205, 229, 232; crops at, 132–133, 138, 189, 198; description of, 174–175; purchase of, 112–113, 118, 126; visitors to, 189, 228, 231
Everitt, Stephen H., 54, 55
evolution, 119, 217, 230

Fairfield Daily Statesman, 181
Fannin, James, 106
Farmington, Battle of, 151
Farragut, David G., 164
fencing regulations, 190, 196

Fenner, E. D., 121
finances, Texas: Smith on, 207
Finlay, George, 206–207
First State Fair of Texas, 127, 128
First Texas Infantry, 148
Fisher, Charles, 10–11, 13, 28, 58, 63
Fletcher, Herbert, 142 n
Foote, Henry Stuart, 67, 68, 83, 200
foreign loan policy, 65
Forshey, C. G., 166
Fort Ashbel Smith, 163
Fort Pemberton, 152
Fort Sumter, 147
Fourteenth Amendment, 171, 172, 174
Fourth of July, 18, 24, 106
Freedman's Bureau, 172
free soil issue, 116
French Agricultural Society, 125
French fleet, 58, 65
French royal family, 82, 90
Friends of Education, convention of, 105

Galveston, 37, 43, 58, 65, 116, 191; defense of, in Civil War, 163–168; and hurricane danger, 192, 211; Union capture of, 152; University of Texas medical branch at, 208–211, 214; yellow fever epidemic in, 60–62
Galveston Bay, 64, 97, 129, 163
Galveston City Hospital, 187
Galveston Civilian, 102, 199–200
Galveston Cotton Exchange, 213
Galveston Historical Society, 190, 191
Galveston Medical College. *See* Texas Medical College and Hospital
Galveston News: attacks Smith, 100, 199–200; publishes Smith's articles, 111, 180, 207, 230, 231; supports Smith, 130, 166, 191
Garfield, James A., 203
Garibaldi, Archbishop Giuseppe, 91
Gentleman of the Old School, The, 59
geologist, state, 136
Gibson, Dr. (acquaintance), 121
Gibson, Randall Lee, 173
Gillette, Henry F., 94, 143, 173, 183, 198, 199
Goat Island, 118. *See also* Hog Island
Godoy, Don Manuel, 228
Goldthwaite, George, 231

Goodrich, Chauncey, 41, 42
Gould, Robert S., 221
Granger, Gordon, 169
Grant, Ulysses S., 153, 155, 158, 181
"Granticism," 181
grapes: in Texas, 177–178
Great Exhibition (London), 122–125
Great International Exhibition (Philadelphia), 192–194
Greek Slave, The, 124
Greeley, Horace, 124, 181
greenbacks, 199, 202, 207
Gregory XVI (pope), 91
Greys, Austin, 218, 232
Guadalupe, 75, 79
Guizot, François, 78, 81

Hamilton, James, 63, 74, 79
Hampton, Joseph W., 28
Hampton, Wade, 178
Hancock, John, 171
Hancock, W. S., 203
Hardee, William Joseph, 149
Harris, Dilue Rose, 58
Harris, Eva, 153
Harris, Ira A., 58
Harrisburg, 38
Hartford Continental Guards, 4
Hartford Courant, 4
Hartford Grammar School, 6
Hartford Retreat for the Insane, 11, 13, 30, 32
Harwood, T. M., 214, 224
Hawes, James M., 163, 164
Hayes, Rutherford B., 197–198
Hays, Isaac, 25
Headquarters (Smith home), 66, 68, 70, 73, 94, 107, 109; crops at, 66, 97; description of, 104; sale of, 141
Hemphill, John, 111
Henderson, Archibald, 12
Henderson, Frances Cox, 65, 143
Henderson, James Pinckney, 92, 102, 104, 106, 139–140, 191; death of, 142–143; and Smith, 34–37, 64, 65, 66; as U.S. senator, 141
Hermitage (Nashville), 47, 67
History of the Republic of Texas, The, 84
Hobby's Regiment, 162
Hogg, Alex, 220

Index

Hog Island, 118, 227, 229
Holland, 85–86
Hollingsworth, O. N., 186
Home and Farm, 195
Hood, John Bell, 148, 173
Hôpital des Invalides (Paris), 20
Hornet's Nest (Shiloh), 150
horse racing, 38, 53
Hôtel Dieu (Paris), 20
Houses of Parliament (London), 86–87
Houston, Margaret Lea, 38, 65, 66, 67, 111, 161
Houston, Sam, 36, 45, 46, 50, 51, 76–77, 79, 81, 87, 121, 141, 191; and annexation, 98; creates Knights of San Jacinto, 88; death of, 161; described by Smith, 38–39, 47, 53–54; drinking habits of, 39, 63, 65, 107; engagement of, 64, 65; and governors' campaigns, 139, 145; and Kansas-Nebraska Bill, 135, 136; and Know-Nothing Party, 135; as president of Texas, 71, 72, 93; and secession, 147; and Smith, 40, 48, 110, 111, 118, 140, 146, 152; in Texas presidential election of 1841, 69, 70; and U.S. presidential campaigns, 69, 107–108, 115; as U.S. senator, 105, 128, 135, 136
Houston, Sam, Jr., 147, 150–151, 161
Houston, William, 67
Houston (Tex.), 37, 38, 44–45, 53, 60
Houston Academy, 143–144, 174
Houston Age, 192
Houston and Great Northern Railway Co., 184
Houston Chamber of Commerce, 172
Houston Dramatic Association, 173
Houston Lyceum, 133
Houston Morning Star, 64–65
Houston Post, 213, 214, 229
Houston Scientific Institute, 173
Houston Star and Telegraph, 132
Houston Telegraph, 165–166, 188–189, 200
Houstoun, Matilda, 84, 104
Hubbard, Richard B., 197, 214
Hudson, Maria, 68–69, 82, 85, 97, 103, 142
Hudson, Radcliffe, 49, 57, 72, 216
Huie, Antoinette, 12, 16, 28, 36, 37, 43;

marriage of, 82; and Smith, 17, 30, 31, 33, 47, 73
Huie, Warren, 12
Hull, Edmund, 197, 198, 213
Hull, Jessie Kittredge, 108, 197, 213
Humboldt, Baron Alexander von, 91, 95
Humphreys, M. W., 219, 226
Hunt, Memucan, 34, 35, 48, 63, 98
Huntington, Collis P., 192
Hutchins House (Houston), 178, 206
Huxley, Thomas, 119
Hyde Park (London), 101
hypodermic syringes, 192

immigration, 50, 72, 77, 80, 83, 84, 116, 193, 197, 207
Indians, 27, 50–51, 57, 71, 89, 170, 180
infectious diseases, 196–197
International and Great Northern Railroad Co., 202
Ireland, John, 221, 224, 232
Irion, Robert A., 45, 50
Irving, Washington, 81, 86
Italy, 91, 92
Ives, Levi Silliman, 29

Jackson, Andrew, 9, 29, 47–48, 63, 67, 98, 105
Jackson, James, Jr., 23
Jefferson, Thomas, 212, 218
Johnson, Andrew, 171, 172
Johnson, Mary, 204, 205–206, 208, 216
Johnston, Albert Sidney, 46, 58, 224, 232; at Shiloh, 149, 150; Smith retrieves body of, 173–174
Johnston, Margaret, 90, 109
Johnston, William Preston, 224
Jones, Anson, 44, 45, 191; as president of Texas, 95–96, 98–99, 102, 103, 104; as secretary of state of Texas, 72, 76, 93; suicide of, 141
Jones, Charles Elliot, 147, 150
Jones, Cromwell, 199
Jones, Mary McCrory, 58, 141, 142
Jones, Samuel Edward, 147
Josephine, 107
Journal of Education, 138, 144, 212
Journal of the Seeings, Sayings, and Doings of the Count de GnawBone, 84

Kansas House, 193
Kansas-Nebraska Bill, 135, 136
Keenan, Charles, 114
Kennedy, William, 77, 83
Kenny's Fort (Tex.), 57
"Key to the Continent, The," 204
Kiddoo, J. B., 172
Kincaid, Jesse, 42, 66
Kinney, H. L., 127, 128
Kittredge, Antoinette Huie, 69, 108
Kittredge, Ashbel Smith, 69, 108, 138; in Civil War, 150, 152, 155–156, 164, 197; on Know-Nothings, 135; Smith letter to, 147
Kittredge, Caroline Smith, 81, 138, 200, 208, 213; and children, 69, 101, 103, 108; at Evergreen, 206; and father's will, 145. *See also* Smith, Caroline
Kittredge, Henry Grattan, 108, 176, 185, 197
Kittredge, Jessie, 108, 197, 213
Kittredge, Thomas, 34, 35, 49, 81, 94, 213
Kittrell, P. W., 140
Knights of Pythias, 218, 219
Knights of the Order of San Jacinto, 87–88
Know-Nothing Party, 131–132, 134–135
Ku Klux Klan, 176

Laennec, René, 20
Lafayette, 21, 22, 23
Lamar, Lauretta, 59
Lamar, Mirabeau Bonaparte, 36, 45, 98, 107, 191, 200; as president of Texas, 52–59, 63
Lamar, Mrs. (Lamar's mother), 59
Lamar, Rebecca, 59
land speculators, 136
Lark, 168
Larrey, Baron Dominique Jean, 20
Laurence, Abbott, 125
Laurens, Levi L., 41, 42
Lavaca (Tex.), 152
Lawrence, D. H., 16
Leavenworth, Elias Warner, 8, 226, 227
Lee, Robert E., 166, 178
legation, Texas, 74, 81
legislature, Texas (state), 141, 184, 191; and TMA, 114, 130, 186; and University of Texas, 140, 209, 217, 220, 223, 224. *See also* Texas Legislature
Leopold I (king of Belgium), 85
Liberating Army of Mexico, 127
Lick Creek, 149
Lincoln, Abraham, 147
Lisfranc, Jacques, 19, 20
loans, foreign, 65
London Herald, 84
Longstreet, James, 173
Louis, Charles Alexander, 20
Louvre (Paris), 78
Loyal Union League, 175, 176
Lubbock, Francis R., 139, 148, 172, 175, 179

Macaulay, Thomas, 21, 24
McCormick's Virginia reaper, 124
McCrory, Mary, 58, 141, 142
McIntosh, George, 78
Magendie, François, 20
Maillard, Nicholas Doran, 84
malaria, 15, 26, 44, 52–53, 97, 101, 106, 111, 163, 178, 198, 199
Mallet, John William, 217, 221–222, 223
manifest destiny, 115
Mansion House (Houston), 42
Mansion House (Salisbury, N.Car.), 9
Marshall (Tex.), 192
Mary Howland, 19
Masons, 144, 218, 219
Matagorda Weekly Dispatch, 84
Matamoros, 106
Maury, D. H., 151, 152
Maxey, S. B., 200, 207
meat biscuit, 120–121, 122, 123, 125, 126, 128, 129, 133
mediation, triple, 81
Medical and Surgical Society of Galveston, 114
medical censors, 43–44, 114
medical examiners. *See* medical censors
medical quackery, 114, 187
Memoranda and Official Correspondence Relating to the Republic of Texas, 142 n
Memphis Medical College, 117
Mexican War, 105–108
Mexico, 72, 111; blockade of, 75, 77, 79, 81
Milam, Benjamin, 106

Index

Miller, W. D., 82
Mississippi River, 158
monopolies, 185
Montezuma, 75, 79
Moore, Dr. Francis, 200
Moore, John C., 149, 150
Morgan, John, 29
Morgan's Point, 46
Mormonism, 69
Morse, Samuel F. B., 23, 25, 37, 48, 94, 101, 119
Murrah, Pendleton, 165, 168, 169

Napoleon, Louis, 125
Narbonne, Count de, 73, 84
Narrative of the Travels and Adventures of Monsieur Violet (Frederick Marryat), 84
National Democrats, 145
National Educational Convention, 119
National Gallery (London), 87
National Institute (Washington), 89
Necker Hospital (Paris), 20, 23, 24
Neuilly (France), 88, 90
New Bethlehem Hospital (London), 24
New England Farmer, 195
Newgate (London), 87
New Orleans Commercial Bulletin, 100
New Orleans True American, 47
New Testament, 27, 117, 230
New York Academy of Medicines, 116
New York Herald, 116
New York Hospital, 11, 17
New York Journal of Commerce, 120, 123, 132
New York Morning News, 100
New York Tribune, 124
New York University, 96
Ney, Elisabet, 221
Nixon, Pat Ireland, 130
Notre Dame, 78
nullification, 28–29, 48

Odd Fellows, 218, 219
Olmsted, Denison, 27
Order of San Jacinto, Knights of, 87–88
Owen, Helen M., 216

Page, L. D., 138
Palais Bourbon, 77

Palo Alto Battlefield, 106
Paris (France), 19, 198
Paris International Exposition, 197
Paschal, G. W., 145
"pay as we go" policy, 202–203
Pease, Elisha M., 137
Peel, Robert, 24
Pemberton, John Clifford, 154, 158
Pennock, C. W., 61–62
Phi Beta Kappa, 8, 118, 119
Phifer, Mary, 30–33, 42–43, 121–122, 138, 142
Philabeaucourt, Mlle de, 72
Philippe, Louis, 77, 125, 191; and annexation, 88, 92, 101; described by Smith, 21, 82
Philosophical Society of Texas, 45
Pierce, Franklin, 128
"pig war," 71, 73–74
Pitié, La (Paris), 20
Planters Mutual Ins. Co., 173
Plato, 31, 112, 231
Playfair, Lyon, 124–125
Poag, W. R., 136
Poinsett, Joel R., 48
Polish Committee, 22, 23
Polk, James K., 98, 108
Pope, Judith, 109
popular sovereignty, 115
Power, Charles, 145
Powers, Hiram, 124
Prairie View State Normal School, 195, 210
preemptioners, 136
Prentiss, Benjamin C., 150
Priceville (Miss.), 151
Prince Albert, 86
Prince of Wales, 123, 198
public debt of Texas, 136
Punch, 126

quackery, 114, 187
quarantine laws, 202, 207

Ragsdale, Smith, 214
railroads, 118, 129, 136–137, 140, 180, 184–185, 192
Rate, Lacklan Macintosh, 77, 87
Reagan, John H., 175 and n, 181, 226
reaper, 124

INDEX

Récamier, Claude, 20
Reconstruction, 170–176, 209
Reconstruction Acts, 177
Red, Rebecca Stuart, 225 n
Red, Samuel Clark, 225 and n
red backs, 66, 71
"Reminiscences of the Republic of Texas," 191
Republic, The (Plato), 231
Republic of Texas. See Texas, Republic of
Richardson, Chauncey, 105
Rio Grande, 105
Roberts, Oran Milo, 171, 202; and University of Texas, 210, 215, 217–218, 221, 224–225
rock salt, 195
Roemer, Ferdinand, 103, 104
Rogers, William, 152
Rose, Dilue, 58
Rosenberg, Henry, 191
Ross, John, 51
Rosseau, Eugene, 19
Rowan House (Salisbury, N.Car.), 9
Royal Geographical Society (French), 90
Royal Society, 101, 217
Rue et Hotel Corneille, 19
Ruffini, F. E., 217, 220, 229 n
Runnels, Hardin R., 139, 140, 145, 209
Rusk, Thomas, 36, 63, 107, 136, 141, 203
Russia, 133
Rutersville College (Tex.), 146

Sabine Pass (Tex.), 152
Saint James's Palace, 86
Saligny, Alphonse de, 71, 73–74, 98
Salisbury (N.Car.), 9, 42, 58, 67, 138
Salisbury Western Carolinian, 11, 28, 36
Sam Patch (horse), 51
San Augustine (Tex.), 63, 99
San Bernard River (Tex.), 57, 162
Sancho, Zicente, 80
San Jacinto, Battle of, 38, 65, 204
Santa Anna, Antonio López de, 191
Santa Fe Expedition, 57, 72, 75
Schilling, Nicholas, 231
Scott, Sir Walter, 21
Scott, Thomas A., 192
Scott, Winfield, daughter of, 89
scrip, military, 44
Sealy, John, 191

secession, 136, 147
Second Brigade, Second Division, Confederate Army, 162
Second Regiment Texas Volunteer Infantry, 148–169, 231
Semmes, Raphael, 178
Seymour, Daniel, 5, 8, 74, 80
Seymour, Horatio, 176
Seymour, Jane, 3
Seymour, John, 18, 19, 48
Seymour, Melancton, 48, 92
Seymour, Ruth, 4
sheep husbandry, 145–146
Sheridan, Philip Henry, 169
Sherman, William Tecumseh, 153
Shiloh, Battle of, 149–150, 152, 159, 173
Silliman, Benjamin (Yale professor), 8, 12, 32, 62, 116
Silliman, Benjamin (classmate), 8, 191, 226–227, 230
Sistine Chapel, 91
Sixty-third Regiment, N.Car. Militia, 33
slavery, 76, 83, 120, 136; Smith on, 29, 114, 134, 147, 231
Smith, Albert, 49, 102
Smith, Ashbel, 12; in agricultural society, 131; on annexation, 35, 90, 92, 97–99, 100, 103; beliefs of, 15, 69, 119, 189; burned in effigy, 100, 132, 227; as chargé d'affaires, 72–95 passim; on constitution, 190; and Democratic Party, 176, 181, 192, 203; described, 14, 83, 194, 232–233; as editor, 28–29, 64–65; on education, 126–127, 131, 137, 186, 194–195, 203; on farming, 131, 195–196; as Harris County superintendent, 185–186; and higher education, 117, 187, 188, 194–195, 197, 206, 207–208, 214, 220–225; in historical society, 178–179; illnesses of, 5, 7, 15, 23, 40, 51–53, 58, 85, 97, 101, 107, 110–12, 150, 163, 198–199, 216, 219, 231; land transactions of, 29–30, 33, 41, 59–60, 64, 112, 118, 127, 141; as legislator, 134–138, 170–174, 199, 202–205; library of, 5, 18, 25, 73, 95, 227; linguistic ability of, 8, 78, 125; as magistrate, 30; in medical association, 211–212, 216–217; in military, 33, 105–107, 147–169 passim; and par-

ents, 110, 144, 183; personal finances of, 9, 11, 27, 34, 41, 46, 49, 60, 85, 97, 112, 146, 170, 198; and political campaigns, 139, 166; positions held by, 12, 122–126, 127–128, 129–130, 144, 192–194, 197–199, 213; on religion, 29, 227, 230; on Sam Houston, 47, 135; schooling of, 5–6, 7–9, 11–13; as secretary of state, 97–103; as slave owner, 29–30, 49, 60, 64, 66–67, 102, 110, 112; on slavery, 29, 76, 114, 120, 134, 147, 231; as surgeon general, 37–56 passim; as teacher, 9–11, 13, 25; writings by, 227 (*see also* specific titles)
Smith, Ashbel Grattan (nephew), 109, 127, 213
Smith, Caroline, 5, 14; and Ashbel Smith, 21, 30; marriage of, 34–35. See also Kittredge, Caroline Smith
Smith, Curtis, 4, 14, 81, 101, 212–213
Smith, Elisha, 4
Smith, Eliza, 49
Smith, George Alfred, 5, 33, 60, 81, 85, 96 n, 201, 204, 232; and Ashbel Smith, 34–35, 70, 94, 96, 216; in Civil War, 150; in father's will, 145; in Salisbury, 28; visits Evergreen, 222, 227
Smith, Harriet Nooe, 200, 201
Smith, Henry, 36
Smith, Henry Grattan, 5, 60, 67, 97, 109; and Ashbel Smith, 16, 33, 94, 102; in Civil War, 150; death of, 200; in father's will, 144–145
Smith, Joseph, 4
Smith, Kirby, 162, 165, 220
Smith, Lydia Huit, 4
Smith, Mabel Seymour, 4
Smith, Moses, Jr., 81; and Ashbel Smith, 10, 11, 14, 15, 16–17; death of, 144; as Hartford constable, 5; ill health of, 138; marriages of, 4; poverty of, 33, 94
Smith, Moses, Sr. (grandfather), 4
Smith, Peter, 49, 94, 97
Smith, Phoebe Adams, 4, 94, 138; advises Ashbel Smith, 9, 10, 14, 34; Ashbel Smith's feelings for, 110, 144, 147; death of, 183
Smith, Robert, 49
Smith, Sir William, 3–4

Smith, Wager, 112
Smith-Cuevas Treaty, 99, 102
snakebite, treatment of, 188
Soisy-sous-Étoilles (France), 88
Somerville (Tenn.), 67, 69
Sorbonne (Paris), 20, 28
Southern Historical Society, 178
Southern Intelligencer, 145
Southern Medical Reports, 1851, 121, 130
Spain, 80
state fair (Texas), 127, 128, 180
steamers, Mexican, 74–76, 77, 79
Stephens, J. H., 144
Stoddard, Soloman, 6, 7
Stuart, D. F., 193 n, 225 n
Stuart Female Seminary, 225 n
suffrage, Negro, 171
sugar cane, 68, 120, 121, 138, 180, 195, 198
Swan, 47

Tallahatchee, Battle of, 153
Tallahatchee River, 153
Talleyrand, 39
Tammany Hall, 116
Taylor, John C., 112
Taylor, Richard, 173
Taylor, Zachary, 107, 108, 115
telegraph, 37, 48, 94–95, 101, 119
Telegraph and Texas Register, 47, 139
Tennessee Volunteers, 35, 36
Terry, Adrian, 8, 32
Texas, Republic of, 82, 103, 104; blockades Mexico, 75, 77, 79, 81; congresses of, 40, 44, 57, 82, 90, 209; currency of, 48, 60, 66–67, 71, 82; described by J. P. Henderson, 34, 36; described by Smith, 67–68; English attitude toward, 74, 76, 77, 93, 95; French attitude toward, 88, 92, 101; immigration to, 50, 72, 80, 83
Texas A&M College, 209, 210, 220
Texas and Pacific Railway Co., 192
Texas and the Gulf of Mexico (Houstoun), 84
Texas and the Texans (Foote), 68, 200 and n
Texas Christian Advocate, 194
Texas Constitution of 1876, 190

INDEX

Texas Grand State Fair (1871), 180
Texas Journal of Education, 210
Texas legation, 74, 81
Texas legislature (state): Eleventh, 170–174; Sixteenth, 202–205; Sixth, 134–138. *See also* legislature, Texas
Texas Literary Institute, 105, 108
Texas-Louisiana border: defense of, 160
Texas Medical Association, 114; meetings of, 130, 178, 179, 186–187, 192, 196, 206, 211–212, 216–217, 223, 227; Smith and, 130, 211–212, 216–217
Texas Medical College and Hospital (Galveston), 187–188, 197, 206, 214, 217
"Texas question," 90. *See also* annexation
Texas State Bureau of Agriculture, 136
Texas State Cemetery (Austin), 173, 232
Texas State Medical Association. *See* Texas Medical Association
Texas State Teachers Association, 176, 217
Texas Veterans Association, 189
Texas Volunteers (Mexican War), 105–107
Thackeray, William Makepeace, 87
Thrall, Homer S., 200
Throckmorton, James W., 137, 140, 174, 210, 214, 216, 226
Thurston, Algernon, 46
Tilden, Samuel J., 192
Tillotson Institute, 229
Times (London), 124, 125, 133
Titania, 124
Todd, Eli, 30, 32
Travis, William B., 106
Trelawny, Edward, 87
Tremont House (Galveston), 72, 100, 163
Tuileries (Paris), 78, 83
Tyler, John, 35, 96

United States Department of Agriculture, 196
United States Navy, 152
University of Texas, 140, 202, 214, 225; construction of, 214, 221–223; faculty of, 215, 218, 220, 223, 229; funding for, 209, 220, 223; law department of, 221, 224; medical branch of, 188, 209, 211, 214, 223; regents and, 210, 214–215,

217–218, 220, 223–225, 229, 232; seal of, 214 n
University of Virginia, 212, 217, 218, 221

Van Buren, Martin, 29, 35, 45, 48
Vanderbilt University, 212
Van Zandt, Isaac, 76, 92
Velasco (Tex.), 43, 57, 67, 161
ventriloquism, 17
Vestiges of the Natural History of Creation (Chambers), 119
Vicksburg, 154–159
Victoria (queen of England), 74, 77, 86; Smith describes, 123
Violet, Monsieur, 84

Waggener, Leslie, 219
Walker, J. G., 165
Wanderer, The, 181
Warrenton (Miss.), 154
Washington, D.C., 48, 96
Washington Chronicle, 47
Washington National Intelligencer, 29
Washington-on-the-Brazos, 97–98
Waul, Thomas N., 179
Waul's Legion, 162
Weeping Confederacy, The, 174
Wellington, Duke of, 74, 86, 123
West Point Board of Visitors, 115–116
Wharf Company of Galveston, 185
wheat, 68, 132
Wheatstone, Sir Charles, 94, 95
Whig Party, 35, 108
Wilkes's Battery, 162
wine making, 89, 177–178, 202
Wooldridge, Alexander Penn, 215, 222–223
Woolsey, Theodore Dwight, 108, 212
Wooten, Thomas D., 214, 222–223, 227
Wren, 167
Wright, Anna Allen, 189, 201, 216, 231–232; family background of, 183–184; marriage of, 208; Smith and, 193, 198–199, 204–205; wealth of, 208
Wright, George, 208

Yale, 7–9, 11–13, 22, 23, 96, 116, 118–119, 185, 212, 226–227

Yazoo City (Miss.), 152
Yazoo River, 152
Yell, Archibald, 98
yellow fever, 26, 116, 117, 187, 211; 1854 epidemic, 132; 1853 epidemic, 131; 1847 epidemic, 111–112; 1878 epidemic, 199; 1864 epidemic, 163; 1839 epidemic, 60–62
Yoakum, Henderson King, 200 and n
Young, Maud Jeannie Fuller, 228

www.ingramcontent.com/pod-product-compliance
Lightning Source LLC
Chambersburg PA
CBHW031236290426
44109CB00012B/317